RIVER *of* DARKNESS

BANTAM BOOKS

NEW YORK

Francisco Orellana's

LEGENDARY VOYAGE

OF DEATH AND DISCOVERY

DOWN *the Amazon*

BUDDY LEVY

RIVER *of* DARKNESS

Published in the United States by Bantam Books,
an imprint of The Random House Publishing Group,
a division of Random House, Inc., New York.

BANTAM BOOKS and the rooster colophon are
registered trademarks of Random House, Inc.

LIBRARY OF CONGRESS CATALOGING-IN-PUBLICATION DATA
Levy, Buddy.
River of darkness: Francisco Orellana's legendary
voyage of death and discovery down the Amazon / Buddy Levy
p. cm.
Includes bibliographical references and index.
ISBN 978-0-553-80750-9 (acid-free paper) 978-0-553-90810-7 (eBook)
    1. Orellana, Francisco de, d. ca. 1546.   2. Amazon River Region—
Discovery and exploration—Spanish.   I. Title.
E125.O6 L48 2011   2010041849
981/.01 22

Printed in the United States of America on acid-free paper

Map copyright © 2011 by David Lindroth

www.bantamdell.com

9 8 7 6 5 4 3 2 1

FIRST EDITION

Book design by Barbara M. Bachman

For my father, Buck Levy,

who first took me to the river

We seldom or never find any nation hath endured so many misadventures and miseries as the Spaniards have done in their Indian discoveries. Yet persisting in their enterprises, with invincible constancy, they have annexed to their kingdom so many goodly provinces, as bury the remembrance of all dangers past. . . . Many years have passed over some of their heads in search of not so many leagues: Yea, more than one or two have spent their labour, their wealth, and their lives, in search of a golden kingdom, without getting further notice of it than what they had at their first setting forth.

—SIR WALTER RALEIGH, *The History of the World,* 1614

There is something in a tropical forest akin to the ocean in its effect on the mind. Man feels so completely his insignificance there and the vastness of nature.

—HENRY WALTER BATES, *The Naturalist on the River Amazons,* 1892

In human terms, Francisco Orellana's is probably the most compelling narrative from the entire conquistador period, for the simple reason that this time it was the Europeans who suffered so desperately, and who needed all their powers of endurance as they battled with a savage environment.

—PETER WHITFIELD, *Newfound Lands*

CONTENTS

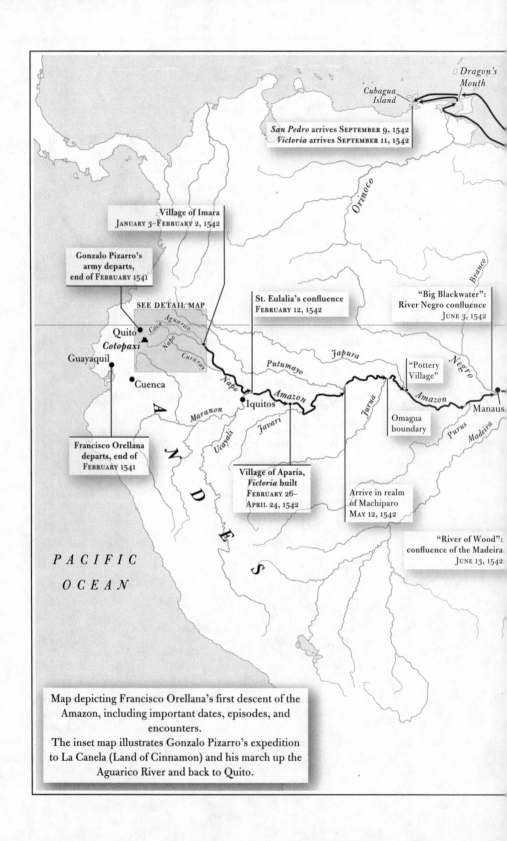

Map depicting Francisco Orellana's first descent of the Amazon, including important dates, episodes, and encounters.
The inset map illustrates Gonzalo Pizarro's expedition to La Canela (Land of Cinnamon) and his march up the Aguarico River and back to Quito.

San Pedro arrives SEPTEMBER 9, 1542
Victoria arrives SEPTEMBER 11, 1542

Dragon's Mouth

Cubagua Island

Village of Imara
JANUARY 3–FEBRUARY 2, 1542

Gonzalo Pizarro's army departs, end of FEBRUARY 1541

SEE DETAIL MAP

St. Eulalia's confluence
FEBRUARY 12, 1542

"Big Blackwater": River Negro confluence
JUNE 3, 1542

Quito
Cotopaxi
Guayaquil
Cuenca

"Pottery Village"

Iquitos

Omagua boundary

Manaus

Francisco Orellana departs, end of FEBRUARY 1541

Village of Aparia, *Victoria* built
FEBRUARY 26–APRIL 24, 1542

Arrive in realm of Machiparo
MAY 12, 1542

"River of Wood": confluence of the Madeira
JUNE 13, 1542

PACIFIC OCEAN

Orinoco
Branco
Negro
Japura
Putumayo
Amazon
Amazon
Coca
Aguarico
Napo
Curaray
Napo
Maranon
Ucayali
Javari
Javari
Jurua
Purus
Madeira
ANDES

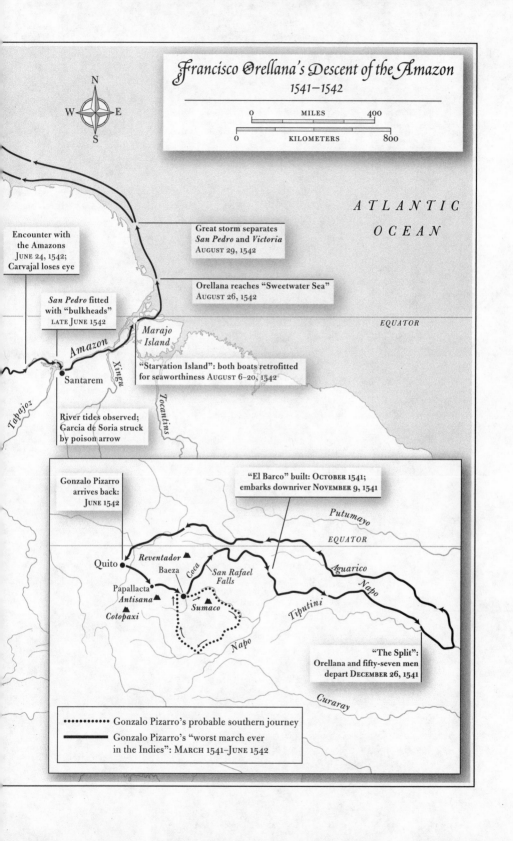

Francisco Orellana's Descent of the Amazon
1541–1542

N
W   E
S

0	MILES	400	
0	KILOMETERS	800	

ATLANTIC

OCEAN

Encounter with the Amazons JUNE 24, 1542; Carvajal loses eye

Great storm separates *San Pedro* and *Victoria* AUGUST 29, 1542

Orellana reaches "Sweetwater Sea" AUGUST 26, 1542

San Pedro **fitted with "bulkheads"** LATE JUNE 1542

EQUATOR

Marajo Island

Amazon

Xingu

"Starvation Island": both boats retrofitted for seaworthiness AUGUST 6–20, 1542

Santarem

Tabajoz

Tocantins

River tides observed; Garcia de Soria struck by poison arrow

Gonzalo Pizarro arrives back: JUNE 1542

"El Barco" built: OCTOBER 1541; **embarks downriver** NOVEMBER 9, 1541

Putumayo

EQUATOR

Quito

Reventador ▲
Baeza
Coca
San Rafael Falls

Aguarico

Napo

Papallacta
Antisana ▲

↑
Sumaco
↓

Cotopaxi ▲

Napo

Tiputini

"The Split": Orellana and fifty-seven men depart DECEMBER 26, 1541

Curaray

••••••••••• Gonzalo Pizarro's probable southern journey

———— Gonzalo Pizarro's "worst march ever in the Indies": MARCH 1541–JUNE 1542

Christmas Day, 1541

CONQUISTADOR FRANCISCO ORELLANA STOOD ON the sodden riverbank and regarded the ceaseless roil of the river, uncertain where the dark waters were heading. In the dying light the water appeared black as it slithered downstream, moving like the skin of some gargantuan dark snake disappearing into an endless jungle. Orellana turned and beheld his bedraggled troops. Some, starving and feverish, their clothes rotted to soiled rags, bent before a weak fire, boiling leather straps from their saddle girths into a bitter broth. Others lay moaning beneath makeshift shelters of palm fronds and ceiba tree bark, their skin sickly white, riddled with bites and stings from mosquitoes, army ants, wasps, and vampire bats. Behind them, from the impenetrable lowland rain forest, sounded the ominous, lionlike roars of red howler monkeys and the piercing calls of macaws.

It was not supposed to be this way. Orellana had fantasized about being fabulously rich by now. He had dreamed, along with his captain Gonzalo Pizarro, of being among the wealthiest men in the world.

Now, all around them was nothing but an infinite river that delivered only death and despair and darkness.

Ten months before, in February, the Spaniards had trekked from Quito over the massive Andes in search of the Land of Cinnamon and the fabled riches of El Dorado, the "gilded man" who, legend held, was daily powdered from head to toe with gold dust, which he would then wash from himself in a lake whose silty bottom was now covered with gold dust and the golden trinkets tossed in as sacrificial offerings.

But the golden dream had proved an unspeakable nightmare. Now, staring at his writhing, starving men, Orellana thought only about how he might get them all out of this death trap alive.

Getting here had nearly killed them. For months they had hacked their way through the dense Andean forests, the forbidding snowcapped Antisana volcano erupting in the distance, rumbling the earth with great quakes and sending shock waves of fear through the exhausted men as the roofs of the abandoned Indian huts they took shelter in collapsed upon them. On their descent from the mountains, rains slashed the hillsides in horrific torrents, sending the men scurrying to higher ground to escape flash floods and engorging the streams so that the conquistadors were forced to cut timber and construct bridges in order to continue forward. The Spaniards suffered attacks by small bands of Indians at the headwaters of the upper Coca and Napo rivers, and all of their native slaves, porters, and guides either died on the freezing mountain passes or fled during the long nights.

The conquistadors had eaten nearly all of the two hundred horses they had brought with them, abandoning others in the dense and roadless forests, which proved impassable for the large animals. Eaten, too, were all of the savage mastiffs and wolfhounds trained to terrorize native populations or to take part in battle. Francisco Orellana, his despondent captain Gonzalo Pizarro, and their few hundred mercenary soldiers were lost in an unknown wilderness, slowly starving to death with scant hope for survival. Progress along the river's dank and decaying shoreline was disastrous. Forlorn, they came to understand that somehow the river must be their only hope for salvation.

So they built a boat, salvaging iron from the shoes of slain horses to fabricate nails, calking the craft with cotton ripped from their own garments and blankets, constructing cordage from tree vines.

Pizarro, glowering and brooding and violent, tortured some captured Indians for information, learning between their screams that perhaps two days' travel downriver was a prosperous village boasting large manioc plantations, enough to keep the men alive, at least for a time.

Francisco Orellana watched the slow and languid movement of the murky river. The waterway appeared hostile and forbidding and alien to him, but he knew what he must do: in this open boat, dubbed the *San Pedro,* he would navigate downstream in search of food.

Orellana, his lips cracked and bleeding, his face blistered from the unremitting equatorial furnace, took Captain Pizarro aside and presented him with his idea: Orellana, second-in-command, and fifty-seven of his compatriots would depart the next morning, boarding the *San Pedro* and twenty-two stolen native dugout canoes and voyaging downstream to find the plantations. Pizarro, despondent and without a better idea, agreed: Orellana should embark at dawn.

As the Christmas sunset poured long skeins of bloodred light over the upper reaches of the Amazon Basin, and the flooded *várzea* forests and swamps reverberated with the eerie twilight *chirrs* and keening of strange animals, both Francisco Orellana and his captain Gonzalo Pizarro gazed at the endless wash of the river. Neither man found it necessary to voice what they both knew: that their only hope of survival lay with Orellana and the fragile wooden craft that would carry him and his small band down the unknown reaches of the twisting, massive waterway.

RIVER *of* DARKNESS

CHAPTER 1

A *Confluence of Conquistadors*

*T*HE VAST AND RUGGED LANDS OF EXTREMADURA, Francisco Orellana's homeland in the kingdom of Castile, produced hard and unyielding men, men who learned the arts of warfare as boys, and who by their early teens could ride their Iberian mounts with panache and wield their Toledo swords with deadly efficiency. Theirs was a temperament forged by eight hundred years of conflict with the invading Moors. To this day, Extremadura is the least populated province in all of Spain, a haunting and land-locked place where seemingly endless tracts of rocky pastureland and burned-out bunchgrass are punctuated by scrubby stands of deep-green encina oak. On elevated promontories, the only respite from the terminal vistas, perch the ruins of castles and ramparts and their crumbling keeps, and the granite remains of Roman arches and bridge columns. The panorama inspired dreams of far-off lands and a better life, as did the stories brought back to Iberia by explorers like Columbus, whose famous *Carta* of 1493 told of innumerable islands peopled by peaceful, naked inhabitants and flowing with spices and gold. The options for men without titles to rise beyond a hardscrabble existence herding swine or cattle were few. They could better their class status through marriage, though most herdsmen or peasants knew that their chances of courting and winning a lady of the elite were less than favorable.

The only other chance for fame, fortune, and titles was a triumphant military career, and this alternative lured many an Extremeño to the ships at Seville headed for the newfound world across the seas.

Such was the lure for young Francisco Orellana. Born in 1511 to a prominent Trujillo family related to the famous Pizarros, Orellana himself declared that he was "a gentleman of noble blood, and a person of honor." Although information on his early years is scant, his upbringing, including early training in the arts of warfare, would have been much the same as that of another Trujillo family to which his was related: the Pizarros, whose eldest son, Francisco, was already winning renown in the New World. Certainly, Orellana's eventual leadership roles and his rapid acquisition of native languages point to a high intellect and distinguished bearing.

Orellana claims to have arrived in the Indies in 1527, at which time Panama was the base from which most of the Spanish expeditions were mounted. Orellana, then still a brash but ambitious teenager, soon signed on as a mercenary soldier, and in the regions north of Panama, likely in Nicaragua, "he performed his first feats of arms as a conquistador." It would have been a thrilling and chivalric time for the young man, fighting alongside veterans of conquest in lands so different from his native Iberia, in lands that very few Europeans had ever seen and that in fact had only recently been discovered by Columbus.* Indeed, the Spaniard's staging area of western Panama lay on the very coast of the Pacific Ocean (the Gulf of Panama) that, after hacking their way across the brambly isthmus, Vasco Núñez de Balboa, with Francisco Pizarro as second-in-command, had discovered just fourteen years earlier.

Over the next decade Orellana would distinguish himself by participating in numerous expeditions and invasions in Central America, and ultimately in the conquests and civil wars waged in Peru. Orellana

---

* Christopher Columbus discovered the coasts of Panama and Honduras on his final (fourth) voyage, 1502–1504.

proudly claimed to have fought "in the conquests of Lima and Trujillo [Peru, not Spain] and . . . in the pursuit of the Inca in the conquest of Puerto Viejo and its outlying territory." Through his efforts and bravery Orellana acquitted himself with great honor and won the admiration of his peers, including the powerful Pizarros. His stature and reputation came not without cost, however. During one skirmish he lost an eye, and from then on he wore a patch, though his loss never diminished his conquistador's focus and vision.

Orellana forever will be linked historically to his kinsman Gonzalo Pizarro through their dual roles in the expedition of 1541–42. Their coming together was hardly a coincidence, given their kinship and common origins in Trujillo. Gonzalo was the second youngest of the five infamous Pizarro brothers,* an ambitious and enigmatic quintet of conquerors sometimes referred to as the "Brothers of Doom," not only for their harsh and duplicitous treatment of the native populations they conquered but for their own rather ignominious ends. Of this deeply loyal band of brothers, only one of the five—Hernando—would die of natural causes. As with Orellana, the details of Gonzalo's early life are sketchy, though his exploits and activities after arriving in the New World with his older brother (some thirty years older, in fact) Francisco, as well as his place of origin, provide much evidence and suggest a great deal about his personality and character.

Described by his chroniclers as exceedingly handsome, a womanizer, an avid hunter, and skilled beyond his years with a sword—"the best lance in Peru" and "the greatest warrior who ever fought in the New World"—he was also known to be cruel and impulsive. Tall and well-proportioned, with an olive-dark complexion and a very long black beard, Gonzalo Pizarro, rather poorly educated, expressed himself in direct, if crude, language.

---

*A more accurate term might be "half brothers," considering that a number of them had different mothers. Their father, Captain Gonzalo Pizarro, fathered at least eleven children with different mothers, and of these, five were sons. Of the sons, only Hernando was legitimate. All of the sons—Francisco, Hernando, Juan, Francisco Martín, and Gonzalo—are associated with the conquest of Peru. The eldest, Francisco, leader and instigator of the capture and overthrow of the Inca ruler Atahualpa, ironically is the only one not acknowledged in his father's will.

To fully understand Gonzalo, we must first consider Francisco Pizarro. Eldest of the Pizarro brothers, Francisco struck out for the Indies in 1502,* and by 1513 he was accompanying Vasco Núñez de Balboa across the Isthmus of Panama to the Pacific. Little more than a decade later, in 1524, the ambitious and skilled Francisco had become a leader himself and put together an expedition to head south from Panama to explore the coast of Colombia in a yearlong venture. There he met fierce resistance from natives and lost a great deal of money, but he remained convinced that there were riches to plunder. In 1524 he formed, with two associates, a private corporation called the Company of the Levant,† which would be devoted to raising money dedicated to further conquest in the New World. For the next two years Francisco Pizarro raised money to sponsor an expedition to the coast of what is now Ecuador. Soon after arriving, they had their first tangible discovery of the riches they sought. Along the seashore's tropical waters they spotted a sailing craft moving steadily along. On closer inspection they could see that the vessel was constructed of local balsa wood, propelled by handmade cotton sails, possessing a woven reed floor and two sturdy masts, and navigated by several native mariners. The sight proved curious and intriguing, for Francisco Pizarro knew of no Indian population who understood and employed sailing ships—not even the highly civilized Aztecs his countryman and distant cousin Cortés had reported so much about.

As the Spanish caravel moved alongside the craft, some of the natives leaped into the ocean and swam toward shore. The Spaniards overtook the remaining crew and questioned them through sign language. The natives indicated that they were from Tumbez, on the northwestern coast, south of Quito, but Pizarro's men were much more fascinated by

---

* Also on this ship, incredibly, was eighteen-year-old Spaniard Bartolomé de Las Casas. Las Casas would later become a priest and the most ardent defender of indigenous rights the native people of the New World would ever know. Las Casas's influence on King Charles V of Spain would eventually bear directly on the life of Gonzalo Pizarro and on the historical outcome of Peru.

† The two men were Diego de Almagro and Hernando de Luque. Almagro would later figure significantly in the history of Peru and the destinies of the Pizarro brothers.

the contents of the craft, which included many wonders, according to a letter later enthusiastically written to Charles V:

> They were carrying many pieces of gold and silver as personal ornaments [and also] crowns and diadems, belts, bracelets, leg armor and breastplates . . . rattles and strings and clusters of beads and rubies, mirrors adorned with silver and cups and other drinking vessels.

After absconding with the contents of the balsa craft and sending the frightened and confused natives on their way, Pizarro took careful stock of the booty. Here was the first substantial evidence that, as he hoped and banked on, somewhere in the vicinity there must surely be an empire, perhaps one as grand and immensely wealthy as the one Cortés had discovered. Francisco Pizarro was almost fifty and had spent nearly half his life searching for just such a prize, but he needed confirmation of its existence. After setting up camp on a mosquito-infested jungle island they later named Gallo, Pizarro is reputed to have assessed his travel-weary troops; many of the men were sick and hungry, some already dying and begging to return to Panama. They had depleted most of their stores. The generally taciturn Pizarro, himself by then gaunt and ragged, is said to have stood before them on the beach and etched a deep line in the sand with his sword tip. "Gentlemen," he bellowed,

> This line signifies labor, hunger, thirst, fatigue, wounds, sickness, and every other kind of danger that must be encountered in this conquest, until life is ended. Let those who have the courage to meet and overcome the dangers of this heroic achievement cross the line in token of their resolution and as testimony that they will be my faithful companions. And let those who feel unworthy of such daring return to Panama; for I do not wish to [use] force upon any man.

With that, Francisco Pizarro stepped across the line himself, indicating that all who followed him would continue south, away from Panama, away from Spain, away from their wives and families and the comforts of home, perhaps forever. Thirteen men, slowly at first, and then with growing conviction, stepped over the line to join him. They would forever be known as "the Men of Gallo." The remainder of the crew, those who refused to cross the line, soon sailed back to Panama on a supply ship that had come to reinforce them.

Those who remained with Pizarro had reason to believe, at least for a time, that their decision had been prudent. They sailed on, and very soon they encountered a coastline that offered open views, unimpeded by mangrove and tidal forest, of the interior. There, at a place called Tumbez, they spotted over a thousand well-made native houses, with wide and orderly streets, a port filled with boats, and thick-coated, long-necked animals that looked like giant sheep being herded about, while hundreds of curious onlookers dotted the shoreline. Francisco Pizarro had discovered the Incas.

The eldest Pizarro brother wasted little time. He hurried back to Spain in early 1528, hoping to gain an audience with King Charles, who was soon to be Holy Roman Emperor. He managed to obtain his hearing, possibly at least partially owing to the king's receptive frame of mind when it came to discussions of conquest—quite an achievement for an illegitimate peasant from Extremadura. Hernán Cortés had only just been at court himself, where his presentation of dancing and juggling Aztecs and his many crates full of golden treasures had garnered him the king's favor and earned him the title of Marquis de Valle, making him one of the richest and most powerful men in the Spanish Empire.*

The king listened attentively to Francisco Pizarro's tales of his first two journeys to this place called Peru,† and to his proposed plan for a third expedition. Then, taking a page from Cortés, as he would do again and again over the course of his conquest, Francisco Pizarro presented the king with fine pottery and embroidered linen clothing from the region. He even paraded a few live llamas before his majesty, highlight-

---

* Cortés had been dispatching treasure ships back to the king from mainland Mexico since 1519.

† A Spanish mispronunciation of "Biru."

ing the value of their wool and their usefulness as beasts of burden. He described the riches he had seen in Tumbez, bringing forth shining specimens of gold and silver. All had the desired impact, and on July 6, 1529, Queen Isabella of Portugal, Holy Roman Empress,* signed the royal license, a document granting Francisco Pizarro the right of "discovery and conquest in the province of Peru—or *New Castille*," as Mexico had been decreed New Spain.

Working quickly as the head of his recently founded Company of the Levant, Francisco scurried to call in favors and raise money, then convened his brothers in Trujillo, rallying them for a long trip across the sea and the uncertainty and great potential that lay ahead. Finally, in January of 1530, the five Pizarros—Francisco, fifty-four; Hernando, twenty-nine; Juan, nineteen; Gonzalo, eighteen; and Francisco Martín,† seventeen— boarded a ship in the harbor of Seville, a ship packed with all the cannons, gunpowder, swords, crossbows, harquebuses, and horses necessary for battle and conquest in foreign lands, and set sail for Peru. Peering over the gunwale and watching his native Spain recede in the distance, young Gonzalo Pizarro could only vaguely imagine the wonders and horrors, the glories and riches, the deprivations and degradations, he would encounter during the next meteoric but star-crossed eighteen years of his life.

THE PIZARRO BROTHERS' infiltration of Peru was much aided by an ongoing civil war waging between the indigenous rival royal Inca brothers Atahualpa and Huascar. The kingdom of Peru the Pizarros marched across in early 1532 was a full-fledged civil war zone; they found formerly great cities like Tumbez reduced to rubble and ruin, abandoned amid the complex civil strife. Looting for riches as they went, the Pizarros cut

---

* Queen Isabella, Holy Roman Empress, also known as Isabella of Portugal. She married Charles V in 1526, and served as competent regent for him during his long absences, notably during the years 1529–32 and 1535–39. She is sometimes confused with Queen Isabella of Spain, who preceded her but died in 1504.

† Francisco Martín was a uterine brother, sharing the same mother but a different father.

a swath south from Tumbez toward the city of Cajamarca, where, they had learned through interpreters, Atahualpa and his large victorious army were encamped. Atahualpa, the Pizarros understood, had defeated Huascar and would now be sole lord of the Inca Empire. What they did not know was that Inca spies and runners had been reporting the Spaniards' movements to Atahualpa since their arrival on the coast, and that the ruler was deeply intrigued by the reports and descriptions: "Some of the strangers, he was told, rode giant animals the Incas had no word for as none had ever before been seen. The men grew hair on their faces and had sticks from which issued thunder and clouds of smoke." The Inca ruler was less frightened by these reports than curious, so he did nothing about the small band of encroaching foreigners—only waited curiously while he planned his own coronation, to see if they might arrive.

Arrive they did. By early November 1532, Francisco Pizarro, his brothers, and his small army became the first assemblage of Europeans to ascend the Andes, climbing a well-maintained roadway to the cold plain of Cajamarca at 9,000 feet above sea level. They were on the Royal Inca Road, the two-thousand-mile network of stone paving connecting the entire Inca Empire, from Carnqui north of Quito all the way to Copiapo on the coast of what is today Chile. Hernando Pizarro had been impressed enough to utter that "such magnificent roads could be found nowhere in Christendom."

On November 16, 1532, Francisco Pizarro and his 167 "Men of Cajamarca"* brazenly confronted the emperor-elect of the Incas, Atahualpa, persuading him to attend a friendly meeting with the Spaniards in the Cajamarca central square. There the Spanish infantry and cavalry lay in wait, hidden inside the empty town buildings. They knew that Atahualpa's army was enormous, with estimates of as many as eighty thousand warriors. Some of the Spaniards were so unnerved that they "made water [urinated] . . . out of sheer terror." Soon Atahualpa arrived

---

* Although Francisco Orellana's name is not associated with records of these men and the events at Cajamarca, he may in fact have been there. The number 168 is typically cited, and this includes Francisco Pizarro.

with all the ceremony attendant on an emperor: borne on a feather-bedecked and gilded litter; preceded by attendants wearing ornate head-dresses, "large gold and silver disks like crowns on their heads," who swept the ground before him; and followed by nearly six thousand troops armed only with ceremonial weaponry. At length, a Spanish Dominican friar, using an interpreter and accompanied by young Gonzalo Pizarro, spoke with Atahualpa in a historic exchange.

Atahualpa, confident in his superior numbers and seeing so few of the foreigners before him, demanded that the Spaniards return every item they had stolen since their arrival in his realm. The friar, holding a dog-eared breviary in one hand and a cross in the other, responded by delivering—as Spanish law required him to do—the famous and insidious *requerimiento,* a self-justifying speech that called on native populations to accept Christ in lieu of their own gods and the Spanish king as their sovereign. Atahualpa listened, but certainly neither comprehended nor much cared about the demands these interlopers were making on someone of his prestige and power. He asked to see the breviary, leafed through it, then angrily and disdainfully tossed it to the ground. The act, interpreted by the Spaniards as a desecration of Holy Writ, was enough to incite an attack, and out flew Pizarro's soldiers from their hiding places.

The spectacle was overwhelming to the Incas, for here came men clad in iron chain mail and shining armor, mounted on giant four-legged animals they had never seen, firing harquebuses and cannons into the ranks of unarmed Inca troops. Explosions of smoke and fire terrified the crowd and soon the Spanish cavalry stampeded into the masses, slashing their Toledo blades with impunity and continuing to fire guns and crossbows at close range. The sounds of the explosions, the percussive bursts of smoke and flame, all were utterly foreign to the Incas, many of whom cowered on the ground or fled in terror. In just two devastating hours, Francisco Pizarro and his men had slashed and stabbed and speared and trampled their way to Atahualpa's litter, still borne by his loyal and courageous attendants. Pizarro himself, bloodied, one hand severely wounded, wrested the Inca emperor from his noble elite and carted him away as a prisoner. As the sun set over Cajamarca that night, nearly seven thousand Incas lay slain or dying, and the balance of power in Peru now lay in the hands of Francisco Pizarro.

Atahualpa, proud ruler of some ten million tribute-paying subjects, was shocked and devastated by his defeat and capture. Not long into his incarceration he began attempting to negotiate terms for his release. He had noticed the invaders' fascination with objects of gold and silver. Anything made of these metals—which were much less valuable to the Incas than to the Spaniards—mesmerized Pizarro and his men. Gold was sacred to the Incas, but it was not used as a monetary currency. Atahualpa determined that his best chance to secure his own freedom and the withdrawal of the Spaniards would be to strike a bargain. He told Pizarro that in exchange for his life and freedom, he would give him as much gold and silver as he wanted—the equivalent of a ransom.

The offer obviously piqued Pizarro's interest. Really? How much, and how soon, he wondered.

> Atahualpa said that he would give a room full of gold that measured twenty-two feet long by seventeen feet wide, filled to a white line halfway up its height, which, from what he said, would be over eight feet high. He [also] said that he would fill the room to this height with various pieces of gold—jars, pots, plates, and other objects and that he would fill that entire hut twice with silver, and that he would do all this within twelve months.

Pizarro immediately agreed to the terms, though he certainly had no intention of honoring his end of the bargain. Pizarro inquired where Atahualpa might get all this treasure, and he was enthralled to learn that Atahualpa's realm stretched a tremendous distance to the south, so far that relay runners racing night and day would take about forty days on foot to reach the end of the empire and return. The empire stretched for thousands of miles, from the top of the continent south to what is modern-day Santiago, Chile. Though he could not have known it at the time, Francisco Pizarro had indeed found a literal and figurative gold mine. He and his brothers were now in control of the greatest empire on the face of the earth.

Atahualpa honored his part of the arrangement, and gold and silver streamed into Cajamarca from all corners of the Inca Empire. Inca guides and bearers were dispatched under Spanish guard and supervision to oversee the taking of plunder at military and civic outposts far and wide, and Hernando Pizarro went on a three-month reconnaissance expedition to learn more about these people and their vast network of roads and military complexes.

Between December 1532 and May 1533, great llama trains bearing finery and antiquities flowed into Cajamarca: gold and silver vessels, jars and pitchers, ornate jewelry, unique sculptures, until as promised the rooms were indeed filling toward the ceilings. Eventually Francisco Pizarro had nine special furnaces built and used Indian smiths to melt these gorgeous masterpieces down so that they could be molded into ingots, officially stamped as legal and weighed, and the Royal Fifth* sequestered for the king in Spain. The initial haul was so immense that the smiths were frequently melting down six hundred pounds of gold per day.

In June 1533, Francisco Pizarro dispatched Hernando in a ship laden with Inca riches, the greatest treasure sent back to the mother country since Cortés's ships bearing Aztec gold more than a decade before. The Inca hoard caused a sensation wherever it landed, and at ports in Panama, Colombia, and Santo Domingo (Hispaniola), Spanish conquistadors lined the docks trying to get a look at the booty and to hear stories of the land of Peru, said to be more magnificent and wealthier than Mexico, causing a renewed gold frenzy. The governor of Panama exclaimed, "The riches and greatness of Peru increase daily to such an extent that they become almost impossible to believe . . . like something from a dream."

BY 1535 FRANCISCO PIZARRO and his partner Diego de Almagro had begun to argue about the division of the spoils and shares, mostly

---

* A royal tax of one-fifth, levied on all profits made by subjects of the Spanish crown in the New World.

because Almagro himself had not been present at the rout of Cajamarca, and though he was technically a partner, he had less claim to the riches. The rift was not only over the disposition of treasure, but of lands and *encomiendas* as well—between the Pizarro and Almagro faithful. *Encomiendas* were royal grants that made captured or subsumed native inhabitants the propertied workforce of a landowner. While these natives were not technically slaves, in reality that is exactly what they were, and many conquistadors were paid not in hard currency but rather by being made *encomenderos,* an added incentive to remain and inhabit the country, with the conquered indigenous people forced to work their land as well as to pay taxes to the Spaniards in the form of goods and services.* Soon allegiances were formed—one was either aligned with the Pizarros or with Almagro and his "Chile Faction," so called because Almagro had agreed in principle to a division of the empire to the south, toward an area called Chile rumored to possess great wealth. The schism between the two factions eventually erupted into an all-out civil war between the Spaniards attempting to control the Inca Empire.

Francisco Orellana, as a loyal relative, was of course on the side of the Pizarros. He had built himself a house in Puerto Viejo, which lies just north of present-day Guayaquil, Ecuador. Orellana's house soon became a waypoint for Spaniards flocking to Peru from Spain and Panama, many drawn by the rumors of the treasure ships and the miraculous wealth of the Incas. It was also a sanctuary for members of the Pizarro faction in the ongoing civil strife, as well as for the resistance insurgencies being waged by Inca holdouts and guerrilla forces unwilling to yield to Spanish rule. While at this house on the coast, Orellana learned that the cities of Lima and Cuzco, which were then the two most important municipalities and Spanish command posts, were under siege by Inca factions. The cities were commanded by Francisco and

---

* An *encomienda* was a royal grant earned through meritorious military service, granting the right of the *encomendero* to use native inhabitants within regional boundaries as a labor force, with the stipulation that the *encomendero* protect the Indians and provide them with religious indoctrination.

Hernando Pizarro respectively, and Orellana felt duty-bound to race to their aid as quickly as possible. Using his own money to finance an army, he bought a dozen horses—a significant expense—and rallied a force of eighty men, providing the best riders with the horses to form a cavalry, and set out for Lima. The two rescue missions were successful, and Orellana reported later with some modesty that he returned home "having left the said cities freed from siege."

Orellana next played a role in the noted battle of Las Salinas, the violent culmination of the struggle for power and Inca spoils. On April 26, 1538, in a marshy plain a few miles west of Cuzco, the two rival Spanish factions faced each other in a decisive battle. Orellana, having been made ensign-general of seven hundred infantry and cavalry, helped the Pizarros achieve a crucial rout, during which 120 of Almagro's men were killed, while the Pizarro troops suffered only nine casualties. Almagro managed to escape on the back of a stray burro, and he made a valiant last stand, but eventually he was overtaken, imprisoned, and then, on the orders of Hernando Pizarro, garroted for acts of treason. It was an inglorious end for the sixty-three-year-old conquistador and former partner, a man who had helped win Peru for the Pizarros. But now that he was out of the way, the Pizarros set about dividing the land among themselves and bestowing titles on those favored supporters, authorizing them to carry out new discoveries in the many unexplored regions of Peru.

For his efforts, Francisco Orellana received from Francisco Pizarro a grant to survey the province known as La Culata, under special commission to settle a city there. The region was well defended by the native inhabitants, and a previous group of Spanish captains had ventured unsuccessfully there. They had been driven back by hostile Indians, and a number of Spaniards were killed. Orellana embarked, as he would say later in a letter of petition to his king recounting his exploits and services, "with the aid of men whom I took along . . . at my own expense and on my own initiative, and at the cost of many hardships on the part of myself and of those who went along with me." Heading north of Lima, they encountered swamps and flood-swollen rivers that were dangerous to ford. Horses and men foundered in the boggy marshes, and all the while, Indians attacked them. Orellana's leadership and tenacity prevailed, however, and soon he had harnessed "the said province under the yoke of Spain" and "established and founded . . . the City of Santiago [de Guayaquil]." Orellana stressed to his sovereign the importance of the city's location and terrain, "a spot so fertile and so rich," he said, and also perfectly situated between Quito and the sea. Here in La Culata, the intelligent Orellana began to develop an interest in the native languages, learning a few regional dialects during his time settling the area.

Francisco Pizarro, El Gobernador, was pleased with developments as he surveyed his new realm and its domains. He decided to further reward Orellana for his valiant efforts, sending him "procurations and appointments, making him lieutenant-governor" of both Puerto Viejo and the newly founded Guayaquil. Francisco Orellana, just thirty years old, had been in the right place at the right time, and he had fulfilled his duties as a leader, a soldier, and a scout. There seemed no limit to what he might yet accomplish.

He did not have to wait long. Soon an opportunity presented itself, an expedition that would test every fiber of his resourcefulness, his leadership, and his courage, an endeavor of danger and discovery that stood to redefine the European understanding of the New World.

CHAPTER 2

Birth of the Golden Dream

ONZALO PIZARRO'S EXPLOITS FIGHTING THE
Inca and battling Almagro were by now legendary, and his
remuneration included the governorship of Quito and
great tracts of land around it, much of it uncharted and
unknown. In late 1540, not long after Gonzalo took up residence in Quito and assumed his mantle as governor, he
began to hear stories swirling about, frenzied rumors that
titillated his already gold-lusty imagination. Most tantalizing were repeated tales about a literal "golden man," the
Gilded One or El Dorado, an Indian king so fabulously
wealthy that daily he charged his subjects with coating his
naked body from head to toe with fine gold dust. At the
end of each day he bathed in a lake, lining its bottom with
gold. Other chiefs, his ancestors, so the story went, had
performed the ritual dusting and bathing for untold gener-
ations. But where were this king and this lake? Spaniards
returning from forays to the north, toward Bogotá, claimed
it was there. Others speculated that the man of gold
and his riches lived over the mountains and to the east, in
the smoldering Oriente, a humid and hostile region lying
east of the Andes that the Spaniards had yet to fully
explore.

Coinciding with all the talk of gold were tales of
another coveted commodity, cinnamon. Since Francisco

Pizarro's first arrival, he had observed that the Incas used in their cuisine a kind of cinnamon said to be acquired from remote tribes dwelling in the steamy forests to the east of the Andes. A countryman of the Pizarros named Gonzalo Díaz de Pineda had recently returned from a venture over the high Andes, where he claimed to have descended to a place called the Cinnamon Valley (La Canela). There, however, a hostile tribe called the Quijos soon repelled him, but not before he discovered from some captives that beyond the Cinnamon Valley there existed a limitless level land peopled with tribes clad in golden ornamentation and jewelry.

The gold rumors in Quito in 1540 became a central catalyst in what would ultimately be among the great chimeras in history—the quest for El Dorado. A number of precedents converged to create the idea—some would call it a myth—and these precursors excited passion and gold greed that took hold of Francisco Orellana and Gonzalo Pizarro as they settled in to their respective governorships.

The first quest was undertaken by Diego de Ordaz, one of the most important captains who had served under Cortés in the conquest of Mexico. His exploits included a heroic climb to the summit of the erupting 18,000-foot volcano Popocatépetl, a climb that impressed King Charles enough to later grant Ordaz a commission to explore and potentially settle as governor the region of eastern South America between the mouth of the Amazon and the Orinoco River.

The mouth of the Amazon itself had been discovered in 1500 by the Spaniard Vicente Yáñez Pinzón, former captain of Columbus's caravel *Niña,* who noticed with great interest that drinkable freshwater had flowed more than a hundred miles out into the salty sea. Attesting to this remarkable phenomenon, he named the river Rio Santa Maria de la Mar Dulce—later shortened to Mar Dulce,* or "sweet sea." By the year 1513 the river was being referred to as the Maranon. He sailed up it a few days' distance, about fifty miles, but by the time Ordaz arrived thirty-one years later, the Amazon remained entirely unexplored by Europeans.

---

* See José Toribio Medina, *The Discovery of the Amazon,* 154–55. The Brazilians call the Amazon the Rio Mar.

Ordaz had become confident that a wealth of gold was there to be discovered, somewhere at the headwaters of a large river, possibly either the Amazon or the Orinoco.

Diego de Ordaz assembled an impressive force for his foray to the Amazon: about 600 men and 36 horses on four ships, including a large flagship and three smaller caravels. In early 1531 they arrived to the north of the mouth of the Amazon, a massive tangle of estuaries nearly two hundred miles wide. During reconnaissance into these estuaries he encountered natives proudly displaying "emeralds as big as a man's fist." The Indians told him, "On going up a certain number of suns [a few days] to the west, he would find a large rock of green stone." Further investigation of these supposed emeralds, which were actually more likely jade, was thwarted by a squall, and rough seas and heavy storms buffeted his armada, ultimately sinking the smaller ships, on which many men were lost. As a result, a rumor began—and persisted for many years—that some of Ordaz's men survived the shipwreck and were living among Amazonian tribes somewhere upriver—no one knew exactly where. Ordaz regrouped but decided to abandon any hope of sailing up the Amazon itself, opting instead to travel northwest for a month and a half, along the coastline toward the Orinoco. Ordaz landed on the island of Trinidad, where he recuperated, stocked the holds with fresh water and grazed the horses, then landed on the mainland across the Gulf of Paria.

Ordaz, three hundred of his remaining men, and all his horses ascended the Orinoco for hundreds of arduous miles, heaving, rowing, and dragging their boats upriver, cutting through the *llanos,* stark plains and savannas and parched, dusty tablelands. They finally came to the confluence of another great river, the Meta, and here were faced with a choice. Indian guides advised Ordaz and his party to take the Meta toward the west, where he would find a civilized, populous nation ruled by "a very powerful prince with one eye," and rich in gold. But eyeing the Meta, Ordaz was dubious; it was rough and shallow, and they would be forced to abandon the boats and proceed on foot.

Another guide pointed south, back up the Orinoco, and began making furious slapping and crashing sounds, and gesticulating with his hands, imitating water hammering down onto rocks. The Spaniards optimistically (and erroneously) interpreted this pantomime to represent goldsmiths hammering away at precious metals, and that was all Ordaz needed to continue his quest up the Orinoco. But in just sixty miles they learned the grim reality of the guide's sign language: they arrived at the violent cascades or rapids of Atures, a violent and impassable defile of rushing white water and falls thundering over rocks, where their boats would be crushed.* The guides now reiterated what they had been try-ing to explain, that the headwaters that Ordaz sought could be reached only by a foot march up the Meta. Ordaz turned his back on his dream for the moment, resolving to return for an overland attempt for this land of the Meta later, with proper equipment and provisions.

The descent began smoothly, the men relieved to be going down-stream for once, but they were soon attacked by Caribs (a rival tribe to the Arawak) wielding bows and arrows. Ordaz dispatched his cavalry to counter the attack, and the sight of charging warhorses clad in armor—the first such animals these tribesmen had ever witnessed—sent them scattering in all directions. Ordaz managed to capture and interrogate a few, inquiring particularly whether there was any gold in the area. He showed the prisoner a gold ring to illustrate what they sought. The Indian responded: "He said that there was much of that metal behind a mountain range that rose on the left bank of the river. There were very many Indians and their ruler was a very valiant one-eyed Indian: if they sought him they could fill their boats with that metal." They also spoke of four-legged animals, describing them as "less than stags, but fit for riding like the Spanish horses." The Indians of course referred to the Andean llama, which Ordaz had heard about from Francisco Pizarro while at court in Spain a few years earlier.

Diego de Ordaz's mind must have been dizzy with the prospect of finally conquering his own empire, just as his countrymen Cortés and

---

* The Atures and the Maipures Falls proved so formidable, in fact, that they prevented Spanish conquistadors and explorers from entering the Upper Orinoco for more than two hundred more years, until 1744, when Jesuit missionary Father Manuel Roman skirted the falls and climbed upriver to the high Orinoco. See Marc de Civrieux, *Watuna: An Orinoco Creation Cycle,* 4–5.

Pizarro had done. Why should the one-eyed ruler of the Meta, who could fill a boat with gold, not be his Montezuma, his Atahualpa?

When Ordaz finally reached the mouth of the Orinoco and the soothing waters of the Caribbean at the Gulf of Paria, he grew single-minded in his quest to return to the headwaters of the Meta, to the land of gold. He needed to return first to Spain, where he hoped to gain an extension on his license to explore and conquer, and to enlist more men and equipment. But the Orinoco had taken a fatal toll on Ordaz, who was harboring an illness contracted somewhere on the river. On his return trip to Spain, Diego de Ordaz died at sea. Afterward, a Spanish proverb surfaced, attributed in no small part to his expedition: "He who goes to the Orinoco," the saying went, "either dies or comes back mad."

But his dream of discovering gold lived on, and foreboding proverb or not, that dream would lure others, including Francisco Orellana and Gonzalo Pizarro, to search for the one-eyed chieftain and his empire of gold.

By late 1540 the myth and legend of El Dorado had reached fever pitch in Quito, fueled in part by other recent multiyear journeys to the north, in what is now Colombia. A well-bred and well-funded lawyer, Licentiate Gonzalo Jiménez de Quesada, set out in 1536 to explore the untracked Rio Grande (since named Magdalena) river to its source, hoping that it would wend its way to Quito and eventually the Pacific Ocean. After a few years of arduous journeying and great loss of men, Quesada had discovered the Muisca (Chibcha) lands (near present-day Bogotá) and people, an advanced civilization that possessed rock salt, emeralds, and finely wrought gold—including a bejeweled and gilded royal litter, very much like those used to carry both Montezuma and Atahualpa. The gold fashioned by Muisca metalsmiths was ornate, pounded into thin sheets and crafted with delicate intricacy and design. Quesada, too, had heard stories about the wealthy land of the Meta, and perhaps believed he had found it—though it was said then to lie farther to the east and to be on a plateau or open plain, less mountainous, perhaps in the wilderness beyond the mountains east of Quito.

All of these tales piqued the adventurous interest of the young and ambitious Francisco Orellana. He then learned, to his great excitement, that Gonzalo Pizarro had organized an ambitious expedition in search of this El Dorado, this Land of Cinnamon. He heard that other competitors were also readying men and equipment for rival expeditions. On the eve of the New Year, 1541, Orellana sped to Quito to offer his services, funds, and men to Gonzalo and to accompany him on his endeavor. But he knew that he must hurry, and that there was no time to lose.

CHAPTER 3

Into the Andes

*F*RANCISCO ORELLANA'S MEETING WITH HIS COUSIN Gonzalo Pizarro in Quito was quick and efficient, for he arrived to find Pizarro already well along in his preparations for departure. Orellana expressed his deep interest in joining Pizarro's expedition, even offering to pay his own expenses and to equip his own force, which suited Pizarro. In return, Pizarro made Captain Orellana lieutenant-general, his second-in-command, and their plan for departure was laid out: Pizarro would complete preparations here in Quito quickly and depart as soon as possible in order to get a head start on any rival expeditions, and Orellana would return to his jurisdictions of Guayaquil and Puerto Viejo to put in order these municipalities, enlist men, and purchase equipment and weaponry. He would then return to Quito, receive written instructions left for him, and follow Pizarro's track over the mountains. The plan was to rendezvous at a place called the Valley of Sumaco, where Pizarro's large army would camp and await his arrival.*

---

* Unfortunately, the exact dates of the meeting between Francisco Orellana and Gonzalo Pizarro, and of their respective departures, are unknown. What is known is that Pizarro departed Quito and Orellana departed Guayaquil (some 165 miles to the south) in late February 1541.

Orellana departed in haste, and Pizarro continued assembling an impressive array of troops for the journey that lay ahead, a foray into the unknown that would one day be described as "the most laborious expedition that has been undertaken in these Indies." By early February 1541, everything appeared in good order.

Pizarro's eagerness to depart was owing partly to his character—he was known for rash and even impetuous behavior—but also to political exigencies. He had at his command a good number of soldiers—numbering in the hundreds—who had been instrumental in aiding Gonzalo and his brothers in the recent civil wars with the Almagro faction, and an expedition of bold scope was one way to employ these idle mercenaries, as well as to reward them, potentially, for their efforts. He was also spurred on by the fact that no sooner had he assumed the governorship of Quito and begun his preparations than he learned that Gonzalo Díaz de Pineda, who had already made one failed attempt to La Canela—the Cinnamon Valley—was back in the city and equipping himself for another attempt, this time enlisting as many of the best soldiers and adventurers as he could find. This was hardly the kind of competition that Gonzalo Pizarro needed, so he immediately met with Pineda and made him an offer that he could not refuse: he granted him numerous *encomiendas* in the region, and, as a bonus, he made Pineda's father-in-law a lieutenant of Quito—a position of significant power. For all this, Pineda had to agree to go with Pizarro, and under his direct command. Pizarro reasoned that, having been over the mountains once, Pineda would prove useful. Pineda agreed to the terms.

Pizarro well understood the importance of trusted men-at-arms, so after placing Orellana second-in-command, he enlisted seasoned veterans of other campaigns to join him, including Antonio de Ribera, who would serve as campmaster, and Juan de Acosta as ensign-general. The force under Pizarro and his captains comprised "nobles of the highest ranks and leading citizens of the realm who, because of the personal prestige of the leader and the great notoriety given to the proposed new expedition of discovery, hastened to enlist under his banners."

The army totaled 220 soldiers (including harquebusiers, crossbowmen, and infantry); nearly 200 horses* armored and fitted for battle; great stores of ammunition and powder; a herd of some 2,000 to 3,000 stinking, snorting swine for consumption en route; highland llamas as pack animals; a snarling horde of nearly 2,000 war hounds, trained not only for battle and intimidation of hostile Indians, but also to herd the swine; and about 4,000 Indian porters, chained and shackled until the moment of departure to preclude escape. These unfortunates would bear the brunt of the expedition's enormous loads, including tons of materials for buildings, bridges, or vessels, while the Spaniards "carried nothing but a sword and a shield, and a small sack of food beneath it." Among the 4,000 porters were a good many native women brought to cook tortillas for the Spaniards and to serve as sex slaves.

On one of the last days of February 1541, Gonzalo Pizarro's bizarre assemblage of nobleman, slave, and animal lurched out of the high, steep city of Quito, over 9,000 feet above sea level, and headed even higher, toward the cloud forests and the Andes Cordillera. Gonzalo Pizarro rode at the front of the main force, proud and upright and confident in his bearing, his compact, war-hardened frame made for the saddle. Antonio de Ribera led the vanguard. They clomped and hoofed up thin tracks on the outskirts of Quito, following human and llama trails that thinned, then diminished almost completely as they entered the misty and sodden cloud forest. They trekked through densely tangled bamboo clusters that slowed progress to a near halt, the sharp thorns tearing at their sleeves and skin. The long train wended through and around thick stands of tree ferns, some arching seventy feet into the vaporous air, and beneath towering *Podocarpus* trees—ancient relatives of pines. After great difficulty they reached the flinty *páramos,* the high Andean valleys that provided somewhat less onerous passages through the mountain range. They were headed for the province of Quijos, a region encompassing the valleys to the northeast of Quito, the most likely location, Pizarro reckoned, of La Canela and El Dorado's kingdom of gold.

---

* Two hundred horses is a staggeringly impressive number, given the cost and difficulty of getting the animals to such remote places. Hernán Cortés, by comparison, landed in Mexico with just sixteen horses.

Though they had begun at the equator, soon they had climbed high enough to see their breath in plumes, and beyond, the forbidding domes of snow-covered, active volcanoes.

As they left the cloud forest and climbed higher, the footing grew slick and mossy, the ground was dotted with prickly *puya* plants, and the temperatures began to plunge further. The native porters, who had begun the forced march nearly naked, shivered in hypothermic agony in the frigid heights. The Spaniards fared better in their thick cotton armor, but the cavalry was forced to dismount and lead the horses up the steep and roadless ravines. Gone were the Inca roads they had grown accustomed to in the lowlands, roads that, though designed for llamas and often difficult for the horses, were paved with stone and included well-planned steps and rest houses every few miles. High up in the *páramo* the ground was trackless, desolate, and bare. Nor did Gonzalo Pizarro and his men have any knowledge whatsoever of the uncharted lands that lay beyond where Pineda had been.

When they eventually reached the province of Quijos, scouts reported that large numbers of hostile Indians were massing and preparing to attack, and Pizarro brought up his troops in tighter ranks. The Indians, apparently intimidated by the large number of armored troops and their horses, withdrew, disappearing into the forest like phantoms.

The ill-clad porters' physical sufferings continued, magnified by emotional and spiritual anguish when, as the entourage was crossing a particularly steep ravine, they were racked by the great roar of an erupting volcano, Antisana to the south, accompanied by an earthquake that roiled the earth underfoot. Although eruptions of great magnitude were common, they were bad omens, and the freezing, naked lowlanders huddled in fear, some attempting to flee. The eruptions and aftershocks sent the Spaniards rushing for cover inside some huts in an abandoned village, but their shelter proved temporary as the roofs caved in from the trembling earth, which rent fissures and caverns in the ground. The sky was charged with electricity, ripped by thunderbolts and lightning. The expedition had traveled less than thirty miles outside Quito, and already more than a hundred Indians had perished from the elements. Others had managed to escape in the night, fleeing down the mountainsides for their homes in the more temperate climes of the equatorial lowlands.

Though the Spaniards were themselves exhausted and cold, they pressed forward for the next month at Gonzalo Pizarro's stern urging. He ordered his men to head toward a place called Sumaco, a village in a valley where he believed, from Pineda's scant reports, that he might reprovision and obtain proper rest. Getting there proved no easy task, not even for hardship-hardened conquistadors. The volcanic eruptions dissipated as their train descended from the mountains, only to be replaced by the torrential downpours of the tropical rain forest. And Pizarro's difficulties were only beginning. They had crossed a high Andean pass—nearly 14,000 feet above sea level—at Papallacta, and then descended into cloud forest again on the other side, still in the midst of the mountains. Though the surroundings were stunningly beautiful— the air was filled with dazzling swarms of hummingbirds—most of the green splendor was lost on Pizarro and his men, who spent each day literally hacking roads and trails with machetes. Pizarro lamented the hardships later, in a letter to his king:* "We came to very rugged wooded country, and great mountain ranges through which we were obliged to open up new roads, not only for the men but for the horses." He added that the rains were a constant problem: "It just rained; it never stopped long enough to dry the shirts on our backs."

As the clouds spat funnels of rain, the streams filled, eroding the canyons and blocking their way. Pizarro ordered carpenters and some knowledgeable porters to build bridges in the Peruvian fashion, using lianas as cordage and cables, then tying cut tree branches in place as flooring or footboards and securing yet more lianas for handrails. Crossing such rickety bridges was a predictably excruciating and nerve-

---

* Conquistadors, as a term of Spanish law, constantly wrote memorials and petitions, sworn statements of their exploits and achievements. These were forwarded to the office of the Indies at Seville, Spain, and there presented to king and emperor. These documents, sometimes composed during expeditions and sometimes after the fact, served several purposes: they chronicled services rendered to God and crown; they recorded events and discoveries and conversions; and they petitioned for future promotions, appointments, and expeditions. Gonzalo Pizarro and Francisco Orellana both wrote memorials of this expedition, and many of their quotes are taken from these.

racking endeavor as they inched their way across a few at a time, until the entire mass of men and women and beasts and baggage had attained the other side. The cavalry led their horses across, the animals perilously bucking and snorting and protesting, and the swine and hounds came starting and stamping next. Last came the heavy crates and barrels of powder and armaments. The work was exhausting and slick and slow. Finally, after building bridges one after another across flooded torrents and hacking their way through the forests, Pizarro's troops and remaining bearers spilled out into the Valley of Sumaco, a lush region that, compared to the country they had just been through, appeared habitable and accommodating.

Mused Pizarro,

We continued our journey till we reached the province of Sumaco, a good sixty leagues [actually, only thirty—or about 110 miles] away [from Quito] and within which it was reported there was a big population, but it was impossible to travel about there on horseback, and there I halted the expeditionary force in order to get it rested, both the Spaniards and the horses, for all were quite worn out in consequence of the great hardships which they had gone through in climbing up and going down the great mountains, and because of the many bridges which had to be built for the crossing of the rivers.

Here Pizarro decided to encamp his motley corps, to replenish supplies as best he could, to discover what he might learn about this Land of Cinnamon, this La Canela and El Dorado as well, and to await the arrival of his second-in-command, Francisco Orellana, who Pizarro had just learned from messengers was not too far behind.

ORELLANA'S EXPEDITION DEPARTURE lacked the pomp and grandiosity of Pizarro's. Though he had tried to make it to Quito in time to leave with Pizarro, Orellana's administrative duties and business in Guayaquil had held him up. He busied himself, too, purchasing gear and equip-

ment for the journey, as well as hiring at his own expense, with paid con-
tracts, as many able soldiers of fortune as he could muster. By the time
Orellana arrived in Quito with his twenty-three companions, Pizarro, as
expected, was already gone. Orellana quickly inquired as to the route
Pizarro had taken, for he planned to follow the same one if possible.
Prominent Spanish citizens of Quito, including government officials
close to Pizarro and those who had watched him leave, took Orellana
aside and counseled him to reconsider, arguing that it would be
extremely dangerous to proceed with so few men and such scant provisions, and that there would likely be hostile Indians en route.

Orellana considered these warnings only briefly. At length he was
given a message Pizarro had left in Quito that reiterated the Valley of
Sumaco as the point of rendezvous. Pizarro would wait for him there.
Orellana vowed to continue, despite the dire warnings. He had, after all,
given Pizarro his word.

Orellana led his contingent up into the foothills, finding the going
arduous and exhausting before they had even reached the base of the
mountains. Soon afterward, as he continued upward, Orellana discovered that the warnings he had been given were well warranted: as he
entered the narrow upland valleys, Indians came forth with spears and
stones and attacked in small detachments. Apparently they found
Orellana's smaller force much less formidable than they had Pizarro's.
The few horses Orellana had brought along were lost, killed, or abandoned in these skirmishes, and though he was indeed ultimately able to
follow Gonzalo's trail and hacked-out roadway, he found scant game or
provisions en route, and what few inhabitants there were had been scattered in the wake of Gonzalo's procession. With some regret, for he had
hoped to join Gonzalo as a kind of reinforcement, Orellana was forced
to dispatch emissaries ahead instead, asking Gonzalo for assistance in
the form of food, lest he and his men perish on the mountainside.

The messengers arrived at Sumaco wan and haggard, but they
found Gonzalo immediately attentive and concerned about his late-
arriving second-in-command and their countrymen. He conferred with
campmaster Antonio de Ribera, ordering him to immediately send a
small relief party. The party backtracked, led by one of Pizarro's trusted

captains, and, according to chronicler Cieza de León, "When Orellana's party saw him they rejoiced at the sight, and still more at the food he brought, of which they were in much need." After resting and rejuvenating for a time, Orellana and his men straggled into the Pizarro camp at Sumaco threadbare and diminished. According to Friar Gaspar de Carvajal, who witnessed their arrival, Orellana came not as a fortifying, fresh reinforcement for the expedition, but rather beggarly, "carrying only a sword and a shield, and his companions likewise."

Gonzalo nevertheless embraced Orellana and his men warmly, immediately took Orellana aside, then called for an assembly of all the captains and commanders to discuss how the next stage of the expedition ought to proceed. After much consultation, Pizarro decided that Orellana and his group should remain in Sumaco to rest and recover as best they could, while Pizarro would lead an advance army of his fittest seventy-odd soldiers, including skilled crossbowmen and harquebusiers and a handful of recently captured native guides, on a reconnaissance mission to the east in search of cinnamon. He chose to forgo horses on this venture, leaving them behind because the terrain was so dense and difficult, still devoid of any roads at all beyond primitive human footpaths. So near the end of March 1541, Gonzalo Pizarro, among the finest cavalrymen in the New World, went ahead as infantry, a foot soldier in a strange land.

Strange it was. The rains continued, pounding and incessant, turning the forest floor into a squelchy bog. Pizarro and his reconnaissance force spent seventy interminable days hacking through clogged and brambly forest seething with vicious mosquitoes and biting black flies, the ground covered with armies of stinging ants. During the sweltering days, drenched equally from the rains and their own pouring sweat, the men cut a swath through the forest with adzes, axes, machetes, and swords, stopping only to drink from streams and swat at swarming insects.

In addition to the lack of trails or roads, fallen ancient trees blocked the Spaniards' passage, forcing them to clamber over the giant trunks or slash their way around, tripping over root buttresses, their faces sliced by vines and thorns and spines of the understory. At night they hun-

kered against ceiba trunks under palm fronds, sharing the soaked
ground with venomous pit vipers, bushmasters, and scorpions. Sleep
came fitfully, if at all, amid the cacophonous croak of bullfrogs, then the
unnerving thrum of cicadas, and the ever-present threat of vampire bats.
These nocturnal mammals fed exclusively on blood and hunted relent-
lessly, navigating by sonar and the heightened vision of their wide eyes,
using their razor-sharp incisor and canine teeth to impale their sleeping
victim's nose or neck or head, and lapping at wounds kept oozing by an
anticlotting agent in their saliva.

Week after week Pizarro and his men plodded on, sometimes aimlessly in great circles and parabolas, skirting flooded areas too deep to
wade, fording swollen rivers, and passing beneath raging waterfalls.
Now and then the terrain would rise and open, and from some elevated
headland they viewed endless rolling mountains plunging steeply to the
river valleys still far below, and occasional high savannas in the distance.

Then, at last, Pizarro began to come across dispersed stands of
canelas, cinnamon trees. The trees, which reminded the Spaniards of
olive trees, had "big leaves like laurels; the fruit consisted of bunches
of small fruits growing in husks like acorns." Pizarro's hopes surged, and
in his wishful state he imagined vast stands of the tree he could cultivate,
sending the coveted spice back to Spain to please his king and compete
with the significant Portuguese trade. "This is cinnamon of the most
perfect kind, and of much substance," exclaimed chronicler Cieza de
León; "no other trees like them have been met with in all the regions of
the Indies. . . . The natives value them highly, and in all their settlements they trade with this cinnamon."

Pizarro soon happened upon small bands of local Indians whom he
detained and questioned, using other captives as interpreters and rely-
ing on sign language. Holding up samples of the trees, he inquired
where there might be more, perhaps whole plains of them. The Indians
shook their heads, saying truthfully that they did not know of any other
trees, or more of them. Pizarro pressed them further, inquiring also of
these poor, naked aboriginals when the land would open up into the
wealthy kingdom of El Dorado, and where might be realms of rich pop-
ulaces and civilizations. Again, they answered that they knew nothing.

This was hardly the response that Gonzalo Pizarro had been looking for. Exasperated, and seeing his dreams of empires of cinnamon and gold dwindling into a sodden nightmare, Pizarro determined to torture a better response from the Indians. Soldier Cieza de León recalled the dark and brutal process:

> So he [Pizarro] ordered some canes to be fixed across poles, like rather thin hurdles, about three feet wide and seven in length, and the Indians to be put on them and tortured until they told the truth. The innocent natives were promptly stretched on these frames or barbecues . . . and some of them were burnt.

Of course, even after having been tortured with flames, the unfortunates could offer nothing but their cries of agony. Disgusted, Pizarro then threw the victims—some from the racks and others, including a few women, torn from their pleading families—to the dogs, "who tore them to pieces with their teeth, and devoured them."

Leaving this abominable business behind, Pizarro mustered his reconnaissance troops and moved out, lurching loudly through this labyrinthine world in which he was essentially lost. The men cursed silently, and Pizarro himself began to grow despondent, though for appearances and for the morale of his men, he said nothing of it aloud. He had believed that by now he would be basking in glorious conquest of some "fertile and abundant province," but instead he had nothing to show for his labors, nothing of merit to report to the throne. It was now painfully obvious that what cinnamon trees he had discovered were too few, and too scattered, to be commercially viable as a crop for Spain. Nor were there roads allowing unencumbered travel to exploit even these paltry specimens. Disillusioned, Pizarro was eventually forced to report to the king:

> We found the trees which bear cinnamon . . . which is in the form of flower buds . . . and these trees were on some mountainsides very rugged, unsettled and uninhabitable; and some of the trees were small and others somewhat larger in circumference,

and they stood at long stretches from one another. It is a land and a commodity by which Your Majesty can not be rendered any service or benefitted in business, because the cinnamon is in small quantities and [would be a source] of even smaller profit.

Pizarro and his men emerged from the forest and could see a large river. He had found the upper reaches of the Napo. The Spaniards felt relieved to at last have open sky above them, and they camped on a wide, level, and sandy beach along the riverside. Their respite was short-lived. That night, it rained so hard that the Spanish sentries stationed around the camp believed the rain pounding the ground, the trees, and the river itself to be the sound of enemy war drums, and they cried out in warning, waking the men, who leaped up and brandished their arms. The river rose and raged ashore in a violent flash flood, carrying away some of their bags and provisions, and they were forced to retreat hastily to higher ground for safety, lest they be swept downstream themselves. In the morning Pizarro surveyed his men, then peered up at a green expanse where "ranges of forest clad and rugged mountains stretched in all directions." Perhaps, though he was racked with doubt, somewhere out there was El Dorado. Pizarro, by now deeply depressed, decided that his only choice was to backtrack the way they had come and return to the Valley of Sumaco, where he hoped, even prayed, that Francisco Orellana and his main force still remained.

CHAPTER 4

El Barco and the San Pedro

*P*IZARRO BACKTRACKED, BUT SOON—PERHAPS DRIVEN to leave the thick, closed-in country—he veered toward the north, away from Sumaco and his main force. At length he and his men came to a large river, and they immediately searched for a place where they might cross. They had found the mighty Coca River, a principal tributary of the Napo. The river was far too wide to cross where they came upon it, a few miles south of two small villages called Capua and Guema, and for a time Pizarro was at a standstill, contemplating what to do.

It was not long before a few Indians materialized, paddling across the wide waters from a village on the other side. They approached in a friendly manner, exhibiting no hostility or show of arms. Remarkably, one of the first to disembark turned out to be their chief, a brave and curious man named Delicola. He had received reports from neighboring upriver tribes—and from his own messengers—of trespassing foreigners and their recently perpetrated atrocities, and he had decided to investigate, to see for himself who these invaders might be and what they might want. Pizarro, learning through crude interpretation that Delicola was a chief, and noticing that he was flanked by fifteen or twenty attendants, received him with as much honor and ceremony as he could, bestowing on him gifts of "combs and knives," which seemed to please him.

The men took a parley. Pizarro inquired, through leading questions that were characteristically devoid of tact, whether beyond, downstream, there might be lands more civilized and richer than these, lands where there might be gold. Perhaps there was even a place and chieftain known as El Dorado? Delicola took little time in answering, for armed with the knowledge of the fate that had befallen his neighbors, he was apparently eager to give these foreigners answers they wanted to hear and thus send them on their way. The clever chief nodded, yes, downstream to the east there were indeed lands and provinces that were very rich, lands ruled by powerful overlords. Delicola was not particularly specific, but that did not seem to matter to Pizarro and his men; they had been gone from Sumaco nearly two months, and were hungry both for food and for the renewed hope of riches. They were ready to believe just about anything that Delicola told them.

The information bolstered Pizarro and his men, and in this way Delicola ensured that he would not be tortured, though he was immediately put under close guard and not allowed to leave. Instead, Pizarro appropriated him as a guide in their quest downstream, for it was clear that the chief knew the country intimately. Though he did not appreciate being taken, in effect, prisoner, Delicola possessed enough wisdom (and certainly a degree of fear) to acquiesce to the arrangement, at least for the time being. Even with Delicola as a guide, the going was rough and dismally slow—at times only a few miles of progress for an entire day—so steep and brambly and cavernous was the terrain. The sheer hills buttressing the river were riddled with landslides, and the men suffered terribly.

During their descent the men began to hear a strange, distant, roaring echo, and they became wary, taking up their arms and remaining constantly alert. The whooshing roar grew louder and louder as they went, and after they had traveled some ten miles the sound was so loud that they could no longer hear one another's voices. They discovered the source of the noise: the San Rafael Falls,* a tremendous rush of

---

* Ecuador's highest waterfall.

water cascading more than five hundred feet into a dark chasm and sending clouds of spray hundreds of feet back up into the sky. It was an awesome, humbling spectacle, and they were forced around the deadly slick vertical walls of its mouth. Not much farther downstream the river narrowed and they approached a natural phenomenon equally impressive: a river gorge "so narrow it was not twenty feet across, yet as far down to the river as the water falls." Here, using deadfall trees they found nearby and cutting others down, the Spaniards made a serviceable but terrifying and dangerous wooden bridge and carefully began crossing the gorge to scout the opposite side of the river. According to one chronicler, the defile was so deep and daunting that it was "rash even to look down, and one Spaniard who dared to look from the brink of the precipice down into the rushing stream in the gorge grew giddy and fell [to his death] into the torrent below."

The harrowing crossing was only one of the Spaniards' problems. Local Indians on the north bank, having seen the Spaniards at work on the bridge, banded together to defend their territory. They dug deep trenches, fabricated forts with wooden barricades, and took up arms, and when the Spaniards reached the opposite side of the chasm they were met with a hail of spears and arrows. Pizarro acted quickly, ordering forward a handful of harquebusiers, who fired on the attackers. Almost instantly a half-dozen Indian warriors were slain, pierced through with metal balls. The shocking, apparently instantaneous deaths confused and terrorized many of the Indians, who struggled to comprehend what had caused their comrades to writhe and bleed and die. "The rest fled in astonishment at so strange a thing as seeing their companions slain at a distance of a hundred or two-hundred paces. They went off spreading reports of the wildness and ferocity of the newcomers, saying they wielded thunderbolts and lightning to kill any who disobeyed them."

Once across the gorge and with the bridge now secure, Pizarro marched in and captured a few of the chiefs of the villages on the north bank and put them in chains. He encamped there at Guema, still guarding the bridge, and dispatched two of his messengers back to Sumaco to retrieve Lieutenant-General Orellana, who was to lead the main force, presumably now rested and recovered, to Pizarro's camp on the north side of the Coca. It was a poor place with very little food to pilfer, but it offered one important geographical advantage: it was on a high savanna, a long, flat area that made for a comfortable camp and offered some vistas over the lands downstream. From here, the plan was to continue descending the Coca along its north bank.

Orellana arrived quickly, ready to serve in any way he was asked. Once the entire expeditionary force was reunited at Guema, the captains discussed their options. They decided to send campmaster Antonio de Ribera and fifty able men downstream to reconnoiter the territory and report their findings as soon as possible, which he did, according to Pizarro:

> He was fifteen days going and coming, and he brought back a story that he had found a great river, that there were houses right on the edge of the water, and that on the river he had seen many Indians wearing clothes, going about in canoes, and that it seemed to him that the province was a thoroughly settled one, because the Indians he had seen wore clothes and were quite civilized.

Pizarro was elated by the prospect of advanced civilization. "As soon as he [Ribera] came with this story," wrote Pizarro, "I set out . . . to this province that is called Omagua."* Perhaps the stories that Delicola had told him were not exaggerated. Maybe he was on the verge of a fantastic discovery, as wondrous as that of his brother Francisco, or the legendary Hernán Cortés before him. Armed now with a concrete vision of a great empire to conquer, Pizarro and Orellana led the expedition down the

---

* Pizarro refers to these people as the Omagua, and he appears to be correct, though there is a great deal of confusion surrounding the name, and there may indeed have been other groups referred to (at least by Pizarro, and later Carvajal) as Omagua or Omaguas. For a modern analysis of the Omagua's range, see Antonio Porro, "Social Organization and Political Power in the Amazon Floodplain: The Ethnohistorical Sources," in Anna C. Roosevelt, *Amazonian Indians from Prehistory to the Present,* 81–83. See also Betty Meggers, *Amazonia: Man and Culture in a Counterfeit Paradise,* 122–30, and John Hemming, *Tree of Rivers,* 30.

thundering and roiling Coca River with renewed purpose. The breath-taking beauty of the river as it churned its way through gorges and cataracts, the lustrous verdure of the foliage against the wet-black rock walls—the wild magnificence was mostly lost on Orellana and Pizarro, so difficult was the travel.

As the expedition descended, they came upon a bluff providing a broader vista of the lands to the east, and they halted to gaze at this wide and wondrous and seemingly never-ending sprawl—a virtual sea of tree-tops—casting outward far beyond the eye's ability to see. The distances before them appeared incomprehensible, but Orellana and Pizarro immediately understood what they were looking at, and they were awed by the implications. They deduced, correctly (based on the little knowl-edge they had from the earlier Pinzón discovery of the mouth and Ordaz's botched upriver attempt at the mouth), that the Coca was an arm of the Maranon (Amazon), and "must flow down to the Sweet Sea." This expedition of conquest was becoming one of discovery as well. For the next few weeks the force continued down the north bank of the Coca, hacking their way through thick forest until at last the landscape began to flatten onto a plain and the narrow current broadened into "a beautiful and abundantly flowing river." They had gone beyond the last of the giant cascades, and the river here was wide and calm, punctuated by lengthy exposed sandbars and a few small settlements that, according to Pizarro, "all have their homes and living quarters right down on the water's edge."

Soon the water was dotted with canoes traveling frenetically back and forth, dashing across, up, and down the river. Before any enemy attacks could be mounted, Pizarro determined to "reduce to a peaceful attitude of mind" these natives. He mounted a preemptive strike, making a show of force with cavalry and armed troops. Almost instantly the vil-lagers in canoes and along the shores were in general chaos, and many of them, including their chiefs, began to flee. "The natives were much alarmed at seeing the horses and so many Spaniards," reported Cieza de León. They were so terrified that "the chief wanted to plunge into the river and to take flight." Thinking this chief potentially useful, Pizarro captured him and had him put in chains alongside the other captive chiefs from upriver.

Upon seeing their chiefs mistreated, a throng of local warriors mounted an offensive in their canoes, urged on by the shouts of the captive chiefs from the shore, including Delicola. The Spanish numbers and firepower proved too much, however, and after a brief skirmish Pizarro had thwarted the attempted rescue and commandeered fifteen of the Indians' canoes.

With all the chiefs, including Delicola, now bound as prisoners and the village taken, Pizarro encouraged his men to learn to use the canoes, as they seemed to be the major mode of transportation along this wider river section. He sent small raiding parties inland on foot and downriver in the canoes in search of food, because stores were getting dangerously low. He cautioned those traveling on the water to remain close by, "because there were frequently on the river as many as a hundred or a hundred and fifty canoes, all warriors; and they are so skillful in propelling these canoes about and in steering them that for this reason no one stands any chance of doing them injury or of being able to defeat them."

The Spaniards were able to do some bartering with a few of the local villages, exchanging the beads and bells and baubles they had brought with them for local yuca (manioc) and fish, but there wasn't enough to sustain the more than two hundred famished Spaniards. The situation was becoming serious. Nearly all the native porters were by now dead or dying, succumbing to the smallpox and venereal diseases that the Spaniards had brought with them. Smallpox, which was initially introduced to the Americas by a slave traveling on a Spanish ship, was particularly devastating and horrific. The indigenous people possessed no immunity to the disease, and the porters broke out in flaming pustules and weals that gouged their faces and bodies. Some welts and blisters were so prevalent on the victims' faces as to render them blind. The sickest were abandoned, moaning and dying in the jungle or along the river's edge.

Pizarro and Orellana contemplated their options. Orellana was put in charge of the prisoner chiefs because of his talent for acquiring languages quickly. He spent time with Delicola and the others, learning the vocabulary of some of the local languages spoken by members of the upper Amazon, including Arawakan, Panoan, and Tupian. Orellana understood the tremendous importance of language and communication as a tool, and he began to keep a dictionary of vocabulary as well as practical words and phrases that would hopefully be useful in time. As he continued on the journey, Orellana would become a highly competent interpreter.* He spent time with Delicola and the other chiefs, trying to find out what he could about what lay downstream. What he neglected to learn, but ought to have, were practical survival tactics, including which forest plants were edible and how to hunt monkeys, tapirs, manatees, or caimans for food.

Pizarro continued to muse. His men were restless, but many were also sick and weak, and as this place was at least habitable, he was reluctant to depart just yet. It was the beginning of October, and they had been gone from Quito for seven torturous months, though they had traveled only some 150 miles. Then one day, while watching the ease of the canoes moving along the river, Pizarro had something of an epiphany: he would build a boat! It was a simple and obvious solution, thought Pizarro, as well as one driven by necessity. First of all, since nearly all the native porters and bearers had perished, there were not enough slaves to carry the Spaniards' heavy equipment. A boat would allow for conveyance of their arms and gunpowder and other stores, and also could carry the sick and injured. Orellana had learned from the chiefs that the river was the central highway or thoroughfare for as far as one could imagine, and that as a result, there were no roads along the way, only sparse footpaths between villages. Boats—especially canoes—were the primary means of travel.

Yes, a boat. Pizarro rounded up his captains and told them of his idea. Some of the captains, including Orellana, favored a retreat to the

---

* Orellana's interpretive skills were documented by Friar Carvajal: "After he came to these Indies, he always made it a point to get to understand the tongues of the natives and made his own elementary primers for his guidance; and God endowed him with such a good memory and excellent natural aptitude, and he was so expert in interpreting that, notwithstanding the numerous and varying tongues that there are in those parts, although he did not understand all the Indians entirely and perfectly, as he wanted to, still, as a result of the perseverance which he applied to this matter, devoting himself to this practice, he was always understood in the end, and he himself understood quite accurately." Quoted in José Toribio Medina, *Discovery of the Amazon,* 72n.

higher savannas, where they might, if fortunate, begin to find some roads or highland llama trails for easier passage, and larger settlements, similar to Sumaco, where they might find food. But Pizarro had made up his mind, and he later justified his decision in a letter to his ruler back in Spain:

> I found it advisable to build a brigantine to protect and accompany the canoes I had captured, and because we were compelled to search for food for the expeditionary force and to cross over the river from one side to the other in order to look for it, and without this brigantine and the canoes the men . . . could not be kept in condition, both from the point of view of food and from the point of view of the problem of transporting their weapons and the munitions for their arquebuses and crossbows and the other things indispensable.

Pizarro's move, while industrious and innovative, was clearly not without famous precedent. He certainly would have recalled the celebrated exploits of Cortés some twenty years earlier, which had now become Spanish (and particularly Extremaduran) legend: how he had harvested timber from the hillside of a dormant volcano, had his porters carry enough wood for thirteen brigantines fifty miles over a mountain pass, then cut a two-mile-long channel into the earth, fabricated the thirteen boats in a makeshift shipyard, and launched an armada onto Lake Texcoco, thus bringing the Aztec Empire to its knees. Gonzalo Pizarro's plan was significantly less ambitious—certainly he and his men could build one boat. But given their condition and the scant resources available to them, building any kind of navigable craft would prove difficult enough.

For the duration of the month of October 1541, the small riverside camp became a center of intense effort and activity. They dubbed the place El Barco, the Boat (which is present-day San Sebastián del Coca, about ten miles above the confluence of the rivers Coca and Napo), named for the ship the Spaniards would build there, which they prayed would be their salvation.

Once the decision was made, everyone, the captains included, devoted themselves to the task. According to one of the priests, Orellana "showed himself more active than anyone else in getting together the material that was needed." He hurried throughout the sodden camp, ordering all iron available, including that from spare horseshoes or those pried from the hooves of dead animals, to be brought forward. He also directed the felling and preparation of the necessary timbers, ordering these brought to selected soldiers from the port cities of Biscay and Andalusia, who had some shipbuilding experience and had been put in charge of the construction of the craft. The boatbuilding process was intricate and time-consuming, and it required the skill and ingenuity of all the men fit and able enough to work. Garcilaso de la Vega described the work:

> They set up a forge to do the riveting; and made charcoal with considerable difficulty, for the rain was so frequent that it prevented them from burning their fuel. They made shelter to cover it, and also huts to shelter from the rain, for though the country is under the equator and extremely hot, they had no way of protecting themselves from the downpour. Part of the riveting was made with the shoes of the horses which they had killed to give the sick food, and also to nourish those who were well when they had no other resources. Another part of the riveting was made of their own armor, which they valued more than gold.

Gonzalo Pizarro, for his part, worked tirelessly in concert with his captains, being among the first to fell trees, and he assisted in all aspects of the building, including the most demanding physical labor. They produced pitch for the boat from resin gleaned from trees, and with the aid of the native chiefs, they scoured the forest for the best lianas for strong cordage. The Spaniards also learned from the natives how to make heavy cordage from the inner bark, or bast, of the *Cecropia* tree, lighter-gauge cord from the fine cuticle peeled from the underside of young palm leaves, and narrow twine from the fiber of wild pineapple.

They calked the boat with stuffing made from their ragged or rotting shirts and cloaks, sealing the gaps with the pitch. Laboring for the better part of a month, by the end of October the Spaniards had built a worthy vessel that was "water tight and strong, although not very large." It was a rowing boat, propelled by six to eight oarsmen, just large enough to carry twenty to thirty men, plus the heaviest of their equipment and stores of food found along the way. They christened the craft the *San Pedro*.

On November 9, 1541, Pizarro and Orellana mustered the newly confident troops and prepared to move down the river, come what might. From up on the savanna, as they cast their gazes far to the east, the green horizon appeared misty and nubilous, their destination uncertain. But Pizarro was now at least hopeful, if not optimistic, and he had a general sense—though he had no idea just how far—of where these mighty rivers were headed. He had determined a course for his men, concluding that "if we did not find any good country wherein to found colonies, of not stopping until [we] should come out to the Northern Sea [the Atlantic]."

They launched the *San Pedro* from El Barco after celebrating mass. Twenty or thirty of the weakest and sickest men rode in the boat, which was captained proudly by Juan de Alcántara, whom Pizarro had charged with her safety. They burdened their new vessel with as much gear as she could safely stow, and flanked the open brig with the fifteen or so canoes stolen from El Barco and its environs, and in this way began to move down the Coca River, with Gonzalo Pizarro and the rest of the crew proceeding afoot along the riverbank, leading what few horses, swine, and war hounds remained. After ten brutal miles, they reached the confluence with the larger Napo River.

In the initial going the Spaniards encountered a few small villages and were able to acquire maize and yuca, and also some sweet-tasting guavas, "which afforded no small help to [the men] in their need." They stored what they could and moved onward, but eventually the villages grew farther and farther apart, then seemed to vanish altogether in the swampy maze. The going was haltingly, painstakingly slow. Deep side creeks frequently forced those on foot to build makeshift bridges, since attempts to leave the river and tramp inland to find crossings proved ineffectual and also risked their losing contact with the *San Pedro*, which

Pizarro had vowed not to do. To keep the party intact, Pizarro ordered that the marchers reunite with the boat each night and carve out a joint camp. "Continuing their journey down the river bank," recalled one chronicler, the expedition

> sometimes wished to diverge in one direction or another to see what the country was like, but the morasses and other obstacles were so great that they could not, and so they were obliged to keep along the river bank, though with much difficulty, for the creeks in the swamps were so deep that swimming the horses through them was an arduous task. Some Spaniards and horses were drowned.

Moving along like this, with the *San Pedro* periodically anchoring to wait for the slow procession straggling alongside, they kept on for "forty-three marches" (presumably forty-three days), encountering not a single day when they did not come upon numerous creeks to cross where they had to wade or swim the horses or construct bridges from felled trees. During these interminable weeks they encountered not a single inhabitant, and so little food that they were forced to consume the very last of their original herd of a few thousand swine. Game was scarce, but at any rate, even had Orellana learned from the natives how to hunt, there was hardly time for full-fledged hunting forays, as all their time and energy were occupied just trying to make it down the river-banks. Then, to make matters even worse, the trusted Delicola and the three other imprisoned chiefs, now far from their homes and fearing their disgruntled captors would eventually kill them, escaped, slipping into the river while still in chains and swimming away before they could be captured. Now the Spaniards were without guides or interpreters in this hostile and alien jungle.

By Christmas Day 1541, they were a threadbare and sorry lot. Gonzalo Pizarro ordered a halt and they pitched a camp. Perhaps he hoped that some respite from their toil might raise morale, which had plummeted to dangerously new depths. They were by now some 150 miles down the river and, according to the chronicles, "beginning to feel the pangs of hunger." This was a serious understatement. In fact, they were malnourished and starving, and perilously weak. Their Christmas meal, instead of roasted fowl or fire-spitted beef, was a thin gruel of boiled saddle leather. Discord and murmurs swirled through the camp, with some of the men even whispering of mutiny, so acute was their distress: "All of the companions were greatly dissatisfied and the talk was of turning back and not going ahead any farther." The friars held a somber mass, and the halting place was named, with a bitter irony, Christmas Camp. After nearly ten months of toil and hardship, the expedition had reached a critical impasse. Their options were running out.

Weakened physically but not altogether broken in spirit, Francisco Orellana called Captain Gonzalo Pizarro aside. They stood by the river's edge, its eternal current lapping at the muddy banks, eroding them away. The night animals began their crepuscular cries, their strange whirring and chirping and screeching, as Lieutenant-General Orellana pointed to the *San Pedro,* then to the river, and spoke honestly to his captain, his cousin and brother to one of the greatest conquerors in the New World. Francisco Orellana had an idea, a proposition, one that—while risky and dangerous and in no way certain—might save them all.

AT SOME POINT before Delicola slipped into the murky waters with the other chiefs and swam to freedom, he had told Orellana that they were headed into a great uninhabited region, a "vast one and that there was no food whatsoever to be had this side of a spot where another great river joined up with the one down which [the Spaniards] were proceeding, and that from this junction one day's journey up the other river there was an abundant supply of food." According to Delicola, this confluence of rivers was some days' journey downstream, and there they would find a place with "plenty of food and rich in gold and everything else they sought." Perhaps Delicola was merely reporting what he thought the Spaniards wanted to hear and thus filling them with false hope. But now, as Orellana looked at the condition of the men, even false hope seemed better than none at all.

It was clear that something different, and drastic, needed to be done. Orellana suggested that he take the *San Pedro* and a group of hand-selected men—some fifty or sixty of the best and fittest—and journey down the river in search of this branching place Delicola had described. Pizarro and the rest of the men would follow on foot and alternately in canoes at whatever pace they could muster. Orellana, after having found and secured food, would return upriver to bring the much-needed sustenance and succor to them. The vague plan appeared, under the circumstances, to be their only hope. Orellana estimated, based on what Delicola had told him, that it would take approximately twelve days to find the food and return.

Pizarro did not take long to sanction the suggestion. "Being confident that Captain Orellana would do as he said," wrote Pizarro, "because he was my lieutenant, I told him that I was pleased at the idea of his going for the food, and that he should see to it that he returned within the twelve days."

At first light on December 26, 1541, Orellana sprang into action. He ushered the sickly, injured, and infirm off the *San Pedro* and ensconced them as comfortably as possible at Christmas Camp. Orellana then began supervising the loading and securing of the brigantine. On board they retained most of the equipment originally carried by the native bearers, including heavy tools for construction; iron and horseshoes and tackle for additional boatbuilding or boat repair, should those be needed; blankets and woolens and any extra clothing and armor; and some harquebuses and crossbows, as well as spare ammunition and gunpowder.

Captain Orellana selected fifty-seven men for the journey, which turned out to be about one-fourth of the entire force. Among the men was Friar Gaspar de Carvajal, who would serve as both priest and recorder of the events, for he would keep a journal of their journey, and a scribe named Isásaga who would compose and execute legal documents. Two African slaves were also brought along. As many men as could fit in the *San Pedro* boarded it, while the rest slid into the canoes appropriated from the upriver Indian tribes (by now the expedition had acquired as many as twenty-two of the worthy craft), and with little ceremony Captain Orellana set out on his food-finding mission, bidding good-bye to Gonzalo Pizarro and the other men with whom he had lived and fought and suffered. The misfit armada cast off down the river, borne by the surging flow to points unknown, and soon the brigantine and the canoes dissolved into the green veil of forest, sweeping around a slow curve in the rain-engorged stream, and then they were gone.

CHAPTER 5

The Split

*T*HE *SAN PEDRO* COURSED DOWN THE SURGING NAPO, the river gaining mass and momentum as other streams and rivers joined it. With each additional river adding more volume and more speed to the current, they made good progress the first day. If Delicola's predictions of what lay ahead proved accurate, Orellana figured there would be no settlements or sustenance for some days, so he planned to course almost continuously, floating by day, only needing to steer to avoid snags and small islands and submerged trees. The first night they tucked into a calm eddy; the canoes pulled ashore and the men slumped in soaked piles on the boat's floorboards and along the banks, inside the canoes or underneath them. Thick swarms of mosquitoes tormented them constantly, so that sleep proved difficult.

On their second day of navigating downriver they narrowly averted disaster. The *San Pedro* was moving along well in the middle of the river when the men were jolted by a violent crash. The *San Pedro*, literally their lifeboat, foundered midstream, impaled by a giant log and in immediate danger of swamping, taking on perilous amounts of water. Fortunately a number of their companions in canoes were nearby and paddled furiously to the *San Pedro*'s side.

With great exertions, the party succeeded in "hauling the boat out of the water and fastening a piece of plank on it," and in miraculously little time they were on their way again, searching for the larger confluence that Delicola had vaguely described as being "some days' journey downstream."

They journeyed continuously for three days, still seeing no sign of human habitation nor an obvious junction, surrounded by forest sounds that grew ever more eerie and frightening—the piercing screams of monkeys and the rasping cries and throaty gulps of bizarre turkey-sized birds, hoatzins and horned screamers, that flew off as the boats approached. Fearsome great caimans lolled like logs in the brown river, slapping the water with their tails when disturbed. Along the shore, as well as in the water, the Spaniards watched warily for the giant constricting anacondas, the world's largest snakes, which can reach over thirty feet in length and which kill their prey (including humans) by coiling around them and squeezing them to death.

By the third day Orellana began to perceive a significant dilemma. The river was rising and moving faster and faster, "owing to the effect of many other rivers which emptied into it." There were so many, and of such size, that it was unclear which one might be the confluence or junction described by Delicola. Orellana now began to realize that returning to Gonzalo Pizarro, a plan conceived under extraordinary duress, would prove difficult, if not impossible, even should they find food. The river was carrying them at tremendous speed, and paddling back up it appeared out of the question. Orellana had already seen how brutally slow land travel was. To return up the river within the twelve-day time frame they had agreed upon now seemed unachievable, nor, at any rate, had they yet found food. According to one of the conquistadors, "the Captain and the companions conferred about the difficulty of turning back, and the lack of food." Their concern growing, the party floated onward.

They had passed impressive river confluences, the Yururi and the Tiputini, but still no trace of any people, hostile or otherwise. For two more days the armada of brigantine and canoes kept on, moving ever farther from their companions upstream, and with no indication of human settlement along their route.*

After nearly a week of their headlong rush downstream, some of Francisco Orellana's men were becoming disheartened, even distraught, and a few were delirious. Orellana ordered a halt to scour the shores for food, commanding the strongest Spaniards to enter the jungle and return with anything they could find. These men wandered about, some eating herbs and roots straight from the ground, grazing like stock animals. Reported Friar Carvajal:

> We reached a state of privation so great that we were eating nothing but leather, belts and soles of shoes, cooked with certain herbs, with the result that so great was our weakness that we could not remain standing, for some on all fours and others with staffs went into the woods to search for a few roots to eat and some there were who ate certain herbs with which they were not familiar, and they were at the point of death, because they were like mad men and did not possess sense.

Captain Orellana, seeing his men in such a state, called on his scribe and friar to say mass as it is said at sea. Friar Carvajal commended to God their persons and their lives, and he asked that "Our Lord deliver us from such manifest hardship and eventual destruction, for that is what it was coming to look like to us now." After mass, Orellana moved about his discouraged men, encouraging them, rallying them, and reminding them to have confidence in their God, for as it was He who had cast them upon this river, "He would see fit to bring us to a haven of safety." Spurred for the moment by Orellana's oratory, the men boarded the boats once again and continued their journey.

---

* One reason for this wide dispersal of settlements was the result of intertribal warfare. On this stretch of Amazonia, tribes lived great distances from each other, periodically going on raiding excursions during which they would take women and children as captives. "On capturing a village they would take the women, also the children whom they enslaved, and would slaughter the men, or drive them into the jungle. The village would then be burnt, and its fields swallowed by the jungle." J. M. Cohen, *Journeys Down the Amazon*, 35–36.

On New Year's Day 1542, a strange and ghostly phenomenon occurred. As the men lay strewn in the boat, listlessly rowing, listening to the languid slosh of the river under the bow or the rush of warm wind across the várzea (flooded areas next to the river), Captain Orellana heard a low and timpanic thumping, like a hollow echo far off in the distance. The sound of drums.

Orellana listened intently, straining to hear and asking for silence, entreating the others to listen as well. He told his men that he believed he had heard the war drums of Indians. Had others heard them, too? Some, perhaps not wanting to disappoint their leader, agreed, saying that yes, they had. Others said they had heard nothing but wind and the sounds of the river, and the coughs and moans of their sick companions. Still, the hope of civilization—even if it was only illusory—bolstered their spirits, and the oarsmen dug into the water with renewed vitality, churning away enthusiastically. Men were put on watch, and they scanned the green horizon with piercing eyes, hoping to see some movement ashore, perhaps children playing by the water or women collecting fruits or nuts. But all that day, and all the next, they saw nothing, and Orellana feared that perhaps the drums had been only a hallucinatory figment of his desirous imagination, his mind now playing devious tricks on him.

A sense of despondency now overtook everyone. "Sick and sound alike, the men lost spirit, thinking that there was no hope left of escaping with their lives." Late on the evening of Monday, January 2, 1542, a week after leaving Christmas Camp and five days from his promised rendezvous with Pizarro, Orellana ordered a halt and brought the armada together, tying the brigantine to trees onshore and landing the canoes. The cooks boiled herbs and roots and saddle-strap soup, and the men slumped and groaned in their anguish. Then, as Orellana sat spooning thin gruel through his parched and cracked lips, he heard it again. The notes came from far away, distant and undefined at first, then clearer, a *bum-bum-bum, bum-bum-bum* that was unmistakably war drums. Carvajal recalled with excitement, "The Captain was the one who heard them first and announced it to the other companions, and they all listened, and they being convinced of the fact, such was the happiness which they all felt that they cast out of their memories all the past suffering because we were now in an inhabited country and no longer could die of hunger."

Orellana was certainly encouraged by the prospect of food, but he was less giddy and more circumspect than his men. As their leader, he was acutely aware of their diminished capacities, and he deeply feared an attack upon the company in their condition. Whatever tribe this was pounding on its drums had certainly already seen the Spaniards and was now preparing for war. He immediately stationed watches at each quarter and rallied the men to stay on high alert. As darkness fell, Orellana became increasingly concerned. "And so that night a heavy watch was kept, the Captain not sleeping." In fact, none of the men could sleep, so piqued were their spirits now with the prospect of food, perhaps as early as daybreak, "for they had had their fill of living on roots."

Sunrise came without incident, and Orellana leaped to action, quietly marshaling his troops, ordering the crossbowmen to prepare their bolts, the harquebusiers to secure dry powder and a supply of balls. All the men, sick and decrepit as they were, now strapped on armor and hoisted shields and swords, exhorted by their leader into battle mode. As stealthily as they could, they loaded into the *San Pedro* and the canoes and cast off to meet whatever foe might lie ahead. They were conquistadors once more.

They did not have to wait long for an encounter. About seven miles downstream, Orellana spotted four canoes ahead, each filled with Indians on what appeared to be a scouting mission. When the Indians witnessed the brigantine coming at them—without question the first such craft they had ever encountered—they turned sharply about and sounded an alarm, calling out and waving their arms, blowing whistles and pounding on drums. Then they disappeared downstream in their canoes, ripples fanning in their wakes.

Within minutes, Orellana and his men heard, now loudly and clearly, the distinctive pounding of war drums, first directly below them, then farther off, like a message or a warning being sent from one village to the next. "We heard in the villages," recalled Friar Carvajal, "many drums that were calling the country to arms. The drums are heard from very far off and are so well attuned that they have their harmonizing bass and tenor and treble." Orellana knew that he had little time to waste, so he goaded the oarsmen to row with all their strength, hoping to reach a village before great numbers of warriors could assemble, against which he knew he and his men stood no chance.

Very shortly, they saw ahead many villagers gathered along the riverbanks, brandishing spears and wooden clubs and chanting. Certainly the natives must have been dismayed by these hairy, grizzled, and bearded white men descending upon them, the first such human beings they had ever seen in a boat of a size and shape that defied explanation. Orellana's men, crazed with hunger as they were, still managed to follow his orders, which he had assured them were the keys to their survival. On they came, and at last they arrived at the first village they had seen since setting out in the *San Pedro* eight days before.

They beached the *San Pedro* just above the village, the mercenary soldiers leaping from the gunwales and clambering to shore in a show of force and in formation, harquebusiers and crossbowmen on their flanks for protection. They were followed closely by the canoes. The aggressive maneuver worked, for as the Spaniards stormed the village the warriors fled, no doubt shocked by these alien beings bearing steel swords glinting in the sunlight, their armor clanking. Orellana first thoroughly searched the village for warriors in hiding, but to his relief he found the huts empty; all the women and children had been evacuated, and the warriors were now congregating along the banks just downstream, as well as in large flotillas of canoes nearby.

Orellana placed his armed guards about the perimeter of the village and ordered all food brought to a central location, where the men could eat in ordered turn while others stood guard. Mercifully, there was plenty. The men showed considerable discipline, given their level of starvation and the euphoria of finally devouring fruits and chugging down gourds of maize or manioc beer called *chicha*. Other food—fish and birds and the meat of monkeys, which the villagers had recently prepared for themselves—was also procured from the various huts and brought forth. For a time the Spaniards ate like famished predators guarding a kill, hunched over, devouring, while the guards stood at the ready, "their shields on their shoulders and their swords under their arms, watching to see if the Indians were turning back on [them]."

The Spaniards satiated themselves in this way for hours, until early afternoon, increasingly watchful of attack. Small bands of warrior canoes paddled back and forth in front of the village, daring to come closer and closer on each pass, and increasing numbers of foot warriors gathered along the banks. Orellana surveyed the situation. A violent encounter appeared imminent.

Realizing that they were outnumbered and that despite the recent sustenance, his men were no doubt still too frail to put up much of a fight, Orellana strode toward the shore and took up a position on the high riverbank. Using language he had learned from Delicola and the other native chiefs and guides, Captain Orellana assured the assembled Indians that they need not fear and urged them to come close, for he only wished to talk. In time, two brave Indians approached, and resorting at times to his rough lexicon, Orellana continued with passive overtures of friendship, proffering some small trinkets reserved for such purposes as well as some Spanish clothes. He asked that they take these and his words of peace to their own lord, for he wished to parley with him.

Almost immediately, an overlord did return. Orellana understood this man to be a chief because, compared to the other warriors, he was attired in more ceremonial garb. The chief appeared peaceful, and he walked directly to Orellana and his captains, all of whom welcomed him with warm embraces. Orellana proceeded with an elaborate presentation of gifts, including Spanish boots and belts, and other items that, though hardly useful, would have been intriguing to the chief. After these formal introductions and pleasantries, the chief asked if there was anything in particular that Orellana and his men needed (he no doubt knew from messengers by now that the Spaniards had been singularly focused on food since their arrival). Orellana was quick in his reply: at present, the only thing they required was food.

The chief issued orders to some of his men, waved them away, and soon food in abundance began to arrive, a bounty in woven baskets: "meats, partridges, turkeys, and fish of many sorts." The Spaniards were elated. Orellana thanked the chief profusely and then asked whether he might persuade other chiefs from the surrounding area to visit, as Orellana wished to speak with them as well. The chief took his leave, saying that indeed he would return with others, for there were thirteen lords in the vicinity, and they, too, would want to meet these Spaniards.

So, Captain Orellana's first encounter with a native village had been a generally peaceful one. It is clear that his approach of using language and diplomacy before violence was effective, at least in this instance, and a diametric departure from the techniques favored by his own captain, Gonzalo Pizarro, who no doubt would already have tortured and killed a good portion of the villagers. Orellana's leadership and tactics—and his skill with oratory and communication—did not go unnoticed by his friar, who claimed "his knowledge of the language was, after God, the deciding factor in preventing us from perishing on that river."

The village was called Imara, and given the apparent cordiality and generosity of their hosts, Orellana thought it prudent to stay for a time, at least until his men could recover their strength. Seven of the Spaniards, despite now receiving regular sustenance, were fatally ill from a combination of starvation, exhaustion, and fevers, and they lay convulsing in tremulous agony. Orellana knew, also, that he must decide what to do about his own leader, Gonzalo Pizarro, and his compatriots awaiting food many days and now hundreds of miles back upriver.*

The village of Imara was a godsend to Orellana's company. It rested on an elevated bank above the river, carved out some distance away from one of the many miasmatic swamps that characterize Amazonia. The people of Imara were probably ancestors of the Huaoranis (or Waoranis), and the village was simple, yet organized, comfortable, and well designed. The tidy huts were framed with strong bamboo stalks, and had thatched roofs to keep out the torrential rains and oppressive sun, and walls of woven plant fibers and strips of leaves. To avoid inundating floodwaters, they were built on stilted platforms so high above the ground (some more than ten feet) that stairs, cut from tree trunks,

---

* Carvajal reports a distance of some 620 miles, which is a considerable exaggeration—but at any rate they were a tremendous distance downstream.

were required to enter the main rooms. Around the huts lay cleared plantations of yuca and maize. Canoes were moored or beached at the riverside, next to fishing nets hung from trees and other gear—javelins and darts and throwers, used for hunting and fishing.

Orellana and his men were hosted there in comfort, and over the next few days, villagers approached these strange foreigners warily, the men mostly gawking with fascination from a safe distance, the women bringing food. Regardless of the hospitality, Orellana maintained constant round-the-clock surveillance of the perimeter, keeping armed guards always at alert. The people of Imara appeared friendly, and gave every indication of tranquillity, but the trust of a conquistador like Orellana only extended as far as his sword point, and he had no intention of appearing vulnerable to an attack.

In due course some of the region's chiefs arrived as well, one after another in ordered succession, coming to show their respect but also out of deep curiosity to see what the Spaniards looked like and to witness firsthand their inexplicable weaponry and their stupendous watercraft. Orellana was happy to oblige, and once all the chiefs had assembled, Orellana decided that the time was right for the standard *requerimiento.*

Despite Orellana's linguistic skills, it is inconceivable that the villagers and their chiefs would have completely understood the far-reaching import and utter affront of the *requerimiento,* which, of course, required they accept Christ in lieu of their own gods and the Spanish king as their sovereign, and that they become vassals of Spain and subject to Christian preaching and education, for which they would receive untold rewards, including peace, prosperity, and everlasting life. If they had fully comprehended, they might well have swarmed the Spaniards en masse straightaway, killing them down to the last man. Regardless, Orellana—as a dutiful conquistador—stood before his gracious hosts and, with his men of the cloth and the Basque scribe Francisco de Isásaga at his side, "spoke to them at great length on behalf of His Majesty, and in the latter's name took possession of this said land." Orellana had a cross erected in the village, but no baptisms or conversions took place just yet, for Orellana had more pressing business matters to attend to.

To ensure the legality of his actions—as was the Spanish custom—Orellana directed Isásaga to draw up the official documents, and that done, he gathered his men together both to rally their morale and to discuss their options, to talk to them "on the subject of what steps it was proper to take in the interest of their expedition and their salvation." Despite the good fortune of their arrival among the nonviolent and generous people of Imara, Orellana well comprehended that their condition remained tenuous. By the rough calculations of some of his men with navigational understanding, since they had left Pizarro at Christmas Camp, the river had swept Orellana and his companions hundreds of miles downstream, certainly well past Delicola's vaguely described confluence. After much contemplation and discussion, Orellana broached the topic of heading back upstream, at the very least sending a small contingent to inform Gonzalo Pizarro of the dire reality—that bringing food in sufficient quantities was not going to be possible.

The men were bolstered by Orellana's speechmaking and impressed with his show of leadership thus far. "The companions were very happy to see the good courage that the Captain had within him and to see with what patience he bore up under the hardships which were falling to his lot, and they spoke to him some very kind words," assuring him that they were united, and behind him, whatever he chose to do. Yet there were murmurs among some that they hoped going back upriver was not among his wishes, so desolate was the uninhabited land that lay behind them. Memories of intense hunger were still very much in the men's minds.

Francisco Orellana fully understood his orders, however, and knew that Pizarro and the rest of the men were no doubt, as had been previously agreed upon, making their way downstream after Orellana, looking for any signs of where he might have camped, or any messages. Pizarro might well have found the junction that Orellana had clearly missed. Dutifully, he offered a monetary incentive to any six able men who would head back up the river in two canoes. He added that they could take with them the two black slaves and some Indian guides from Imara as oarsmen, and asked that these volunteers carry with them letters describing the "news of what was happening."

The men hemmed and grumbled, discussing Orellana's proposal. They mulled it over, some arguing that the length of time it would take to go back upstream would result in certain death, so that no amount of money would be worth it. Others reasoned that by now Captain Pizarro had probably turned back anyway, or gone off in search of food on his own. They had come eight days downstream. Who could even begin to imagine how long it would take them—should they miraculously survive the ordeal—to go back? It was certain suicide.

In the end, only three volunteers came forward, perhaps hoping to endear themselves to their captain with a show of bravado. However, they eventually balked, too, by adding an impossible contingency: they would go only if some of the crossbowmen and harquebusiers came along. Orellana, as fair and diplomatic a captain as he was, could not afford to spare his only weaponry, and in any event neither the cross-bowmen nor the harquebusiers had any interest in going. They were at a stalemate. Tension hung as thick as the humid air around them. It was, of course, well within Orellana's power at this moment to simply order at swordpoint certain men to make the voyage. But he was of a different mien and temperament; he was a different kind of leader. Orellana's priest would later say that his captain believed, both in his dealings with the natives and with his own men, "that kind treatment was the proper procedure to be followed."

Orellana stood on the banks of the Napo and on the brink of a momentous decision. From just beyond, in the village, came the raspy sound of women grating manioc on boards, the pulp from the tasty tubers falling into long wooden urns. Squealing children scurried about naked, their tiny feet squelching in the mud. Orellana knew that once he decided to continue downstream, there would be no turning back. He also knew how his actions would be perceived: as insubordination at the very least, as mutiny or treason at the worst. The man he would be disobeying was the brother of the richest and most powerful man in the viceroyalty of Peru, perhaps—it could be argued—among the most pow-erful and influential men in the world. Gonzalo Pizarro's reputation for violence, cruelty, and harsh punitive measures was legendary—he was known to have stolen the imprisoned Manca Inca's wife for his own sexual pleasure, and he indiscriminately tortured ruler and peasant alike. There was no benefit to being on the wrong side of the Pizarros, and Orellana fully comprehended that the Spanish penalty for treason was death. Depending on how the ruthless Gonzalo Pizarro interpreted his second-in-command's actions, Orellana risked finding himself at the receiving end of a garrote or a sword blade.

But great leaders must make difficult decisions. Orellana made up his mind, though he told no one of his exact plans just yet. They would not attempt to go back upstream, but would rather remain in Imara for a time, to see if Gonzalo or any of his men or messengers arrived from Christmas Camp. In the meantime, Orellana called forth a few of his trusted men and, under the thrum of the forest canopy, gave them their new orders: some were to gather the remaining horseshoes stored in the holds of the *San Pedro;* others he dispatched to the interior to begin felling trees. While they waited for any news from Pizarro—news that both Orellana and his men suspected would never come—they were going to build a forge and a nail-making factory right there in the middle of the Amazonian jungle. The men turned resolutely to their work, and every one among them knew exactly what this meant.

They were building another boat.

CHAPTER 6

The Plight of Gonzalo Pizarro

*A*FTER GONZALO PIZARRO AND HIS MEN—SOME TWO
hundred of them—had waved good-bye to Orellana and
the *San Pedro* back on Boxing Day at Christmas Camp on
the Middle Napo, they had waited a few days, mired in
hunger and inactivity. Pizarro knew that men of action
grew depressed when sedentary, and at any rate the agreement with Orellana had been for Pizarro to begin making
his way downstream on land, thereby shortening the distance Orellana would be forced to return. A place of
potential rendezvous—roughly, for this had never been formally worked out and none of them had ever been there—
was the confluence of the Napo with what Chief Delicola
had described as a very large river, the Aguarico, as it is
known today. So Pizarro rallied his men and what horses
remained and prepared them for a series of difficult day
marches.

Just as it had been from El Barco to Christmas Camp,
the jungle trekking was slow and arduous, with the fittest
men breaking trail, hacking and swinging with machetes
and swords through the sultry days, the muscles in their
shoulders and forearms burning with every passing hour
and every excruciating mile. According to Cieza de León,
"There was not even any track to follow. To enable them to
proceed and bring along the horses, the strongest men went

ahead, opening a road with axes and wood knives, never ceasing to cut through that dense wild in such a way that all the camp could pass and journey eastward." Moving on foot and leading the horses through these jungle and rain forest landscapes, the Spaniards averaged no more than three miles a day, forging and scything their way down the tangled banks of the Napo, scrambling over slimy downed ceiba trees or crawling through the tangled roots of strangler figs, the roots and branches seething with spiders the size of a man's hand. During the long, dreadful nights, they shared the ground with hordes of army ants and the dreaded conga ants, whose sting is among the most painful in the world, causing hallucinations in some victims and reducing even the toughest men to agonized writhing.

To make conditions even worse, according to Cieza de León, "the heavens poured down water from their clouds in such quantities that for many days, including nights, the rains never ceased." After a few days of such toil, including wading and swimming across deep tributaries and marshy areas, Pizarro and his men halted and looked out across a giant swamp, with a huge island far in the distance. It appeared to be, on first observation, impassable. Assessing the predicament, Pizarro sent out a few scouting parties, some to forage for food and others to assess any alternatives for crossing the swamp from an inland route.

The food scavenging did not yield much, mostly fruits and plants utterly foreign to the Spaniards, but there was one significant stroke of luck, which Gonzalo Pizarro described as "a miracle," in which he "personally captured . . . five canoes from the Indians."* Because no skirmishes or encounters with Indians were recorded, it seems likely that Pizarro had happened across canoes abandoned by Indians who had vacated the area. Regardless, the windfall provided Pizarro with at least one option: he would send Captain Alonso de Mercadillo across the swamp and down the river "with a dozen Spaniards . . . to see if there was any sign of Francisco de Orellana, and to seek for some fruit or roots by which the Spaniards might be sustained."

---

* Although the records do not explicitly clarify this, Gonzalo Pizarro's delight at acquiring these five canoes suggests that Orellana and his men had taken with them all 22 canoes that the expedition had obtained when Orellana departed Christmas Camp on December 26, 1541.

Mercadillo's party left immediately. Pizarro kept the remaining men occupied with periodic food forays, though by now he must have understood what a mistake it had been not to learn about edible forest foods from his native captives when he had had the chance. The tribes throughout Amazonia are expert in living off the land, and millennia of coexistence in the tropical jungles taught them how to differentiate safe plants from poisonous ones, how to collect and drink rainwater with palm leaves, and even ways to extract salt from specific types of plant buds. This last would have been vitally useful, as all the men suffered from salt depletion by then. As it stood, the Spaniards bided their time, catching and eating lizards and snakes and even some grubs and insects, deciding to hold their remaining horses and dogs in reserve in case things got even worse. Said Pizarro, "We were forced to eat the little buds of a plant, like a vine stalk."

After eight days, Mercadillo and the small scouting force returned bearing bad news: they had found nothing. No food, no villages, no sign of Orellana. Pizarro was beginning to wonder what might have befallen Orellana and whether he would ever see his captain again. Had they been attacked by Indians farther downstream, killed in some godforsaken place along this unmapped river? Was Orellana lost up some circuitous tributary? Or—and this thought was perhaps the most repugnant and vile of all, almost unthinkable—could Orellana have intentionally deserted them? Reduced now to eating nothing but "wild herbs and coarse fruits never before seen or known" (at least not to them), Pizarro cast his gaze out at the great swamp and the island looming like a mirage beyond, and pondered the idea of building another boat.

Gonzalo Pizarro consulted with his captains, and while they agreed that a boat would be a tremendous help—indeed, might even save their lives—there were problems with the plan. Building the *San Pedro* had taken a Herculean effort, and the men were now even weaker, if such a thing were possible, than they had been then. What was more, Orellana had with him most of the tools and the salvaged iron horseshoes, iron necessary for making the nails to hold a boat together. Right now, Pizarro conceded, building a boat would be too difficult. Food was the essential thing.

Gonzalo Pizarro called forth his trusted countryman Gonzalo Díaz de Pineda, the battle-hardened veteran who just a few years earlier had led the initial expedition from Quito over the Andes in search of the Land of Cinnamon. Now Pineda's services, skills, tenacity, and spirit came to the fore, for Pizarro counted on him to succeed where Mercadillo had failed. He must descend the river far enough to find Orellana, and failing that, he absolutely must return with food. These were essentially his only options, lest they all perish here on this river of darkness and death.

As Pineda and his scouting party pushed off in canoes, their emaciated countrymen were eating the carcasses of dead dogs and horses, "without wasting any of the entrails, skin, or other parts, for all was food for the Spaniards." Pineda crossed the swamp, so focused on the import of his responsibilities that he would have been oblivious to the chatter of wattled jacana birds squawking off of their lily pads as the men paddled past, or the graceful silhouettes of resplendent scarlet macaws flying overhead. Pineda steered the canoes back out onto the Napo River, imploring his men to dig with deep purpose in every stroke.

For days they raced downstream, going well beyond where Mercadillo had been before, arriving finally at a river the chroniclers described as "larger and mightier than the one they had been navigating, the two becoming one." The Aguarico is also known today as "the gold-bearer" for the iridescent speckles of gold that sparkle in its sands. Reasoning that this must be the place that Chief Delicola had originally told them about, Pineda drew into an eddy and pulled the canoes ashore to do some reconnaissance.

Along the banks they began to see telltale signs—"cuts made by wood knives and swords"—of Orellana's passage. The marks on the trees, the trodden banks, areas cleared for sleeping, all were indications that Orellana had camped there, but there was no sign that he remained in the vicinity. It was obvious to Pineda, given the size of the river, that here was the place where Orellana should have waited after going up the Aguarico to find food—this was a likely rendezvous spot. But Orellana and his men had left nothing but transient traces—no letters or messages nailed to trees, no canoes left for support, no food, nothing. Pineda and his men were racked with discouragement, convinced now that, unless by some miracle Orellana had headed up the Aguarico River and was still there or making his way back down, their esteemed lieutenant-general was not coming back.

Armed with only the remote hope that Orellana was somewhere up the Aguarico, though this seemed extremely unlikely given how much time had passed, Pineda convinced his men, disconsolate though they were, that they themselves must ascend this other river in search of food. To sustain themselves for the difficult upriver journey, the men ate "palm shoots and some fruit stones which had fallen on the ground from trees, together with all the various kinds of noxious wild beasts which they had been able to find."

Pineda and his compatriots had by now learned to use the tippy native dugout canoes with serviceable skill, and they began their labored ascent. The work was backbreaking, as well as mentally exhausting, the current strong enough in places to make them feel as though they were paddling in place. Still, upstream they stroked, steadfast in their toil, until they had gone what they estimated was thirty miles. Finally, as they lurched their way upriver beneath the sun's furnace, they spotted something different along the bank line ahead. Beyond the shore, toward the interior, were clearings, and rows of what appeared to be crops, evidence of habitation. The men shook themselves alert, landed, and, swords brandished, went ashore to meet whoever might still be there.

To Pineda's great relief—for he and his men were in no condition to do battle—the place was abandoned. And to their delight—and, for some, salvation—it had been a large, well-organized, and highly productive yuca plantation. The fields were overgrown and looked untended, but still they found evidence of a once thriving farm, with "many very thick patches of yuca so large that the stems that came from their roots looked like a small forest." The plantation extended for a number of miles along the river, though any huts or dwellings the Spaniards encountered had been deserted long ago. Realizing that they were safe from enemy attack, the men fell to their knees in praise to their merciful God, then, despite Pineda's exhortations to restrain themselves, fell upon the yuca in a feeding frenzy.

Some bent over and some crawled around, pulling the bulbous tubers from the ground with as much zeal and excitement as they would have shown had they discovered a rich gold vein. Pineda must have had the wherewithal and good sense to start some fires for roasting the yuca, or even rooted around for abandoned cooking pots, for not all ate the raw plants. After the members of the scouting party were satiated they loaded their canoes high with as many of the roots as they could carry and hurried back down the Aguarico to where it met the Napo, then began the difficult upstream paddle, made even harder laden as they were with the yuca.

By the time Pineda returned to Gonzalo Pizarro and the wretched swamp camp, nearly a month had passed. For twenty-seven long days Pizarro and his men had waited, with each passing day their condition growing more and more hellish and their hope of survival diminishing. Wanting to preserve the last of their precious horses, they had subsisted on "nothing but saddle and stirrup leathers, boiled in water and afterward toasted over the ashes." Then, with nearly all hope lost, Pizarro and his men looked across the swamp and saw vessels approaching. They might have imagined or hallucinated hostiles at this point, but instead, as the boats drew closer, they "saw the canoes and learnt what they brought, and they all wept for joy."

After a brief reunion, the captains divided the yucas among the men, who tore at the vegetables, eating them unwashed and uncooked, many biting into the crunchy flesh with clumps of dirt still sticking to the tubers. Given the number of men and their level of hunger, they mowed through the few canoeloads of yuca in a very short time. Pineda reported to Pizarro that up the Aguarico River were vast plantations of the food stretching for many miles, and it was agreed that they should all make a concerted effort to hurry there.

During Pineda's absence, Pizarro had not been entirely idle, and the ablest men had built a few rafts by lashing downed trees together with vines and creepers. In this way they also lashed the canoes together with cords, and with the vision of the Aguarico yuca plantations having replaced their dreams of gold, they crossed the great swamp in shifts, swimming the remaining horses, some of the men clinging for their lives to the sides of the canoes. It took Pizarro and his men eight days to trample downstream to the Napo's confluence with the Aguarico, where they were confronted with another problem: the river was very deep here, and the yuca plantations, according to Pineda, were all on the other side. They would have to cross.

They spent the next week crossing over, using the tied-together canoes as rafts to ferry the men and remaining dogs, and again swimming the horses—though as Pizarro noted, not without loss. "I determined to take the expeditionary force across the large river in the canoes, in which crossing much difficulty was encountered, accompanied by a loss of horses due to the great size of the river and the depth of the water." Once across, Pizarro saw the blazes and tree marks left by Orellana, then turned and resolutely marched his troops upstream for thirty miles, making an average of three miles a day with difficulty, wading across creeks and streams and snake-filled bogs, sometimes sinking as high as their armpits.

On the tenth day they arrived at the abandoned plantations, famished beyond reason once again. They staggered through the fields of umbrella-shaped plant leaves. "As all came in an exhausted state," reported one chronicler, "not having eaten anything for so many days, they did nothing but pull up yucas, with the earth still sticking to the roots, and began to eat them at once." One Spaniard, a man named Villarejo, sat chewing on a "root of white color, and rather thick." According to his comrades, he had hardly even tasted it when he stood, then became delirious and unintelligible, then "lost his reason and became mad."

Not long afterward other compatriots, including some of Pineda's men, started falling sick, their bellies distending grotesquely, some flopping about the ground and moaning in agony. Nevertheless, Pizarro ordered camp made—they would stay for a time where there was a guaranteed food source.

Surely Pizarro, or some of the other men, had seen the elaborate sequential preparations of yuca conducted by the people of El Barco during their lengthy stay there, for yuca—as the Spanish call it—or manioc (*Manihot esculenta*), the "super-crop that enabled man to evolve from foraging to farming," was ubiquitous throughout the river populations of the Amazon. As it was the region's most important food source, great and systematic care was adhered to in its preparation. What Pizarro was coming to understand, through the hard experience of his sickening men, was that eaten raw, yuca was deathly poisonous.

There are two main types of manioc, bitter and sweet. Both are toxic in varying degrees, and unfortunately for Pizarro's men, the two varieties are extremely difficult to tell apart, especially for the uninitiated. "Subtle morphological traits differentiate the deadly 'bitter' from the innocent 'sweet' plants, and their recognition is literally a matter of life and death." Sweet manioc, though slightly poisonous, may simply be boiled or baked or roasted and eaten. Even consumed raw, though it will make one sick, it is not typically lethal. Bitter manioc, on the other hand, is full of cyanide (prussic acid) and requires elaborate preparation and leaching out of the cyanide before it is safe for consumption.

Certainly, throughout their stay in El Barco, the Spaniards had seen the villagers coming from the manioc fields, burdened by large carrying baskets strapped to their backs, the baskets brimming over with tubers. Once the manioc was harvested and collected and brought back to the village, the women loaded baskets full of the tubers, took them to the river, and submerged them, shaking them vigorously to clean the manioc tubers of dirt before peeling them of their outer skins, cutting the sweet manioc into chunks or slicing them, and leaving the poisonous manioc whole. Then began the essentially never-ending process of grating, using ingenious hardwood boards studded either with stone or hardwood, or with animal-based teeth, palmwood thorns or flecks of hardwood, or fish bones or bone splinters.

The women bend over these graters, or sit on the ground with the grater between their knees, and then, holding a tuber in each hand, grate vigorously back and forth until the tuber is mashed into a pulp.

The manioc pulp or mash is transferred to a *tipiti*, a long, tubular woven basket that closes at one end. About six or seven feet long, the *tipitis* hold the watery manioc mash, and, with a stone or heavy log tied to one end, compress it in order to leach out the poisonous prussic acid, making the manioc safe for consumption. Who knows how many people died from eating yuca tubers before this process was discovered? At any rate, the *tipitis* and the process proved a "groundbreaking invention," allowing varying forms of manioc—it is used as a porridge, as bread, as beverages both fermented and fresh—to become the essential mainstay carbohydrate diet throughout the Amazon, second only to rice as a crop of global significance.

Pizarro and his party remained at the yuca plantation camp for eight days, during which time the place became a macabre, almost ghoulish scene: men grew jaundiced and weak from vomiting, their stomachs bulging grossly, and they fell to the ground from dizziness, only to find themselves racked with terrible and incessant bouts of diarrhea. The men were described, with some understatement, as "very sick and sore, wan and wretched, and in such an afflicted condition that it was very sad to look upon them." Seeing his men sickening in their food lust, Pizarro and other captains must have realized the cause, for they are said to have "themselves grated the yucas by means of very sharp thorns that grow on certain trees in those forests, and made bread of the meal, finding it to be . . . wholesome." In this way, after cooking the yuca correctly, the men began to recover their strength, though a few died from cyanide poisoning and from overeating.

There was certainly no shortage of the croplands, which extended for many miles along the Aguarico River. Pizarro and his men reported that the plantations went on for 120 miles. The cultivated areas had likely been the domain of ancestors of the Siona-Secoya peoples, who once held sway up and down long reaches of the river but were apparently driven off by enemies, ironically providing Gonzalo Pizarro and his band with unlimited feasting (once they employed proper preparations and cooking techniques).

While at this camp, during which time Pizarro noted that he and his men "rested after a fashion, and . . . laid in a supply of food for another uninhabited stretch," the captain now understood with certainty that Francisco Orellana was gone. He had taken the brigantine, most of their weaponry, and the bulk of their tools and abandoned the main force.

Gonzalo Pizarro had been brooding about his vanished second for weeks, both while he had awaited Pineda's return and now, as his fury smoldered at the camp. He had been going over in his mind the agreement that he and Orellana had struck. The essential details of the plan appeared clear enough, and in fact both Pizarro and Orellana agree, in writing, on most of the particulars, though their renderings do differ in several crucial respects.* Pizarro would later record his version of their pact in a letter to his king:

> Captain Orellana told me that in order to serve Your Majesty and for the love of me he was willing to take upon himself the task of going in search of food. . . . And being confident that Captain Orellana would do as he said, because he was my lieutenant, I told him that I was pleased at the idea of his going for the food, and that he should see to it that he returned within the twelve days and in no case went beyond the junction of the rivers but brought the food and gave his attention to nothing else . . . and he answered me saying that by no means would he exceed what I had told him and that he would come with the food within the time that he had stated.

One can imagine Gonzalo Pizarro, whose temper is well documented, fuming by the fireside as he thought about Orellana. Words like *traitor, deserter,* and *mutineer* would have run through his mind, over and over, slapping him from sleep under the humming jungle canopy. Pizarro grew more incensed the more he thought about it, later adding in the missive,

> Paying no heed to what he owed to the service of Your Majesty and to what it was his duty to do as he had been told by me, his captain . . . instead of bringing the food he went down the river without leaving any arrangements for the aid of those who were to

* Orellana's version of their vague agreement, recorded by Carvajal, suggests that Pizarro was to await his second-in-command's return "as long as he should see fit, and that, in case [Orellana] did not come, [Pizarro] should not be concerned about him; and thereupon [Pizarro] told [Orellana] to do whatever he thought best" under the circumstances. José Toribio Medina, *The Discovery of the Amazon,* 170.

follow on, leaving only signs and choppings showing how they had been on land and had stopped at the junction of the rivers and in other parts . . . he thus [displayed] toward the whole expeditionary force the greatest cruelty that ever faithless men have shown.

Indeed, Gonzalo Pizarro now considered Francisco Orellana a mutinous traitor, and he resolved to deal with him as such. In the meantime, he had men to lead. As he saw it, they now had only one option, and in this respect the future, though dark and unknown, lay before him in simple clarity. He would abandon his quest for El Dorado and strike a retreat for Quito. He would rally his men, take what food they could, and continue up the Aguarico River, hopefully to its headwaters in the lower Andes, and then, God willing, he would make a final push back over the rugged mountains and descend into Quito.

If he ever saw that villainous rebel dog Francisco Orellana again, he would take justice into his own two hands, in the form of a razor-sharp Toledo sword.

CHAPTER 7

St. Eulalia's Confluence—The Amazon

*D*OWNSTREAM IN THE VILLAGE OF IMARA, FRAN-
cisco Orellana and his men labored on at their forest factory. Orellana had quietly determined, having seen that
downstream river travel was their only viable alternative,
that the salvation of his men and their expedition
rested not only on the continued seaworthiness of the *San
Pedro,* but on the construction of another boat. Moreover,
he had the vision to look many miles down the serpentine
and unexplored river, an astonishing distance he would
have had no way of truly comprehending or believing, to
imagine navigating all the way to the sea. According to
Friar Carvajal, Orellana knew that the *San Pedro* and the
canoes would not be enough to take them all the way to the
ocean:

> The Captain, seeing that it was necessary to
> make plans for what was ahead . . . [advised] that
> for this reason it was necessary to apply our wits to
> building another brigantine of greater burden so
> that we might sail on the sea . . . in spite of the fact
> that among us there was no skilled craftsman who
> knew that trade, for what we found most difficult of
> all was how to make nails.

Orellana's men worked diligently, following both his orders and his example, for rather then merely sitting idle and delegating, Orellana participated in all the various tasks that he asked of his men. Meanwhile, to Orellana's eternal relief and appreciation, their good hosts the Imarans offered workers to assist and continued to bring the Spaniards abundant quantities of food, which enabled them to work long and productive days.

Orellana and Friar Carvajal, who was always at his captain's side witnessing and recording the events as they transpired, observed that the chiefs and higher caste members went about wearing "jewels and gold medallions." The sight of gold certainly piqued Captain Orellana's interest and imagination, as it had been the expedition's primary goal, but he showed considerable restraint. One imagines that the likes of Hernán Cortés or any of the Pizarro brothers would have found a way to quickly appropriate the native treasure, but instead, Orellana chose an entirely different tack. "Never did the Captain permit that anything be taken away from them," it was reported, "or even merely looked at, in order that the Indians might not conceive the idea that we valued such things, and the more indifference we showed in this matter, the more gold did they put on." Orellana knew that his life and the lives of his men depended on the hospitality of his hosts, and he chose not to jeopardize that relationship, despite the Spanish propensity for gold lust.

One of the gold-wearing chiefs of the area, a man the Spaniards referred to as Aparia the Lesser, came forward to meet with Orellana. He was an elderly chief, quite talkative and forthcoming, and he had a fascinating story. He said that farther downstream there existed villages of wondrous wealth, and there was even a kingdom, ruled by a powerful overlord called Ica, located many miles inland up a tributary (perhaps the nearby Curaray), a kingdom rich in gold. Then Aparia the Lesser mentioned something even more compelling. He said that as a boy, he had visited a place far downriver that was peopled by fierce women warriors whom he had seen with his own eyes.

For Orellana and his men, stories of women warriors or "Amazons" would not have seemed fantastic or unbelievable, for it had long been believed that such women of legend—whose origin in classic mythology was north of the Black Sea—would be found in the New World. Columbus himself, back in 1493, had made reference to an island peopled only by women, women who periodically took men from nearby islands for procreation and who kept only female offspring. The grand conquistador Hernán Cortés had written to the king in 1524 about a place in the province of Ciguatan, south of Panama, "an island inhabited only by women, without a single man . . . and many of the chiefs have been there and have seen it." This island, according to Cortés, was also rumored to be rich in pearls and gold. Similar tales persisted among the conquistadors exploring throughout the Orinoco (Venezuela) as well as in the Colombian *llanos* (vast plains) between 1536 and 1538.

Orellana listened intently to the stories related by the chieftain Aparia the Lesser, filing them away in his memory. Perhaps spurred by the possibilities of wealth and exotic lands, he pressed upon his men the need to pursue their work with renewed enthusiasm and speed. Two men, Juan de Alcántara, a stout hidalgo, and Sebastián Rodriguez, a Galician, volunteered for the duty of nail fabrication, which greatly pleased their captain, who promised them payment and extra reward for their efforts. Orellana delegated others to continue with the forge and the charcoal:

> He ordered at once some bellows to be made from buskins, and all other necessary tools also. And he ordered other comrades to form groups and prepare good kilnfuls of charcoal. All this was promptly done. Each man took up his axe and went into the forest to cut wood and bring it on his shoulders to the village, a distance of nearly two miles. Then the pits were built with very great toil indeed, since our men being feeble and not expert in this kind of work collapsed under their loads; those who were too weak to cut wood worked the bellows, while others fetched water.

Orellana and his contingent, which was now down to fifty men—seven having perished since their arrival in Imara—spent three hard weeks at this work, toiling through incessant rains, oppressive heat and humidity, and clouds of mosquitoes. The mosquitoes were so thick and bothersome, in fact, that during certain times when the swarms were at their worst, each Spaniard had to be paired with a partner whose sole job was to use a coat or shirt to fan away the insects, or swat them from his companion so that he might continue using his hands. Despite these hardships, in under a month Orellana's makeshift industries had managed to produce "two thousand very good nails" as well as hardware to rig masts for an oceangoing vessel.

Near the conclusion of their arduous labors, Captain Orellana noted that the food deliveries from the people of Imara and the surrounding villages now came with decreasing frequency. Fifty hungry working men consume a great deal of food, and the Imarans were apparently giving their guests a hint that it was time for the Spaniards to be on their way. The locustlike consumption of food and resources, plus the noise and clanging of constant metalworking and the attendant smoke and stench from the forge fires, all disturbed the bucolic villagers. Sensing that they had overstayed their welcome, the Spaniards began storing food for departure, as Carvajal reported: "We laid in what foodstuffs we could, because this was not the time to stay any longer in that village, on the one hand, because, so it seemed, this was beginning to become irksome to the natives." They would have to build the second boat somewhere down the river.

Orellana wished to leave while relations with the Imarans were still cordial, and he ordered the men to begin readying for a prompt departure. There were, however, a few matters of political expedience to attend to before he left. Orellana, an ambitious and visionary dreamer, had certainly not forgotten why he had come here, why he had left the comforts of his home back in Puerto Viejo and risked his life. Before he had departed from Guayaquil, Orellana had been careful to lay out, in "memorial" documents that were legally registered with and signed by magistrates, the duties and services that he had already performed in service of the crown, all with a political eye toward someday becoming the independent governor of a region or province somewhere in these newfound lands, with the requisite legal and royal consent. He had yet to find the right place, but with the optimistic vision of a conquistador, he would continue to seek such a domain. But what he needed to do now was take the time to document his actions from his initial separation from Gonzalo Pizarro as well as from this point onward, being careful to address how his actions would be perceived and scrutinized back in Quito, as well as far away in his homeland of Spain.

His plan to send canoes back upriver to try to find the main force had met with a negative response. Aside from the few reluctant volunteers, most of the men had flatly refused, saying that they "feared certain death in view of the long time it would take them to make the journey," which they estimated at a few hundred miles against a very stiff current. Their refusal, Orellana now figured, might just work in his favor, providing a documented rationale for his decision to continue down the river system. Probably prompted by Orellana himself, the scribe Francisco de Isásaga, who had earlier been put in charge of recording everything of a legal nature that "may occur and come to pass" in his presence, now brought forth a petition and went about the camp, asking for signatures from the men.

The petition—written to Captain Orellana himself but clearly aimed at a higher audience, namely the king—claimed that despite Francisco Orellana's desire and entreaties to go back up the river, the men, for various reasons, pleaded otherwise. The petition reiterated the great distance they had come, the impossibility of "so up-hill a journey," and pointed to "how much more danger of death there would be for us were we to go with Your Worship back up the river!" Peppered with much beseeching and begging, the document ended by pleading that Orellana not place his men in the difficult position of having to obey him or otherwise appear as traitors, but assuring their captain that they would happily follow him by an alternate route "by which at least their lives might be saved."

Both of the priests present, as well as Isásaga and all the other members of the expedition (save two, who were either dying or too feeble even to mark an X with their hands) signed the document, which Isásaga folded and stored securely with the other important legal papers. The petition was a shrewd move by the politically savvy Orellana, for it provided written proof that his men had overruled his desires, and it essentially justified his decision to continue downstream on what was clearly now a "strange and hitherto never experienced voyage of discovery."

On February 2, 1542, after hearing mass and saying prayers for their fallen compatriots, Orellana and his captains bade farewell to the chiefs of Imara, including Aparia the Lesser, whose fanciful tales still hung in the air and fired the Spaniards' imaginations. Loaded with as much food as they could safely store in the *San Pedro* and the canoes, and the heavy nails and ironwork they had manufactured, the Spaniards lumbered out into the Napo River, riding its swift southeastward current once more.

The *San Pedro* and fleet of canoes had gone only a short distance when they reached the junction of another impressive river pouring into the Napo from its southern shores, coming at them with terrifying turbulence. It was the mighty Curaray River, a magnificent tributary that thunders its way from the eastern slope of the Andes and runs roughly parallel to, but south of, the Napo. Where the rivers met, the waters boiled like a muddy cauldron, and the oarsmen of the *San Pedro* and the men paddling the canoes dodged rolling and bobbing tree trunks and enormous knots of gnarled vegetation. The light canoes struggled, close to overturning, in violent whirlpools. Orellana directed the laden *San Pedro* to a safe eddy away from the dangerous confluence and paused to contemplate an upstream reconnaissance in canoes.

While the Spaniards were staying in Imara, one of the chiefs who came to pay a visit and bring food had said that he lived up a nearby river and was an important overlord of that domain, and Orellana suspected that this, the Curaray, was that river. Could it also be the river of Ica's realm that Aparia the Lesser had described? Orellana was tempted to explore the region, and in fact some of his men reported hearing drums emanating from up the river and then seeing "many Indians in canoes ready to defend the landing place." The prospect of encounter was tantalizing, but Orellana knew that getting the *San Pedro* up that river would be impossible. Even the canoes had almost been sunk in the tumultuous confluence of currents, some of his men having barely escaped drowning. Reluctantly he opted to continue on their way, assuming that they would reach other villages and people soon enough.

Food being a constant concern, Orellana diligently scouted the riverbanks all along their way for signs of people, crops, or even harvestable animals, though neither he nor any of his men had yet learned how to effectively hunt the local fauna, which would in any case require a time-consuming and exhausting detour. At its lowermost reaches the Napo River grows wide and braided with huge channels, the lands between the braids appearing as islands. Once, Orellana allowed a party of eleven Spaniards in two canoes to reconnoiter some such islands, looking for fish in the shallows, but by the end of the first day apart there was no sign of the smaller group. After two days, Orellana grew deeply grieved, "expecting never to see them again." Late on the second evening the canoes returned, and there was rejoicing and storytelling and backslapping among the reunited men. Afterward, Orellana ordered that all vessels remain within sight of one another at all times.

The canoes and brigantine sailed on, passing through what one chronicler described as "many hardships and extraordinary dangers," though he gives no details of these travails. They passed ominous-looking burned villages, recently torched and still smoldering. They arrived at a few small abandoned settlements, then reached a sparsely inhabited village of about sixty huts, most of whose population had vacated in advance of the Spaniards' arrival. Orellana assured the Indians whom he met there that he and his men meant no harm, and Orellana took pains to remind his men that under no circumstances were they to molest or mistreat the Indians in any way. Shortly thereafter, his diplomacy was rewarded: "They brought back turtles of the very large variety . . . and they also brought parrots, which food was sufficient to enable the companions to dine plentifully that night."

On February 12, 1542, Francisco Orellana and his fleet noticed a truly great river coming in to meet them from the south bank. The incoming flow from the right impressed and even frightened the men, for it was far bigger than the river they were on, bigger than anything they had ever seen.

> The one which came in on the right side as we came downstream . . . did away with and completely mastered the other river, and it seemed as if it swallowed it [the Napo] up within itself, because it came on with such fury and with so great an onrush that it was a thing of much awe and amazement to see, such a jam of trees and dead timber as it brought along with it . . .

it was enough to fill one with the greatest fear just to look at it, let alone to go through it.

Francisco Orellana had reached the confluence of the Napo and the Maranon, the origin of the Amazon River proper. Though he certainly could not know it at the time, Orellana and his crew were the first Europeans to experience the world's largest river. The Spaniards grew awed by the stupefying scope and scale of the river, a grander and more inspiring body of fresh water than any of them had ever encountered, or ever would again. "It was so wide from bank to bank," they recounted, "that it seemed as though we were navigating launched out upon a vast sea."

Indeed, the Amazon River is so immense that superlatives fall short of doing it justice. More than 4,500 miles long, the Amazon discharges one-fifth of all the freshwater that flows into the earth's oceans, about sixty times the amount contributed by the Nile, its closest rival in size. Snaking across an entire continent in a languid west-to-east flow, the immense river drainage is fed by some five hundred tributaries, a number of which themselves, were they located anywhere else in the world, would be the largest river on their continent. In places the Amazon sprawls a remarkable fifty miles wide; it can vary in depth with floodwaters or tides by as much as fifty feet; and, near its terminus at the Atlantic, it contains an island the size of Switzerland.

Orellana and his men saw trees many times the size of the *San Pedro* twisting violently in the river's whorls, and they knew they must stay always on alert to avoid being struck and wrecked. Here, too, they encountered floating islands, some more than a mile wide, great rafts of moving meadows, wondrous and bewildering to behold. The banks of the river teemed with wildlife that they viewed fleetingly as they sailed on: brown capybaras, giant rodents up to four feet in length, that dived from the banks into the muddy water to escape predators, and huge tapirs—hoofed animals related to rhinoceroses and horses—with their short, bristling neck hair and downward-curving snouts, that wallowed through the mucky bog lands, disappearing into the marsh as the expedition came near. Numerous felines, black-spotted jaguars, pumas, ocelots, and margays, lurked in the shadowy forests along the river as well, their predatory eyes luminous in the moonglow at night.

The Spaniards encountered more villages, learning from their chiefs that they were now in the outer realm of a powerful overlord called Aparia the Great. Orellana and his men paused in one of these villages, but marauding mosquito swarms literally drove them away and they packed up and sought refuge farther downstream. They pulled ashore and rested for a few days, where Indians "came with peaceful intent to bring us large quantities of food."

On Sunday, February 26, rested and reasonably fed, Orellana started off again, coming soon to a large, two-forked channel in the river. Almost immediately they saw four or five canoes approaching them from below, paddling hard upriver. The Spaniards readied for possible confrontation, though up to now the Indians of the region had not been warlike. As the canoes drew closer, Orellana could see, to his continuing good fortune, that these craft were laden with foodstuffs, and as they came alongside, the Indians spoke to Orellana, who, after a bit of trial and error, began to converse back, and they exchanged introductory pleasantries. Friar Carvajal once again marveled at Orellana's gift for language, saying, "The Indians remained very happy to see the kind treatment that was being extended to them and to see that the Captain understood their tongue, a fact which was of no little consequence with our getting to a haven of clear understanding."

Orellana produced a few gifts for these men, who he learned were prominent lords under vassalage to Aparia the Great. In exchange for Orellana's trinkets, the lords proffered delectable foods, including "many partridges like those of our Spain, save that they are larger, and many turtles, which are as large as leather shields, and fish also of various kinds." This convivial exchange completed, the Indians offered to guide Orellana and his men downstream to the main village where Aparia the Great resided, and Orellana agreed, following the canoes down one of the channels in the river.

A few of the Indian canoes sped off, vanishing downriver, and as Orellana rounded a curve he saw a large settlement, and only minutes later witnessed an alarming sight: "It was not long before we saw many

Indians come out of the aforesaid village and get into their canoes, in the attitude of warriors, and it looked as if they were getting ready to attack us." Orellana felt certain that he had fallen into a trap.

Quickly barking out commands to his men, Orellana ordered the crossbowmen and harquebusiers to ready their weapons, and the rest of the soldiers brandished their blades. Orellana directed the oarsmen of the *San Pedro* and the Spaniards in canoes to row at full strength for shore above the village, and in minutes they were storming the banks. "The Captain leaped out on land all armed, and after him all the others, and at this the Indians became quite frightened." The Spaniards stood their ground, defiant and at arms, while the Indians pooled in their canoes in the shallow bank waters, in a tense standoff.

At length Orellana called out for some of the Indians to come ashore, waving to them. A few did so, and Orellana spoke calmly to them, assuring them that they need not fear harm, that he and his men came with peaceful intentions. The Indians apparently comprehended Orellana's message, for they conveyed it to the many canoes that remained waiting there on the water, and moments later they began coming ashore, including, to Orellana's amazement, Aparia the Great himself:

> The overlord leapt out on land, and with him many important personages and overlords who accompanied him, and he asked permission to the Captain to sit down, and so he seated himself, and all his followers remained standing, and he ordered to be brought from his canoes a great quantity of foodstuffs, not only turtles, but also manatees and other fish,* and roasted partridges and cats and monkeys.

* The Spaniards in the New World mistakenly considered the manatee a fish, when it is in fact a mammal. Believing it to be a fish allowed them to consume the manatee on Good Friday, though this caused some controversy. Father José de Acosta, who wrote *The Natural and Moral History of the Indies,* mentions his reservations when served manatee one Friday in Santo Domingo: "The so-called manatee [is] a strange kind of fish, if one may designate a fish an animal which brings forth its young alive and has teats and milk with which it nourishes them, and feeds on grass in the fields; but the fact is they ordinarily live in the water, and that is why they eat it as fish. . . . In color and in taste the chops from this fish do not seem to be anything but slices of veal, and in part of ham: it is as large as a cow." Quoted in José Toribio Medina, *The Discovery of the Amazon,* 239.

The stalemate had merely been a misunderstanding. The people of Aparia (as the Spaniards called the village—which lay just below present-day Iquitos, Peru) had come to welcome, not fight, the Spaniards. Orellana thanked Aparia the Great for the food, and he took the formal opportunity to launch into his *requerimiento* speech, his friars at his side, adding that the Christians "worshipped a single God, who was the creator of all created things, and not like them who walked in the paths of error worshiping stones." Orellana explained that he and his companions were servants of a great emperor and master, who commanded the Christians and, in fact, "to whom belonged the territory of all the Indies and many other dominions and kingdoms existing throughout the world."

The implications of this last bit of information must surely have been lost in translation, for Aparia the Great continued in good and cordial spirit, listening intently to the words and accent of this eloquent stranger. The chief then paused to offer a rather compelling bit of advice. He told Orellana that if he happened to be going downriver to visit a people called Coniupuyara, which in their language meant "grand mistresses," then the Spaniards should proceed with great caution and try to avoid them altogether, for they seriously outnumbered the Spaniards and would kill them all. Orellana assured Aparia the Great that he would pass them at a distance, if only to record his findings and discoveries and report them back to his master, the emperor Charles.

These initial dealings completed, Aparia the Great suggested that Orellana and his men take lodging in the village, as many huts were being vacated and prepared for them; he added that they might stay as long as they like—everything they needed would be provided for them, including daily food. Delighted by this kind treatment, Orellana asked Aparia the Great to have all the chiefs of this surrounding principality (there were apparently twenty-six of them, all his vassals) to come and visit when they could so that Orellana might present them with a gift. Clearly Orellana intended to appease his hosts to the best of his ability, thereby avoiding an eventual cessation of food offerings such as had occurred in Imara. And as he had done in Imara, Orellana also ordered that a very tall cross be erected in the village, which drew interest from the Indians and became a point of conversation, if not comprehension or reverence.

Orellana's men now had roofs over their heads and the promise of steady meals. After scouting around the interior, Orellana noted that there was also an ample supply of workable timber, though some of it at a good distance away. He thus decided that "since there was a good supply of materials here as well as good will on the part of the Indians, it would be well to build a brigantine, and so the work got underway."

Orellana sought the wisdom and knowledge of the chief Aparia the Great in those first few days in the village, learning everything he could about the river's course, its condition and temperament, and the lands they would face in their continued journey. Orellana listened with fascination and trepidation to what the chief had to say. The people of Aparia, he learned, traded a long distance downriver, and their lands extended some 250 miles to the east. While on this river section, Orellana was assured, he and his men would be treated well and allowed to pass unmolested. But then came the ominous news that just beyond the land of the Aparians the Spaniards would invariably encounter the kingdom of Machiparo, overlord of a hostile and warlike people who were archenemies of the Aparians. Once the Spaniards entered their realm, Aparia told Orellana, they were sure to be attacked.

Orellana had only just begun to ponder the implications of this daunting prospect when the chief continued. If they managed to escape the lands of Machiparo, and this was by no means guaranteed, they would next encounter an even more powerful and much larger tribal federation: the Omagua. Fearsome warriors, the Omagua lived in a constant state of war with interior forest tribes. They raided far and wide, and they protected their riverside villages by building them on islands, making them inaccessible to their enemies. They built wooden stockades around their huts, too. Even more chilling, Orellana learned, the Omaguas took prisoners and kept them as slaves. "Old men and women not suited for slavery were killed immediately, while captives of high status or outstanding courage (the Spaniards surely qualified), and who therefore constituted a potential danger if left alive, were put to death during ceremonies. The heads were kept in the houses as trophies."

Given this last bit of information, Orellana ordered his men to redouble their efforts. They must repair the *San Pedro* and immediately begin work on a second brigantine, a bigger, more powerful, seaworthy warship. It would need to hold many oarsmen for ramming speed, and have masts for sailing the large open freshwater bodies and eventually the ocean. The ship would have to have places for the crossbowmen and harquebusiers to fire from the decks.

Where they were going they would not be welcome. They were headed for battle.

CHAPTER 8

The *Victoria*

*T*HE FIRST BOAT, THE *SAN PEDRO*, HAD BEEN BUILT with the labor and combined expertise of the entire expeditionary force, under the direction of the harsh and unforgiving Gonzalo Pizarro. Orellana, who operated with a different, more reasonable and democratic leadership style, canvassed the men for those with carpentry experience. Eventually Diego Mexía came forward. He hailed from Seville, and while he was not actually a woodworker by trade, he had been a woodcutter and stonecutter, and he knew something of woodworking. He offered to serve in the role of foreman, overseeing the ship's construction.

Orellana then ordered certain able-bodied and trustworthy men to take on managerial positions and others to follow suit with hard labor:

> And thereupon the Captain ordered an appointment of the work among all the companions whereby each man in one group was to bring one frame and two futtocks,* and others in another group to bring the keel, and others the stem pieces, and others to saw planks, so that all had enough to occupy themselves, [though] not without considerable toil.

* Futtocks are the curved timbers that form the ribs in the frame of a ship.

One immediate impediment and source of toil was the fact that the requisite wood was located "very far away" from the village, combined with the Spaniards' perceived vulnerability during this time. Despite Chief Aparia the Great's peaceful demeanor and generous treatment of them, Orellana continued to exercise caution. No doubt advised by the chief as to which types of wood were most suitable for making canoes or other watercraft, Orellana sent the woodcutters to the forest in small detachments, with some men designated as cutters and the others as guards. Once a team had cut its allotment, the cutters would carry the timbers on their backs to the distant village while others formed a rear guard for them, to ensure that no Indians, "friendly" or otherwise, could harass them. Working in organized teams, within a week Orellana's crews had brought in enough wood for the second brigantine.

That done, Orellana promptly assigned other important tasks, including the making of a forge for more charcoal, as they needed still more nails (in addition to the two thousand they had made in Imara) and other metal objects for the boat's construction. Here, near camp, the work was once again impeded by horrifyingly large and persistent mosquito swarms, which drove the men to the edge of insanity. According to one account, the insects were so troublesome that in order for the men to get anything at all done during certain times of day, they had to operate in hour-long shifts, one man working and up to two men whose job it was to "drive the mosquitoes away from him by means of a pair of fans made out of feathers which the Indians gave us." The Spaniards called these fans "fly shooers," and they were incredibly useful and even necessary—it was said that a man could not sit long enough to eat unless one of his comrades was busy fanning the mosquitoes away from him.

Orellana's choice of the village of Aparia as the place to build the second brigantine was both wise and fortunate, perhaps a combination of luck, good leadership, and decisiveness. For one thing, the chiefs around Aparia, especially Aparia the Great, were not only generous, but they also seemed to be increasingly fascinated by the Spaniards and their ways, and particularly intrigued and inquisitive about their guns, armor, and metal tools. The Spaniards were in this village from February 26 to April 24, and during those two months many chiefs from the vicinity came to pay their respects, speak with Orellana, and exchange gifts. Orellana must have been growing increasingly sheepish about the meager gifts remaining to him, baubles like bells and Spanish combs and a last mirror or two. Then one day a delegation of Indians arrived who, more than any before them, captivated and engaged Orellana and his men:

> There came to see the Captain and his men four Indians, who approached us, and they were each of such a stature that each one was taller by a span than the tallest Christian, and they were quite white and had very fine hair which reached down to their waists, and they came all decked out in gold and splendid attire; and they brought much food; and they approached with such humbleness that we were all amazed at their manners and good breeding; they took out a great quantity of food and placed it before the Captain and told him how they were vassals of a very great overlord, and that it was by his command that they came to see who we were and what we wanted or where we were going.

Orellana was mesmerized by the appearance of these natives and also by the gold they wore. Especially of interest to him was this "very great overlord" they described, who must have been a person of significant wealth and power. As was his usual approach, Orellana listened politely, exchanged formal pleasantries, and then told them that he, too, was an emissary of a great leader, a ruler who held dominion over all these lands. Orellana told them a little about his Christian God, the one true God, at which point the tall white men asked permission to depart, for they had much to report to their overlord. After the exchange, Orellana gave them "many things to present to their principal overlord, and asked them to tell him that the Captain earnestly requested that he come pay him a visit . . . and they said that they would do so, and they left."

Unfortunately, for whatever reason, this chief overlord did not come to meet the Spaniards, and the Spaniards were never to learn where the distinctive natives were from, or anything else about them. Were they shamans, albino giants, or both? How could their physical characteristics be explained? One possibility is that the men were pituitary giants, a condition characterized by prepubertal excess of the growth hormone. It has been suggested that such a condition of so-called gigantism might also be the result of ritual childhood castration, though none of the chroniclers make any mention of ever seeing such a ritual. Certainly, earlier Spanish accounts of indigenous peoples included plenty of genetic anomalies and wonders. Cortés reported more than once that Montezuma kept in his court, and was attended daily by, "misshapen hunchbacks and dwarves and albinos." The bone-white skin patina described by Orellana and his men might well have been a result of albinism, or perhaps it was artificially achieved with powders or paints or dyes, or some combination thereof, used in ceremonial ritual, for Orellana and his men later described seeing "sorcerers, daubed with whitewash."

It is also not beyond the realm of possibility that these men were from one of farther-reaching tribes, such as one of the various Arawak groups located up the Ucayali River. These groups were very sophisticated, which would explain their regal bearing, humility, and fine manners, as well as their formal regalia. It has been argued that the Arawak were the nexus from which these "culture bearers" branched out.

Wherever they were from, the tall and mysterious gold-clad men fascinated Orellana, confirming once again that wonders abounded everywhere in these vast regions, and that up one of the main river's mighty tributaries must be realms and kingdoms of unfathomable wealth—it was only a matter of finding them.

While working on the brigantine, itself a huge undertaking, the Spaniards tried to impress their religion upon the people of the village, and at any rate, as it was the time of Lent, both Friar Carvajal and Friar Gonzalo de Vera of the Order of Mercy were busy hearing confessions daily from the men. Orellana well understood the dangers of conquistadors at rest: they tended to grow edgy and impatient, for they were men of action. In sedentary conditions the men were more likely to transgress, to rape the local women or mistreat their hosts, so Orellana kept all of them busy every waking hour with tasks connected to the boatbuilding, and when those were finished, with mandatory worship services. Morale, Orellana understood intuitively, was crucial. But he also seemed now to comprehend that his voyage, and that of his men, had assumed even greater importance: they were in the process of great new discoveries, of seeing places never before witnessed by white men. According to Friar Carvajal,

> I preached every Sunday and every feast day, and Maundy Thursday, Good Friday, and Easter. . . . I endeavored to lend assistance and encouragement, to the best of my ability, in keeping up the good spirits of those brothers and companions, reminding them that they were Christians and that they would render a great service to God and to the Emperor in carrying on the enterprise and in patiently bearing up under the present hardships and under those to come, until they should complete this novel voyage of discovery.

Francisco Orellana himself was never idle. While overseeing the construction of the new brigantine and the repairs to the *San Pedro,* which had begun to rot, the shrewd captain also saw fit to further his political positioning vis-à-vis Gonzalo Pizarro. In order to do this correctly (and from his perspective, legally), he needed to formally dissolve his captaincy under Gonzalo Pizarro and formally assume his own captaincy over the men he now led. There were certain Spanish precedents for such a controversial action, not the least of which was Cortés's famous 1519 dissolution of his commission under Diego Velásquez, governor of Cuba, under whose aegis Cortés had gone to mainland Mexico in the first place. In a shrewd strategic coup, Cortés officially resigned his command under Velásquez as he simultaneously founded a new city on Mexico's eastern shore, naming it Villa Rica de la Vera Cruz (the Rich Town of the True Cross). Within minutes he had himself "elected" chief justice and captain-general of the town that only moments before he had conjured into existence. Francisco Orellana would certainly have known of this fabled political maneuver.

The scribe Isásaga now prepared yet another document on behalf of the company, this one similar to the recent appeal that begged Orellana not to take them back up the river. The wording of this new document was critical, too, for it once again suggested that it had been orchestrated and driven by the men themselves and not by Orellana (though it is certainly not hard to picture Orellana leaning over Isásaga's shoulder as he penned the document). The missive Isásaga wrote summarized the efforts and exploits of Orellana's men, calling them "cavaliers and hidalgos, comrades, able-bodied men" in order to portray them as being in possession of their faculties and not under duress. The document recounted again Orellana's insistence that they attempt "to go and search for the Governor [Gonzalo Pizarro] dead or alive," and the men's outright refusal to follow. The document reiterated their current situation, including their great distance downstream, and expressed that they personally assumed responsibility for the desertion of Gonzalo Pizarro. They had witnessed Orellana's resignation of his previous post, and now they petitioned him directly:

> We, perceiving and realizing the evil effects and great disorders that can prevail . . . among men being without a captain in these forest regions and lands of infidels . . . summon you, the honorable Francisco Orellana, to keep and protect us in all peace and tranquility, as you did keep us and command us before, and as in other parts you have kept and commanded Spaniards in greater numbers than we who are here at the present time; because we appoint you now to be our captain again in the name of His Majesty, and so we wish to swear to it, and we shall swear to it, and for such a captain we wish to have you and obey you until . . . His Majesty shall decree otherwise.

The document went on to delineate all the inevitable "harmful evils, tumults, homicides, and other outrages" that would surely occur should Orellana refuse the captaincy, so he really had no choice but to agree, which of course he did, with his hand placed firmly on the mass book and in the presence of both friars, swearing by God "and the Holy Mary, by the sign of the cross, and by the four sacred Gospels." The petition, a crucial legal document, was signed by all members of the expedition, either by their name or, for the illiterate, by an X mark.

Now that he was officially their captain-general, Orellana's first order of business was to make Alonso de Robles, a fellow Extremaduran, his lieutenant. Robles had won Orellana's favor along the way through deeds, actions, and demonstrated leadership temperament. The plan was to use the competent and courageous Robles for reconnaissance and food-gathering missions as they continued downstream. In addition to Robles, Orellana could count on Cristóbal de Segovia, a hardened and daring soldier nicknamed Maldonado who was known to be trustworthy in the field, for he had been one of Sebastián Benalcázar's lieutenants. In the chronicles of the expedition, Segovia would also sometimes be referred to with the title of "captain," suggesting he was a man of power and command.

This business taken care of, it was back to the boats and the preaching, the latter about which Orellana instructed his friars specifically: "The Captain requested of me that I preach and see to it that all attend to their devotions with great fervor, as persons who had very great need of asking God for his mercy." Evidently, Orellana had taken the warnings of Aparia the Great to heart, and to soul. He and his men would need all the help they could get, where they were headed.

By now the *San Pedro* had been repaired, and Orellana made sure that it was fitted for eventual sailing, suggesting—as evidenced by the seagoing design of the newer boat—that he now fully intended to cross the continent in these ships and sail to the Northern Sea (the Atlantic). The brand-new boat, which was considerably larger than the *San Pedro,* would allow all the men to travel in the two boats, dispensing with most of the canoes from this point onward, retaining just a few for stealthy and fast tributary reconnaissance. They calked the new ship with cotton and tarred her with pitch (perhaps resin from local rubber trees or black beeswax), all brought at Orellana's request by the people of Aparia. When finished, she measured, at waterline, nineteen *joas,* making her "quite large enough for navigating at sea." Wide-beamed, with nine thwarts to accommodate eighteen oarsmen, she would be the sturdier, more defensible, and less vulnerable of the two vessels, Orellana hoped. She would need to be something of a battleship.

They named the new craft *Victoria,* showing a blend of bravado and hopefulness, honoring the great victories they would no doubt win by her means.

The boats ready, and now with legal documents sealing his past and securing his future, Orellana "ordered that all the men be ready and make up their ship-stores," because it was time to depart. The two months the Spaniards had sojourned in Aparia had been a blessed respite, as they had dined on delightful fresh fish, turtles and manatees and forest fowl with hot peppers, yuca in all its styles, with *chicha* to drink. But now it was time to move on.

By sharpening his language skills and vocabulary during his extended stay, Orellana had learned much from Aparia the Great and all the other chiefs he had met. The consensus was clear: for the next 200 to 300 miles, they would continue to sail through the tranquil dominions of Aparia the Great, where they would not be attacked and food would be readily available. But beyond the lowermost reaches of Aparia the Great's chiefdom,* they would confront the warlike Machiparo, and they had best be well prepared when they reached this powerful overlord and his warriors.

Orellana, now in command of a small fleet, approached their departure with order, organization, and definitive leadership. The gunpowder—which up until this point they had hardly used but which might ultimately prove their salvation—was loaded and packed with extra caution, the kegs well wrapped to protect them from tropical deluges or splashing river water. The harquebusiers readied their matchlocks, which relied on dry powder, breaking them down, cleaning them, and reconditioning them until the bronze barrels and hook triggers gleamed in the sun. The crossbowmen tended to their weapons in turn, making certain that the nuts and windlasses were in proper repair and that they

---

* There is considerable debate regarding the extent and organization of these "chiefdoms" or multivillage polities. The term "chiefdom" was first coined by Kalvero Oberg in 1955. The evidence for the existence of Amazonian chiefdoms gathered by archaeologists and anthropologists such as Anna Roosevelt and Robert Carneiro suggests more organized, structured, and complex societies than had been previously believed to inhabit the Amazon River Basin. See Robert Carneiro, "The Chiefdom: Precursor to the State," 37–79, in Grant D. Jones and Robert R. Kautz, *The Transition to Statehood in the New World*.

had plenty of steel-headed "bolts" or arrows, with their feather flights sleek and streamlined.

Although Aparia the Great and the neighboring chiefs had assured him that food would be available for a time, Orellana remembered all too well their recent near-starvation and took no chances, stocking the holds of the ships with as much food as his hosts would provide and the boats could safely carry.

On the eve of St. Mark's Day, April 24, 1542, Orellana and his men bade farewell to Aparia the Great and his people, leaving what paltry parting gifts they could. The Spaniards boarded their boats, eighteen oarsmen having been selected to power the virgin *Victoria*. Unsure of what lay ahead, but steadfast in his goal now, which was to "complete this novel voyage of discovery," Orellana set off with his men into the mysterious waters of the massive Maranon, the soon-to-be-immortalized river of the Amazons, adrift once more.

CHAPTER 9

River of Darkness, Brothers of Doom

WHILE FRANCISCO ORELLANA AND HIS MEN FEASTED daily on succulent manatee steaks, roasted partridges, ducks, and turtle meat, their countrymen, led by Gonzalo Pizarro, were experiencing a living hell. Gonzalo, described by contemporaries as "a lover of warfare and very patient of hardship," was certainly having his patience tested now.

His dreams of El Dorado had been replaced by a nightmare on the banks of the Aguarico, his sick and bloated men moaning against the faint crackle of the campfire. All through the long night the remaining dogs, stick-thin and skittish, whined and howled, their own famished yips swallowed by the infinite forest understory. How far was Gonzalo Pizarro now from those exalted days when he and his brothers claimed the Inca Empire as their own, watching the emperor Atahualpa fill entire rooms with gold. He had been to the farthest reaches of that empire, won it for crown and country, won fame and riches and honor, and now here he lay, on the sodden ground, riddled and swollen with insect bites, his once stout frame gaunt as a vine. He was already wealthy beyond measure—had it been ambition or avarice or ego that had led him here, or some dire combination of these?

Whatever his current regrets, Gonzalo Pizarro remained

first and foremost a well-respected captain and a conquistador, a proud Extremaduran, and he would behave as such. He and his men must move, and move now. A few of his soldiers had already died, their ravaged bodies laid to rest with a prayer in the soft earth near the yuca plantation, and others now "swelled in such a way that they could not walk on their feet." Pizarro ordered that these hobbled men, and the others who were too weak to walk, be hefted onto the backs of the remaining horses and tethered to the saddles with leather cords and forest lianas, their splayed feet lashed together beneath the horses' midriffs so that they would not fall off as the pack animals plodded upstream. A few of the fitter men mumbled complaints, calling these mounted men laggards and weaklings for not walking on their own.

Captain Pizarro and a handful of his healthiest men led the main bedraggled body, hacking away through the dense forest with wood knives and axes. By now many of the men went forward in bare feet, their boots having long since rotted off or been lost in the squelchy muck or cooked into broth along with saddle leather, girth straps, and reins. Pizarro placed a trusted man or two in the rear guard to keep the train of men moving along; sometimes they had to pick up the fallen, or prod forward those who slumped among the ferns. The horses, lank and knobby-kneed and rib-bare in their weakened state, struggled mightily.

At least there was food. For nearly a hundred miles they remained among abandoned yuca plantations and foraged as they went, and this sustained them until they at last noticed some footpaths in the forest and came upon a small populated village. The natives, seeing the horses and the ghoulish men strapped to their backs, fled into the dark and shadowy forest or leaped into canoes and paddled away on the river. Eventually, some curious men returned by canoe with food, which they threw onto the banks from a safe distance. Grateful for the food, Gonzalo Pizarro tossed in return "hawks' bells, combs, and other trifles" that he always kept for barter, and he tried to communicate with his benefactors through sign language. Desperate to discover where they were and for direction on where they wanted to go, he must have deeply resented Orellana at that moment and envied his linguistic skills.

Pizarro's ignorance of language again proved detrimental, for he was able to glean no useful information from these villagers. Frustrated, without guidance, he drove his men headlong upriver in an extended forced march through the thinly populated terrain of the region, but after eight consecutive days the trails and paths connecting villages—likely of the Secoya peoples—became sparse and indefinite and then disappeared altogether. Finally, "there were no longer any Indians, nor any track leading in any direction, because the natives from this point used the river as their only road." The last peaceful Indians they encountered had indicated, through signs, that beyond—farther upriver—there would be no roads and no more food. Learning this, Pizarro had taken all available food from the villagers, lashing the pilfer to the backs of horses, each man carrying as much as he could without toppling over.

The once proud leader of conquering armies, Gonzalo Pizarro now verged on despair, for "he knew not in what land he was, nor what direction to take to reach Peru or any other part where there were Christians." He called together his best leaders, among them Juan de Acosta and Gonzalo Díaz de Pineda, and they talked among themselves, trying to reach a consensus on their next move. They decided that the best course of action would be to send Pineda ahead upriver. He would bring with him a crossbowman, a harquebusier,* and a few of the local Indians for their paddling expertise. Pineda and this small group would work their way upriver in two canoes they lashed together for stability, seeking for populated villages with food and shelter and making blazes and cuts in trees to show where they had been. Meanwhile, Pizarro would march the remaining force upstream along the banks, following the blaze marks to the camp Pineda would strike, where they planned to meet up each night. This march, which would come to be referred to as "the worst march ever in the Indies," would take them nearly two hundred miles on foot through lands Pizarro himself described as "mountainous, with great ranges, and characterized by ruggedness, and uninhabitable."

---

* The documentation that Gonzalo Pizarro's men had crossbows and firearms directly contradicts his charge against Orellana, which claims that Orellana took or carried off "all the arquebuses and crossbows and munitions and iron materials of the whole expeditionary force." See Gonzalo Pizarro, letter to the king, September 3, 1542, in José Toribio Medina, *The Discovery of the Amazon*, 248.

The "worst march" claim appears not to have been hyperbole. Gonzalo Pizarro did his best to lead by example, but with each passing week he grew more and more despondent, watching the condition of his men disintegrate further each day. Many of them were now racked with dysentery, and most were barefoot, limping slowly and painfully forward. Some attempted to fashion *alpargatas,* grass woven shoes or sandals similar to those worn by the Basques, using remnant saddle leather and straps to tie them to their feet. Their leggings had long since rotted off, and vines and thorns tore and cut at their unprotected thighs and calves. They were a morbid and ghastly corps:

> In this condition they went on, nearly dead with hunger, naked and barefooted, covered with sores, opening the road with their swords; while it rained so that on many days they never saw the sun and could not get dry. They cursed themselves many times for having come to suffer such hardships and privations.

In such a destitute condition Gonzalo Pizarro and his men lurched slowly up the Aguarico River under heavy rains, the lands now utterly devoid of natives. Pizarro gazed up through the treetops each night, or along the river horizon, for signs of smoke coming from Pineda's signal fires, which he had promised to build daily. The wisps of smoke curling like vapors into the air were all Pizarro and his men had to look forward to each day, for the fires meant that at the very least their compatriots were just ahead, and they would be stopping for the night, scouring the campsite together, in shared suffering, for any edible fruits they might pick off the ground or from trees.

Ahead in the canoes, Pineda rowed valiantly upstream with his party, worried daily that his captain and comrades would die of hunger unless he found prosperous habitations. The upriver paddling became more and more strenuous the higher they went, as the Aguarico was joined periodically by other raging tributaries, and one day the river poured so violently against their makeshift canoe-raft that they were forced to run the boat aground and leap ashore. Pineda discussed the situation with his mates, trying to figure a way around the heavy confluence, concerned that Pizarro and the rest would find it especially difficult or even impossible to get through "owing to the density of the forest and the large affluents that came to join the river."

As they discussed their options, Pedro de Bustamante stood to survey the river ahead and alerted Pineda and the others to what appeared to be a canoe eddying in the water just beyond a bend. It was indeed a canoe, very shortly to be joined by fourteen or fifteen more of them, each bearing eight or nine warriors armed with shields, spears, and *atlatls*, or spear-throwers. They eddied calmly in the slack pool, defiant in their home waters.

Pineda acted quickly and struck flint to steel, igniting the match of his harquebus. Bustamante followed suit, loading his crossbow with a shaft and standing at the ready as the canoes eased downriver toward them, seemingly unafraid of the Spaniards. Just as they came within range, Pineda lowered the harquebus and fired, hitting one of the Indians squarely in the chest. The unsuspecting warrior crumpled, dropping dead in the river. Bustamante, spurred by Pineda's blast, fired the crossbow, his arrow impaling one of the Indians in the flesh of his arm. Stunned—and no doubt confused by the thunderous explosion that had left one of his brothers dead and bleeding in the water—the Indian pulled the arrow from his arm and hurled it back at the Spaniards, prompting loud screams and a violent barrage of darts, spears, and arrows by the other Indians.

Pineda and Bustamante, both battle-hardened and skilled in warfare, reloaded quickly, firing in unison and felling dead another pair of Indians, then took up their swords and shields, readying for hand-to-hand combat. These Indians had never before experienced the booming percussive echo of a harquebus blast, nor smelled the acrid, sulfurous scent of spent gunpowder in the air. With three of their warrior companions slain in the span of only a few seconds, the Indians grew frightened, tucked in, and sped off downriver in their canoes, steering wide of Pineda, Bustamante, and the others.

The Spaniards, thrilled by their effective offensive and the flight of the Indians, swung into their canoe-raft and followed in hot pursuit, firing the harquebus at them as they closed the gap. Once again the loud explosion of the gun confused and terrified the Indians, who now leaped from their canoes and swam ashore, scattering. The Spaniards managed to reel in and retrieve some of the canoes, a few of which, to their delight, were loaded with food, including fish.

Pineda and his men ate the newly won food with gusto, relishing something different, "for it had been many days since they had tasted anything but roots and herbs which they found on the banks of the river." After they had finished, Pineda took out his sword and cut a series of crosses into the bark of trees along the riverbank, so that Pizarro, in following up, would know his scouts had been there and gone.

Later that afternoon, invigorated by the fighting and the food, Pineda and Bustamante continued their reconnaissance upriver, working hard to push against the boiling current. By dawn the next morning the continuous rains abated and fog lifted off the river, exposing their surroundings bright and clear, and they could see, beyond the swaying green canopy of primary rain forest, what appeared to be the outline of high mountain ranges looming far in the distance. The river here was rapid and they saw rocks, according to Pineda the first they had seen in more than a thousand miles. They had reached the headwaters of the Aguarico, to the north of the Coca River. Hardly able to contain their excitement—for this must assuredly, they believed, be the Andes Cordillera—they stashed some food in the recently acquired canoes and hid them in the forest for their return. Then they climbed back into their double canoe and raced downstream to report the news to their captain. They were no longer lost, and, God willing, they would soon be among Christians again.

GONZALO PIZARRO, MEANWHILE, continued his death march up the Aguarico. The expeditionary corps of friends and countrymen, comrades in arms, men with wives and families back in Quito or the Indies or the mother country, courageous Spaniards who had dreamed of *encomiendas* of their own, working mines, crates filled with gold borne to their loved ones in treasure-laden ships—these men were now barely recognizable. Wan and jaundiced and skeletal, many simply dropped dead in their tracks. When they had marched proudly and gallantly out of Quito more than a year ago, they had had more than two thousand strong and snarling war hounds at their heels; by now they had eaten all but two, Gonzalo Pizarro's own personal dog and the one brought along by the original campmaster, Antonio de Ribera.

The rains had drenched the men and reduced what clothes they had left to tattered rags that hung from their bodies like torn bandages. Many of the men were so weakened by famine that they could walk for only a few minutes at a time before slumping again to the forest floor, sometimes crawling along on their hands and knees like wounded animals. During the interminable nights they could hear the padding footfalls of tapirs and capybaras and agoutis and deer feeding in the forest, but these animals could only be slain by skilled and patient hunters trained to stalk them. The Spaniards were reduced to fantasizing about eating them as they starved.

Only a few horses now remained alive, and these poor animals were subjected to a most gruesome survival tactic. The men had begun slicing slabs off the horses' sides as the animals clomped along; they would eat the meat and then dress the horses' wounds with mud and river clay, packing it on thick to stanch the flow of blood. Later, when hunger overtook them, the men would remove the mud and clay plasters, letting the blood flow again and draining the thick red liquid into their helmets, to boil and then season with herbs and peppers, making a ghastly blood soup.

Gonzalo Pizarro was himself barely hanging on. He would write of this anguished march, which included wading through leech-filled swamps and creeks for miles, in water and mud that was sometimes knee-deep, often armpit-deep:

> All the remaining horses, more than eighty in number, were finally eaten; and in this uninhabited stretch were found many rivers and creeks of considerable size . . . and there were many days when there were built in the course of advancing two leagues [about five miles] twelve, thirteen, fifteen and even more bridges to take the expeditionary force across.

Still Gonzalo led his men on, bludgeoning a slow trail through the land, encouraged and drawn forward by finding Pineda's marks as he went.

Just as Pizarro's situation was most dire, Pineda and Bustamante returned in their canoe-raft. Amazingly, it had taken them only a day and a half to descend the stretch of the Aguarico that had required eleven days to ascend, so strong was the current. Pineda and Bustamante found their captain at the rear guard, spurring the stragglers on and trying to keep their morale from flagging. It was a joyous reunion in the forest, though one tempered by the deaths of many of their compatriots in the intervening weeks.

Pineda dutifully and enthusiastically reported his encounter and clash with the Indians, the likelihood of small villages upstream, and, most important, the great high mountains they had seen, beyond which he believed "they would find inhabitants, or a road which would lead to the land of Christians." At this point, after all that he and his men had been through, Gonzalo Pizarro was content to have any kind of hope to cling to, and he cheered at the news and shared it with his men, extolling their courage and bravery and asking that they make speed now, for their troubles would soon be over.

But Pizarro had enough of his wits left about him to know that his men were terribly vulnerable, and he feared an attack by the very Indians that Pineda had encountered, who now knew the Spaniards were in the area and would have had time to organize and prepare for a battle. Captain Pizarro called upon Juan de Acosta to take eighteen of the healthiest Spaniards, "armed with their swords and bucklers," and forge ahead, defending themselves at all costs.

After a few days of marching, Acosta indeed came to a village, which to his alarm sat on an elevated promontory and was well defended. Reasoning that surprise and a show of force was their only option, Acosta led what he could mount of a foot charge, battling hand to hand with the few armed Indians who had been stationed to protect the perimeter of the village. Although Acosta and two other Spaniards suffered deep wounds during the encounter, their assault paid off, as the villagers fled, leaving behind a good deal of food. This haul of food sustained them as well as Pizarro and the rear guard, who arrived later, though eight more of his men had died in getting there.

Rejuvenated, they now looked beyond the canopy and could see that Pineda had been right—the Andes indeed loomed in the distance. They could even see the smoldering dome of the nearly 12,000-foot Reventador volcano spewing blackened cloud plumes, for it had erupted just the year before and remained active and angry. Although they were encouraged by the prospect of finding Quito, they also remembered how difficult climbing over the high Andes passes had been the first time, when they had been fresh, strong, and well fed. The return over the pass would test the very limits of their will.

They slogged upward, steadily gaining elevation as they climbed through the mountains. By a stroke of good fortune they came to a village of friendly Indians who took them in and fed them, and here Pizarro decided to rest for ten days for a final push over the mountains. Through sign language and much gesticulating Pizarro learned that there was a shortcut to Quito, which he determined to take. But the shortcut proved no bargain, for along this track they arrived at rapids much too swift to wade. Pizarro knew his men would not have the strength or will to backtrack or go around. Instead, they spent four days building a bridge to cross the churning current, sleeping on the cold, hard ground at night, or staring up at the flickering stars. During one of these nights, guards reported seeing "a great comet traversing the heavens," and that morning Gonzalo Pizarro awoke to describe a bizarre nightmare that he had experienced the night before: a fierce dragon had attacked him, tearing his heart from his chest with its sharp teeth.

Superstitious, as many of the Spaniards were, Pizarro called on one of his men, Jerónimo de Villegas, who dabbled in astrology and could read dreams. Pizarro described the dream to Villegas and asked him to interpret it. With vague but ominous foreboding, Villegas told him that he would soon discover that "the object he most prized was dead." At the time, Gonzalo Pizarro could only shudder and guess at its meaning.

Pizarro rallied his men to finish the bridge, which they did, and then they made one final surge over the mountains and reached the outskirts of Quito. Word of their return traveled fast throughout the city, and people came out to meet them, bringing pigs and horses and clothes for Pizarro and his captains, who were a dreadful lot to witness. They came, according to officials who watched their arrival, more like animals than men. Agustín de Zárate, a Spanish official, recorded what he saw as Gonzalo Pizarro and his miserable band arrived at the end of June 1542:

> They were traveling almost naked, for their clothes had rotted long ago with the continuous rains. All they wore was a deerskin before and behind, some old breeches and leggings and caps of this same skin. Their swords were sheathless and eaten with rust. They were all on foot, and their arms and legs were scored with wounds from the thorns and bushes. They were so pale and disfigured that they were scarcely recognizable.

Of the nearly two hundred men who had parted ways with Francisco Orellana's group, only eighty made it back to Quito. They had traveled, mostly on foot, more than two thousand miles, and literally everything they had started the expedition with—200 horses, 2,000 to 3,000 swine, 2,000 dogs, and more than 4,000 native bearers—was gone, dead and gone, along with the 120 of their companions who had perished en route.

As Gonzalo Pizarro, now nearly bereft of his dignity, approached Quito, he was offered a horse, but he refused to mount, wishing to show the suffering shared among infantry and captain alike. Instead he walked, leading the pathetic, salt-deficient, half-crazed remnant of his "expeditionary force" into the heart of Quito. Arriving at the gates of the city, Gonzalo and his men knelt to kiss the ground, then proceeded straight to the church to thank God for delivering them from their hardships.

As he walked toward the cathedral, now more like a common foot soldier than a decorated captain and celebrated cavalryman, Gonzalo

Pizarro might well already have been plotting revenge on Francisco Orellana. Then someone whispered to him the disastrous news. While he had been away, his brother—knight of the Order of Santiago and marquis of His Majesty's kingdom of New Castile, Francisco Pizarro—had been murdered.

CHAPTER 10

The Assassination of Francisco Pizarro

*A*FTER HEARING MASS AND RECOVERING AS BEST they could, Gonzalo Pizarro and his men met with some of the Pizarro allies of Quito, who initially wept to see their countrymen in such a pitiable condition and to learn that so many of their friends would never return to them. They showered the members of the nearly two-year expedition with food and other comforts, and the company "began to eat with such a desire to stuff themselves that they had to use restraint so as not to burst." The men fell on any salt they could get their hands on with particular voracity, claiming that "what they had lacked most had been salt, of which they had found no more than a trace" for more than one thousand miles. All of them, Gonzalo Pizarro included, suffered from salt deficiency, or hyponatremia, whose symptoms—muscle cramps, severe headache, nausea, disorientation, seizures, even coma—many of them exhibited.

Taking precedence over all else, Gonzalo pressed his friends for the precise details of his brother's downfall. He discovered that Francisco had died nearly a full year before, in late June 1541, while Gonzalo had searched for gold and cinnamon under his brother's aegis. At that time, Francisco Pizarro had been governor and military commander of New Castile, essentially having been granted a personal appointment by the king to serve as representative of all Spanish power and dealings in Peru "and to govern the millions of new vassals that the king had acquired by virtue of Pizarro's own sword."

But rather than sit idly by like the moneyed marquis that he now was, and enjoy the leisure he had earned through his labors, the sixty-three-year-old conquistador instead spent much of his time in the field, working wheat crops right alongside native laborers, for Francisco loved the physicality of the work, and he eschewed the standard pursuits of Spanish nobility, pastimes such as falconry or game hunting. And of course he governed his newly won realm to the best of his abilities, though from the outset his reign was contested and beset with political impediments and challenges.

Highest on the list, there was the unsavory and politically complicated Almagro business to contend with. Brother Hernando Pizarro, thirty-eight and ambitious, had recently traveled to Spain to make his case before the king, a case aimed at defending his actions of 1538 during the notorious Spaniard-on-Spaniard Battle of Las Salinas. In that pitched battle between the rival factions, 120 Almagro men fell to only 9 of the Pizarro faction (700 infantry and cavalry, it will be remembered, had been led by Francisco Orellana), and Diego de Almagro himself had been captured, imprisoned, and ultimately ruthlessly garroted by Hernando Pizarro for acts of treason. Hernando arrived with a ship full of gold and other Inca treasure, hoping the booty might bolster his case with the king, but an Almagro captain named Diego de Alvarado had beaten him there and had already filed legal charges against Hernando for what he characterized as Almagro's unjust assassination.

As a result of this poor timing, Hernando was denied the chance to plead his case to the king and was instead immediately arrested and thrown in jail, where he would remain for the next twenty years, not knowing freedom again until he was sixty. Though he would live for nearly another twenty years after his release, he was by then a broken and pathetic half-blind man who walked with a cane and was unable to assist his brother Francisco's cause in Peru. He never returned there again.

With Hernando then imprisoned in Spain, and Gonzalo Pizarro off on his expedition to the land of La Canela and beyond, the Almagristas—about two hundred men who had fought alongside Diego de Almagro—seized their opportunity. Though they had traveled to the farthest southern reaches of the Inca Empire, as far south as Chile, thinking they had won lands and *encomiendas,* their efforts had thus far garnered them little. The Pizarros denied them the kinds of rights and privileges required to raise their station, such as holding political offices, and thus they were barely making suitable livings in Peru, hardly better than the natives. As long as Francisco Pizarro remained in power, they could see no chance for a change in their economic situation.

So in June 1541, with two of the Pizarro brothers at least temporarily out of the way, a small group of Almagristas met in Lima and began rather brazenly hatching a plot to rid themselves of Francisco Pizarro. Living in Lima at the time was Diego de Almagro the Younger, the nineteen-year-old son of Pizarro's former business partner. While young Almagro was said to be brave enough and not lacking heart, he was also thought "so boyish that he was not adapted for personally ruling over people, not to command a troop." Still, he proved a useful symbol and rallying point, and the Almagristas used him as incentive and further justification for their plans, claiming that they would avenge his father's murder. They planned to use the young Almagro's house as their base of operations. Their plan was dangerous, dark, cold-blooded, and calculated. They would murder Francisco Pizarro.

The group of about twenty of the so-called Chile Faction, the coconspirators in the plot, decided that on Sunday, June 26, 1541, while Pizarro was on his way to attend mass and therefore most likely to be unarmed and lightly guarded, they would fall upon him and kill him.

But the Almagristas did not count on one of their own losing his nerve. As it happened, the day prior to the deed, while Francisco de Herencia, one of the plotters, was at confession, he developed a conscience and spilled the entire plan to his priest, who in turn relayed the assassination plot to the marquis himself.

A man in Francisco Pizarro's position of wealth, fame, authority, and power certainly knew he had plenty of enemies, and death threats were commonplace. Pizarro even knew that the disgruntled Almagristas had been meeting in secret, for he had spies all over the land, constantly reporting back to him. Still, this plot appeared sufficiently real to Pizarro that rather than leaving his house to attend mass the morning of June 26, he asked that the priest come to his house instead. He would hear mass at his home, then proceed with an elaborate feast for his many guests, such as he often hosted on Sundays.

At dawn that morning, while Pizarro dressed and prepared for mass, the would-be assassins strapped on their armor and chain mail and armed themselves with swords and daggers, just as they would for battle. As they were set to depart, some of their spies arrived with word that their plan must have been discovered, for Pizarro had remained at home, claiming that he was too ill to attend mass.

The plotters barely paused before they made their crucial decision. Their leader, Juan de Herrada, explained that their choice had practically been made for them:

> If we show determination and . . . kill the Marquis, we avenge the death of [Almagro] and secure the reward that our services . . . merit, and if we do not go forward with our intention, our heads will be set on the gallows which stand in the plaza. But let each one choose the course he prefers in this business.

If they failed to kill Pizarro, they stood to be hanged publicly for plotting to do so anyway, they reasoned. So, like men inflamed with patriotic duty, heavily armed with crossbows, halberds, and at least one harquebus, they rushed into the streets shouting "Death to tyrants!" and "Long live the king!" They stormed past the plaza and ran directly toward Francisco Pizarro's home, a few of their men mounting horses and riding after them in support. Shouts echoing the name "Almagro!" rang through the streets as they went.

For his part, whether he had believed the death threats or not, Pizarro had gone about his daily routine at home, first hearing mass and then proceeding as planned with the noontime repast. About twenty of his friends, as well as his half brother Francisco Martín de Alcántara, had assembled upstairs in the great dining room and were enjoying their meal when they first heard the ruckus below in the streets. Francisco Pizarro's page, having seen the men charging across the plaza, burst into the dining room shouting "Arm! Arm! The men of Chile are coming to murder the Marquis!"

Alarmed, Pizarro and a number of his guests leaped up and rushed to the top of the stairway to see what was happening. At precisely this moment, the first of the Almagristas arrived in Pizarro's courtyard, fully armed and with weapons waving. There, they instantly stabbed one of Pizarro's pages, impaling him and heading for the stairs into the main house.

Pizarro turned, grabbed his brother, and sped for one of the nearby rooms to procure weapons. His guests, meanwhile, showed considerably less courage. Some ran back through the house seeking escape routes, and a number leaped through windows into the garden below, "most of them," recorded Cieza de León, "showing great cowardice and taking to flight in a dastardly way." A huddle of terrified dinner guests remained in the dining room.

By then, Francisco Pizarro, Francisco Martín, and another friend were nearly armed, and they were joined by two more pages, Vargas and Cardona. Pizarro threw off the purple robe he was wearing, grasped the sword that had helped him to win Peru, and unsheathed it.

He did not have to wait long. The Almagristas quickly made their way to the dining room, where they were met by one of Pizarro's guests, a man named Chávez, who tried reasoning with them, begging them not to attack their fellow Spaniards. Their answer was to run him through, stabbing him repeatedly with their broadswords and daggers, then tossing his bloody body aside. "He instantly fell in a death struggle, and his body went rolling down the stairs and into the courtyard."

The Almagristas pushed their way into the dining hall, shouting now for the tyrant Pizarro to show himself. Francisco Pizarro, certainly no coward, appeared in the doorway to the adjoining room; his breastplate had been hurriedly half buckled, and he was flanked by Francisco Martín, the two pages, and the only guest who had chosen to stand and fight. The five stood in the doorway, swords brandished.

Though the numbers were uneven—twenty of the Chile Faction to only five for Pizarro—the clever marquis knew how to make a battle of it, and he and his supporters held their ground even as wave after wave of the Almagristas surged forward, swinging their swords wildly. In the first few violent skirmishes Pizarro and his men mortally wounded two of the attackers, who fell to the ground moaning in agony, clutching at their gushing wounds. "At them, brother!" Pizarro shouted. "Kill them, the traitors!"

Finally, some of the Chile Faction grabbed one of their unfortunate mates and, using him as a human shield, rushed forward, the rest pushing him from behind like a battering ram. Pizarro managed to run the first man through, but as he did so, the rest of Almagro's men swarmed the sides and overwhelmed the five defenders.

The Pizarro brothers fought valiantly, trading sword thrusts and parries, the clang of steel on armor ringing through the halls, but in the end they were outnumbered. First Francisco Martín de Alcántara fell in a heap, slain. Then, one after another, the two pages and the remaining friend of Pizarro collapsed from their wounds. At last it was Francisco Pizarro alone facing his challengers:

> Those of Chile . . . delivered blows on that Captain who had never tired of discovering kingdoms and conquering provinces, and who had grown old in the Royal service. . . . At length, after having received many wounds, without a sign of weakness or abatement of his brave spirit, the Marquis fell dead upon the ground.

At just before noon on June 26, 1541, the sixty-three-year-old conqueror of Peru and governor of New Castile passed away. It was recorded that before he died, a strange and wondrous celestial event took place, a sign in the heavenly skies that was witnessed by many of the townspeople: "The moon, being full and bright, presently seemed on fire, and changed colour, one half of it becoming blood-red, and the other half black. Then there was seen to dart from it certain shimmerings also the colour of blood."

The body of Francisco Pizarro, wealthiest man in Peru, was later hurriedly dragged to the church, while his attackers went about the city, shouting and celebrating and declaring Diego de Almagro the Younger the new governor of Peru. At the church, a man named Juan de Barbarán, a fellow native of Trujillo who had once been a servant to the marquis, offered to furnish both Marquis Francisco and Francisco Martín with proper burials. In fact, Pizarro should have been clothed in the cloak of the Order of the Knights of Santiago, but there wasn't time. Barbarán and his wife, who had offered to help, learned that the Almagristas were coming to cut off Pizarro's head and display it on a gibbet. So Barbarán dressed the marquis hastily, "put on his spurs after the fashion of members of the order," and buried him, paying for the cost of the funeral mass and the candles from his own pocket.

GONZALO PIZARRO LEARNED about all of this sordid business during his first few hours back in Quito, and his blood boiled with rage while his heart pounded for revenge. He was now one of only two Pizarro brothers remaining alive, and Hernando was locked up outside Madrid. There was much to do. The country remained in political turmoil, the control of it still up for the taking. Gonzalo knew of only one course, and that was to bide his time, rest his weary body, recover his health, and then win the empire back—for himself, and in the name of his family, his brothers, and his king.

Gonzalo Pizarro licked his substantial wounds—his brother dead, the Pizarro political influence in question, and his grand expedition a devastating loss of men, of personal finances, and of his dream of El Dorado and a cinnamon empire. He had explained to the men of Quito his version of the details surrounding the building of the *San Pedro,* the split of the expedition, and Francisco Orellana's abandonment of him and his men. Gonzalo began planning to write a letter to his king describing the events that had taken place on the river. For the time being, however, dealing with Francisco Orellana—assuming that the traitor and his men were even still alive—would have to wait.

CHAPTER 11

On the Maranon to the Realm of Machiparo

RANCISCO ORELLANA AND HIS MEN IN THE *SAN Pedro* and the *Victoria* now navigated along the mightiest river in the world, though at the time they would not have known exactly what to call it and they could only estimate roughly where it was heading. At this point on the river, which was less than two hundred miles below modern-day Iquitos, Peru, the massive width of the glassy waterway now encompassed great incoming streams like the main Maranon and Ucayali from the south and the Curaray from the north. This staggering breadth would have over-whelmed and confused them, likely tricking them into thinking they were much closer to the river's terminus at the sea than they in fact were. In reality, Iquitos is a jaw-dropping 2,300 miles from the river mouth at the Atlantic, and is the "furthest inland deep-ocean port in the world."

Orellana would certainly have been aware of the famous journeys connected to this region, and as a result would likely have believed the river he was now on was called the Maranon, formerly the Santa Maria de la Mar Dulce (sweet—that is, freshwater—sea). The exploits, expe-ditions, and discoveries of Spanish compatriots were well known and admired—as were those of their rivals, the Portuguese—so Orellana would have known that in 1500, Spaniard Vicente Yáñez Pinzón, who had captained the

Niña on Columbus's voyage in 1492, sailed near the mouth of a great river and miraculously discovered freshwater more than one hundred miles out to sea. He decided to investigate, and following the freshwater brought him to the true mouth of the river, which he ascended some fifty miles, anchoring there. Pinzón soon ran into fishermen, reporting that they were "many painted people who flocked to the ships with as much friendship as if they had conversed with us all their lives."

Pinzón, rather than reciprocating the peace, captured thirty-six of the native inhabitants and took them as slaves, leaving the river before exploring any farther and before having to deal with the repercussions of his actions. The tides near the river mouth proved violent and unpredictable, sending waves crashing against his craft and threatening to swamp him, so he departed the river system, but he thereafter referred to it either as the Rio Grande (which made sense, since he estimated the river's mouth to be more than one hundred and fifty miles wide, and he was right) or the Mar Dulce. By 1513, other Spaniards, including Diego de Lope—who eventually sailed past the mouth—began calling the river the Maranon, after either a captain of that name or, more likely, the *maran-i-hobo* or cashew tree (called in Peru *maranon*), which thrives on the banks along the river mouth. From this time, and up to Orellana's journey, the river was referred to as the Maranon.

AFTER DEPARTING FROM the village of Aparia the Great on April 24, 1542, Orellana and his men descended the wide river, moving and exploring steadily downstream. Although they did not possess even a compass, they would have been able to orient themselves by reading the stars, as well as from the basic observation of the sunrise and sunset. They were heading essentially due east, which supported Orellana's supposition that the river would eventually lead them to the sea.

Orellana had no concrete idea of what he might encounter downstream. He believed Aparia's predictions that he would encounter hostiles, and to that end he adopted the tactic of remaining in the middle of the river so as to avoid attacks from shore. There was also the wealthy kingdom of Ica the chiefs had described, which presumably lay to the north of the main river but a long way from it. He had learned of the legendary warrior women, and he still harbored dreams of lands of great riches and high civilizations. Certainly his knowledge of the world's greatest civilizations, and their proximity to famous rivers, predisposed him to this hope, "for along the great rivers of the Old World, the Nile, the Tigris and Euphrates, the Indus, the Ganges, the Yellow River, had sprung up the world's greatest and richest civilizations." There was every reason to think that a river of the Maranon's magnitude and wonders, of which they had yet seen only a glimpse, would possess such high culture and wealth.

They moved along for many days without encountering any hostile Indians. In fact, word had been sent downriver by Aparia the Great to afford the Spaniards safe passage, and Orellana found villages that had been abandoned so that they might sleep there comfortably, where the inhabitants had sometimes left the Spaniards food. This trend was short-lived, however, and after a time, Orellana "recognized that we were now outside the dominion of the tribal domains of that great overlord Aparia; and the Captain, fearing what might come to pass on account of the small food supply, ordered that the brigantines proceed with greater speed than had been the custom."

One morning, having just departed from an uninhabited village, Orellana's brigantines were approached by two Indians in a single canoe. They appeared friendly, and Orellana invited them to board his boat so that he might converse with them. The older of the two men claimed that he knew the country well, knew the intricacies of the waterways and braids and channels, and Orellana ordered that he remain on board so that he might guide the Spaniards, while he sent the other man home in his canoe. Very soon it became evident, however, that the elderly Indian had overstated his knowledge of the region downstream, and he was in fact quite ignorant of the river. Orellana offered him a canoe and sent him back upstream to his own village.

From that point on, according to Father Carvajal, they "endured more hardships and more hunger and passed through more uninhabited regions than before, because the river led from one wooded section to another wooded section and we found no place to sleep and much less could any fish be caught, so that it was necessary for us to keep to our customary fare, which consisted of herbs and every now and then a bit of roasted maize."

By May 6, already running low on the foods brought from Aparia, they came to a place that appeared to have been recently inhabited and was also naturally elevated, providing safe lookout advantages. Orellana decided to stop there to scout around on land for food, while a few others were to try their luck with some hunting and fishing in the slower-moving estuaries. At this place, Father Carvajal recorded an incident that was so remarkable that he said that he would not have dared to write it down "if it had not been observed by so many witnesses who were present."

Not long after the hunting and fishing party had commenced, Diego Mexía of Seville, the man who had volunteered to take charge and oversee the building of the *Victoria,* spotted a nice fat bird perched in a tree at the river's edge. He deftly pulled back and aimed with his crossbow, firing at the bird. The crossbow misfired, however, suffering mechanical failure as the nut—the all-important projection from the lock of the bow, which holds the string ready until the trigger releases it—popped off and plopped into the river. Though small, the nut is a key component of the crossbow, and its loss would have rendered that weapon useless.

Just a few minutes later another man named Contreras began fishing in the same spot, casting out with one of the group's handmade poles, and by good fortune he snagged a large fish that swallowed his hook. As hooks were few and scarce, Contreras decided to gut the fish in order to retrieve it, and miraculously, "the fish, being opened up, in its belly the nut of the crossbow was found, and in that way the crossbow was repaired, for which there was later no little need, because next to God it was the crossbows that saved our lives."

Orellana and his men might yet need a few more miracles. By May 12, six days later, they reached the first village of Machiparo's territory, and Orellana ensured that all the crossbows were in excellent working order.

Just as Aparia the Great had predicted, the Spaniards were greeted not with offerings of food, but with a welcome of quite another sort, according to Carvajal:

Before we had come within two leagues of this village, we saw the villages glimmering white, and we had not proceeded far when we saw coming up the river a great many canoes, all equipped for fighting, gaily colored, and the men with their shields on, which are made out of the shell-like skins of lizards and the hides of manatees and of tapirs, as tall as a man, because they cover them entirely.

Orellana had cause for great concern, for Machiparo was rumored to be a tremendously powerful overlord with numerous tribes under him. Within his chiefdom, which extended some 200 to 300 miles downriver and was heavily populated, there was scarcely a space between settle- · ments, with the largest group of villages, according to the reports, possessing a full twenty consecutive miles of houses. Most daunting of all, Machiparo, who ruled from headquarters on an elevated bluff just off the river, had the capacity to organize huge armies quickly—many thousands of warriors young and old. And now, large numbers of these warriors came straight at the Spaniards, paddling furiously in well-organized squadrons, screaming battle cries and accompanied by the menacing pounding of war drums and the high-pitched wail of wooden trumpets, "threatening as if they were going to devour" Orellana's entire party.

Orellana had only moments to organize his defensive tactics. He called for the *San Pedro* and the *Victoria* to join together, rowing abreast to present effectively one large, wide craft, so that each vessel might support and defend the other.*

The attackers closed on the Spanish boats, holding their tight and orderly formations and surrounding the brigs in a pincer movement. Orellana bellowed for the crossbowmen and harquebusiers to make ready, but he soon discovered devastating news: the gunpowder in the harquebuses had gotten damp, rendering the guns temporarily useless. It would be up to the crossbowmen to repel the attack, and they immediately rallied to fire away on the Indians, who were right upon them.

---

* The aggressive Indians were part of the powerful Machiparo division of the Omagua chiefdom, at the time the most complex tribe in the entire Amazon.

These men wore thin, dark mustaches, different from any the Spaniards had seen previously. The crossbowmen sent their bolts whirring at these warriors, killing some and wounding others, and reloading with their customary celerity. Although the damage they inflicted momentarily stunned and halted the first waves of canoes, countless reinforcements were right behind in support, attacking the Spaniards so violently and at such close range that "it seemed as if they wanted to seize hold of the brigantines with their hands."

This floating fight raged on, Orellana and his men leaning over the gunwales to deliver blows with their swords and lances while the cross-bowmen reloaded, the Indians swinging back with wooden clubs and slinging spears from deadly handheld throwers. The combined flotilla drifted into close proximity of the village, where the ferocious attack continued. More Indian warriors poured into the water from the shore, their canoes surging toward the Spanish boats from all quarters. Orellana noted later, with some understatement: "There were a great number of men stationed on the high banks to defend their homes; here we engaged in a perilous battle."

Despite the dangers involved, Orellana determined to change tactics: they must try to land. The crossbowmen fired, furiously reloaded, and fired again, and Orellana charged the oarsmen to dig with everything they had. As the two boats powered into the shallows, half of the Spaniards leaped overboard, landing waist-deep in the river and charg-ing violently with their swords flying, scattering many of the Indians into the trees and behind the houses of the village. Meanwhile, the rest of the Spaniards remained on board the beached brigantines, defending the boats from Indians still attacking from their canoes.

The uppermost portion of the village now momentarily under con-trol, Orellana dispatched Lieutenant Alonso de Robles and twenty-five men to race through the settlement, driving out any lingering Indians and searching for food—for if they might hold here for at least a few days, he hoped to reprovision and rest. Robles drove his small force into the village, fighting all the way, for though the Indians appeared to be retreating, they still defended their homes. Robles could see that the vil-lage went on and on—it was enormous, impressively organized, and well stocked with food. He thus decided, rather than pressing forward, to return to Orellana at the landing site and explain "the great extent of the settlement and its population . . . and tell the Captain what the situation was."

Robles returned to the landing area and found Captain Orellana and some of the other men temporarily ensconced in a few of the houses, though the attacks from the Indians on the water persisted. Other than tending to various wounds, there was no rest. Robles took Orellana aside and told him what he had seen as he had raced through the village: "There was a great quantity of food, such as turtles in pens and pools of water, and a great deal of fish and biscuit, and all this in such great abundance that there was enough to feed an expeditionary force of one thousand men for one year."

Robles's account of Machiparo's land of plenty appears not to have been an exaggeration, for these people were highly sophisticated and industrious, raising a variety of crops including manioc, maize, beans, yams, peppers, pineapples, avocados, sweet potatoes, and peanuts. They kept "large quantities of honey from bees" and fished successfully for manatees, using the hides for shield covers and drying the meat on racks for storing. The manatee was not only a delicious delicacy, but highly nutritious. Noted one Spanish chronicler, "with a small amount [of manatee] a person is more satisfied and more energetic than if he had eaten twice the amount of mutton."

Their turtle farms were extensive and elaborate: controlled corrals or tanks surrounded by wooden fences, the nutrient-rich waters holding thousands of turtles, whose high-protein meat was delicious and much prized by the natives. The turtle farming technique was highly developed and well orchestrated. During breeding season, the Machiparo people released females into the sandbanks along the river, where they would lay their eggs. When the baby turtles hatched and began moving along on foot, the Machiparo tossed them on their backs, drilled small holes in their shells, strung them through with long lianas, then towed the strings of young live turtles behind their canoes, taking them back to their holding ponds at the village. Here they would be fed and fattened with leaves and other forest vegetation for later consumption. Each turtle was said to be "larger than a good sized wheel," and one turtle could feed an entire family.

Given its abundance and advantageous position, Orellana and his captains very much wished to stay in this village if they could manage to, but that was questionable at least, given the constant attacks against them. Capturing the entire village, given its apparent vast size, was out of the question, but they had managed to win a few families' worth of huts, and the brigantines had a solid, well-protected, and defensible anchorage. At the very least, Orellana determined that gathering and securing food should be their primary objective. Orellana called upon Cristóbal de Segovia— nicknamed Maldonado—and directed him to lead a dozen or so companions on a food-raiding sortie, gathering everything they could safely carry back to the landing site. He told them to hurry, because Robles had reported having seen villagers removing their foodstuffs from the houses.

Maldonado and his men set off immediately, and as they penetrated deeper into the village they discovered that Robles had been right—the Indians were indeed running off with as much food as they could carry on their backs, in baskets, and bundled in their arms. Maldonado turned his attentions to the turtle pens, collecting more than a thousand turtles from their elaborate holding corrals until armed warriors began to appear, looking fierce and severe and, to the Spaniards, grotesque, for their foreheads had been flattened, a feature distinct from other tribes the conquistadors had encountered. This effect was achieved in infancy by "applying to the [babies'] forehead a small board or wattle of reeds tied with a little cotton so as not to hurt them, and fastening them by the shoulders to a little canoe, which serves them for a cradle." The Spaniards described the distorted heads as looking "more like a poorly shaped bishop's miter than the head of a human being."* Their appear-

---

* Apparently, the Omaguas took their appearance very seriously, wearing their flattened heads as a source of great pride. According to Father Samuel Fritz, who visited the Omagua region extensively, "The distinguishing peculiarity of this tribe is the wearing their forehead flattened and level, like the palm of your hand, and of this they are exceedingly proud; the women especially to such an extent that they jeer at and insult women of other tribes by saying that they have their head round like the . . . skull of a savage from the forest." Samuel Fritz, *Journal of the Travels and Labours of Father Samuel Fritz in the River of the Amazons Between 1686 and 1723*, translated from the Evora manuscript and edited by the Reverend Dr. George Edmundson, 47.

ance, with their heads compressed like those of hammerhead sharks, coupled with their bloodcurdling shrieks and the pounding of drums and blowing of whistles, much terrified the Spaniards.

Having only just procured the stock of turtles, Maldonado found himself dangerously outnumbered. Fighting in tight ranks, protected by their metal armor and wielding steel blades, he and his dozen companions fended off attack after attack, pausing during any lulls to continue gathering whatever food they could in adherence to Orellana's order. But the Indians constantly re-formed and replenished their ranks, and during the second wave of attacks two Spaniards suffered serious injury, which seemed to invigorate the Indians. They

> came back at Cristóbal Maldonado so resolutely that it was evident that they sought (and actually started) to seize them all with their hands, and in this assault they wounded six companions very badly, some being pierced through the arms and others through the legs, and they wounded the said Cristóbal Maldonado . . . piercing one of his arms and giving him a blow in the face with a stick.

As the waves of Indian reinforcements seemed to be unceasing, and with more than half of their men badly wounded, a few of the Spaniards now considered themselves as good as dead should they continue to fight, and one or two appealed to Maldonado to retreat to Orellana's position. Maldonado barked at these men, imploring them to fight on for their honor and reminding them their retreat would only serve to further inflame the Indians and signal their victory. Instead, Maldonado rallied the least injured of his comrades, and he "fought so courageously that he was the means of preventing the Indians from killing all our companions."

While Maldonado and his group fought for their lives, Orellana had problems of his own. After he had dispatched their raiding party, Orellana and his own small army had noticed a lull in the fighting around them. Fatigued from fighting and from the heat, he and his men in a moment of poor judgment stripped off their armor and retired to the huts to rest. Unbeknownst to the Spaniards, small bands of Indians crept back through the forest and now came at them in a silent surprise attack. Before the Spaniards even noticed or had time to react, the Indians were upon them and among them, felling four of the conquistadors with grave wounds before Cristóbal de Aguilar, a handsome young man with experience fighting in Peru, sounded the alarm. At the same time, he assumed an aggressive stance, facing the enemy, and fought with courage against the Indians who surrounded him.

Hearing the alarm, Orellana leaped to see what was happening, sword in hand. The sight was daunting: the houses were completely flanked by warriors, and the upper village square teemed with more than five hundred chanting, angry Indians. Orellana cried out his own alarm, and with that all the remaining companions rallied behind, as he led an all-out attack on the main Indian squadron. They fought continuously, hand to hand, for two straight hours. One experienced fighter named Blas de Medina charged straight into battle with nothing but a dagger, rushing in among the throng of Indians with such passion and bravery that his friends were astonished, and were inspired to fight even harder when they saw his thigh pierced clear through. After the two hours, Orellana had managed to rout the warriors, but at a cost of nine Spaniards grievously wounded.

This intense battle over—at least for the moment—Orellana led the fittest of his men to find Maldonado if they could. By good fortune, they met on the same path. Maldonado had been returning with his beleaguered men, and Orellana could see that Maldonado himself, and all the rest, were bludgeoned and bleeding. One of these men was so badly injured that he died of his wounds eight days later. Remarkably, Maldonado had managed to get away with many turtles.

Looking over his troops and assessing the situation, Orellana ordered that the eighteen injured men receive immediate medical treatment back at the huts. The number of wounded was devastating, constituting a full one-third of his force. The two priests were charged with their care, though they could offer little in the way of medicine, having along with them "no other remedy but a certain charm." Father Carvajal, who helped attend to the wounded, does not specify what this "certain charm," was, exactly, but it is possible that the men had learned something of Amazonian medicine having to do with plants and herbs, or even connected to sorcery and shamanism, during their long months in Aparia.

It is conceivable that they had learned and acquired some of the botanical (or spiritual) treatments for injuries while there. Carvajal would have been well aware that the Holy Inquisition in Lima, Mexico City, and Cartagena established charges against acts of superstition and charms, but under the circumstances, this far removed from civilization and without any of their own medicines, these rules and writs could respectfully, and of necessity, be ignored. Whatever "charm" Carvajal employed, he believed it had positive results, for within two weeks "all were cured except the one who died."

While the priests were attending to the wounded, sentries arrived short of breath, reporting to Orellana that the warriors had begun to return, and that many were now hiding in a gully, preparing for yet another attack. Orellana quickly dispatched sixteen men, under Cristóbal Enríquez, with orders to dislodge this new force from the creek bottom. Some of the gunpowder had dried by now, and Enríquez brought with him a harquebusier, but that unfortunate was soon impaled through one of his legs, rendering his services useless. Without the firepower of the harquebusier, the small detachment failed to make any impact on the large force of natives, and Enríquez sent a messenger to apprise Orellana of his difficulties, asking for more men because the number of Indians, already impressive, was growing by the minute.

Orellana now came to a decision. Instead of sending more men, he sent back the messenger, ordering Enríquez to fall back little by little, without giving the impression of a forced retreat, which would only incite an attack. Rather, Enríquez and his men should steal back stealthily, undetected if possible, and immediately begin helping to load the boats, for Orellana planned to depart as soon as they could. He would not allow a single Spaniard to die in this village. When all were once again safe on the shore near the brigantines, Orellana gathered the men together and made a resounding speech, "recalling to them the hardships already endured and bolstering them up for those to come."

Orellana had something of an epiphany in the village that day. He told his men that there was no need for any of them to die here or now, since they were not presently on a mission of conquest, but rather on a journey of discovery and exploration. It was true, he reminded his men, that God had brought them down this river. But Orellana exclaimed that his intention was to "explore the country in order that, in due time and when it should be the will of God . . . and of his Majesty, he might send him to conquer it." Orellana was bent on returning, but he now knew that it would take a much bigger and better-equipped army to conquer the kingdom of Machiparo. For now, he must cut his losses and flee.

Orellana ordered the men to work quickly, and in orderly fashion. First they loaded the food, including maize, manioc, many turtles, and stolen dried meat from the natives' racks. Then, in a clever ploy, Orellana commanded that any men too wounded to walk without limping be carried aboard the ships on the backs of the others, wrapped up in blankets to appear like sacks of maize or manioc. He insisted that no men be seen limping to the ships, for he wanted to maintain the impression that the Spaniards were not vulnerable to the Indians' weapons, or susceptible to wounds of any kind, let alone death.

As the sun set, sending bloodred streaks across the darkening sky, the last of the men climbed aboard, and the oarsmen, some of their hands broken and bleeding, took painfully to their posts. Orellana called for the brigs to be unmoored, and in the dim evening light the tired and beaten men pushed off, the oars dipping silently into the murky Maranon. But this would be no silent or secret departure, for the moment the brigantines moved out into the main flow of the river, Orellana looked ashore and saw thousands of warriors on land raising their spears and screaming and chanting. But most worrisome, hundreds and hundreds more, even as darkness was falling, were leaping into canoes and racing toward the *San Pedro* and the *Victoria*.

CHAPTER 12

Among the Omagua

*T*HE OARSMEN OF BOTH THE *SAN PEDRO* AND THE *Victoria* rowed furiously, their backs straining against the pull of their long and frantic strokes, but try as they might, they could not distance themselves from the inflamed canoe warriors of the Machiparo. Darkness descended around the boats so that the water and the hulls of the ships became eerie shadows, and the oncoming warriors were less seen than heard, their arrows whizzing over and into the boats with the sound of beating bird wings. They attacked continuously, "again and again, like men who had been wronged, with great fury."

The spears came at the ships with stupefying force, and from considerable distances, forcing the Spaniards to duck below the gunwales and fasten tight their armor and helmets. The native warriors achieved their distance and velocity by employing spear-throwers—level boards or planks of wood about three feet long and three or four inches wide, with a bone hook at one end to secure the spear or arrow, whichever was being thrown. The wooden spears could be up to six or seven feet long, tipped with a deadly sharp point or arrowhead made of very hard wood such as the black wood of the chonta palm, or sometimes animal or fish bone. Some of these arrowheads were intentionally detachable, allowing them to remain in the victim after the shaft of the spear was retrieved. To shoot with this instrument, according to chronicler Cristóbal de Acuña, "the arrow is taken in the right hand, with which the spearthrower is held by its lower end, and placing the arrow against the hook, they launch it with such force and accuracy that they do not miss at fifty paces."

Even amid the rain of whistling arrows* and spears, the Spanish crossbowmen and harquebusiers did their work, firing back with their own skill and accuracy, felling many natives in the closest canoes, the flaming belches of the harquebuses and the acrid stink of the spent powder frightening others so that they backed off for a time. Orellana ordered the boats to move to what he believed was the center of the river, hoping at least to limit the attacks from shore by staying out of range.

That night proved eerily long and spooky, for the Indians in canoes pursued the Spaniards throughout the night, attacking intermittently, their only warning the ghoulish war cries and the onrushing whistles of swarms of airborne spears. At sunrise Orellana and his sentries peered over the decks, deeply concerned by what greeted them: "We saw ourselves in the midst of numerous and very large settlements, whence fresh Indians were constantly coming out, while those who were fatigued dropped out."

Orellana had no such luxury of begging off, and his men were flagging. Since their arrival in Machiparo's domain, they had been fighting for their very lives almost continuously for over twenty-four cruel hours, with no time to eat or drink. Almost too exhausted to row, the oarsmen hung slumped on their benches, their palms blistered raw. Orellana took stock of the situation, eyeing the sacks and baskets of pilfered food. He knew that he and his men must eat soon, or they would lack even the strength to protect themselves. At about midday, Orellana spotted an island midriver, which appeared from a distance to be uninhabited. He

---

* Anthropologist Robert Carneiro observes that "a number of Amazonian tribes have 'whistling arrows,' made by attaching a perforated nut to the foreshaft of the arrow. When one of these arrows is shot into dense foliage, it whistles on its downward trajectory, making it easier to locate when it lands." The whistling would have been quite unnerving to Orellana and his men.

exhorted his men to head for the nearest shore of the island and to land there if they could.

Orellana had only just put his ships to shore, and his cooks were preparing to strike fires for a meal, when another series of attacks came at them, this time from both the water and the land. Indians had swung downriver, beached their boats, and now swarmed forward on foot, while others struck in surges from the water. They mounted and sustained a series of three concerted charges, forcing Orellana to relinquish the beachhead. He ordered his men back into the boats, which they took to in full retreat. Orellana figured rightly that they were safest inside the protection of the boats, and off they moved again, famished and forlorn, pursued all the while by ever-growing numbers of Indians. Orellana must have doubted whether his men could withstand another day of this, for as they went, more canoes issued from each successive village, as if the invaders' arrival had been announced well in advance.

Ahead, Orellana and his crew witnessed along the banks a truly daunting sight: the shoreline was thickly settled with houses and structures, and "on the land the men who appeared were beyond count." One chronicler said that there came at them more than 130 canoes, and that there were more than 8,000 Indians in this village. Then, as the floating battle raged on, the Spaniards noted a strange and foreign phenomenon, for the Indians had resorted to a different sort of weapon altogether, one that Orellana, his men, and his priests would have had no idea how to combat:

> There went about among these men and the war canoes four or five sorcerers, all daubed with whitewash and with their mouths full of ashes, which they blew into the air, having in their hands a pair of aspergills,* which as they moved along they kept throwing water about the river as a form of enchantment, and after they had made one complete turn about our brigantines . . . they called out to the warriors, and at once these began to blow

---

* Aspergilla, a brush or instrument for sprinkling holy water.

their wooden bugles and trumpets and beat their drums and with
a very loud yell they attacked us.*

Given Machiparo's great numbers and the relatively few Spaniards,
and the difficulty the Indians were having vanquishing this mysterious
foe, it is hardly surprising that the natives would have employed assault
sorcery, shamanism, or witchcraft, practices which played significant
roles in their daily lives. Shamanism was often inextricably linked with
warfare and tactics, and it would have been an obvious means to combat
these unannounced and uninvited interlopers. The Spaniards were
unlike anything these Indians had ever seen: white-skinned and hairy,
with long, grizzled beards. They came in enormous high-sided canoes,
and their weapons launched fire and spit smoke and searing-hot balls
that killed from great distances. Their swords flashed fiery in the sun,
blinding and cutting, able to cleave a man with one overhead blow.
Machiparo and his people would do whatever it took—constant warfare
or witchcraft—to banish them from their land or, better yet, kill them.

Warfare shamanism sometimes employed particular spells aimed
directly at enemies, either known intertribal enemies with whom a group
had long-standing animosities, or foreign, unknown marauding hostiles
like the Spaniards. The "assault sorcery" spells "possess devastating
power that veteran light shamans employ, not just to cause pain . . . but
to kill." The shamans, as part of their complex and highly ritualized
assault sorcery, used effigies (wooden figurines, and sometimes quartz
pebbles, that did the shaman's bidding) to attack or decimate enemies
directly, or even whole enemy villages:

> To perform assaultive sorcery, the master . . . awakens the
> effigy by fumigating it with tobacco smoke and makes it stand and

---

* Richard Muller, in *Orellana's Discovery of the Amazon River,* 50, offers an alternate translation to the encounter with the sorcerers: "The pursuers were continuously on our trail, accompanied by four or five sorcerers who by means of long tubes filled the air with clouds of smoke
and sprinkled water all around in the manner of witchcraft. After completing a turn around our
vessels, and, so they thought, having freed the atmosphere of bad spirits, they exhorted the
natives to fight, and the noise of their cornets, drums, and shouting was frightful." The blowing
of tobacco smoke is associated with much assault sorcery, including spells cast during warfare.

sway on the palm of his cupped hand. Suddenly, the figurine lifts off with the roar of a hurricane and flies to the targeted village, whose residents can hear the missile approaching but not see it. Only the local white shaman beholds the flying image and warns the people of the dying days that lie ahead. When in the air, the quartz pebbles surge in a triangular formation closely followed by the figurine. Hovering over the village . . . the intrusive foursome selects its victims, swoops down, and kills the enemies one by one in quick succession. The pebbles tear into their bodies like an arrowhead, allowing the effigy to penetrate deeply into its victims. The siege may last for four days, until many have succumbed as if to an attack by . . . a war party.

Orellana and his company must have wondered if the spell these sorcerers had cast on them was working, because downstream, just ahead, the river narrowed. They had been driven into an enemy-lined gauntlet that they must pass through, a slender branch of the main river where they would be steered dangerously close to the shore. It looked like a planned ambush, and as they approached they saw that a chieftain stood onshore among his warriors rallying them forward, as well as encouraging those still chasing and attacking the boats from all sides. "Those on the water resolved to wipe us out," the Spaniards recalled.

Sensing the gravity of the moment, Orellana called on his finest marksman, a harquebusier named Hernán Gutierrez de Celis, and gave him orders to shoot. They might have only one chance to save their lives now. Celis readied and steadied, took careful aim, and fired just as they floated near the bank. The firearm exploded and concussed, shocking the Indians with its thunderous boom, and the ball struck the chieftain square in the chest, tearing him open and killing him instantly. The explosion of the gun and sudden death of their chief sent the assembled warriors into panicked confusion, and they stood over their lord with wide and frightened eyes, not knowing what to do. Seeing them in this state of shock, Orellana charged his oarsmen to row for their lives, and they churned through the narrows and into the open water beyond the channel, gaining again the safer center of the widening river.

The Spaniards managed to escape that ambush, but the canoes continued to pursue and attack the brigantines for the next two full days and nights, giving Orellana's men not a moment's rest nor time to eat. They were weak with hunger, racked with thirst—their tongues swollen and their lips cracked and bleeding—and now the delirium of sleep deprivation overcame many of them. Orellana knew that they needed to land and recover soon—but where?

Extending over three hundred miles down the Maranon, the territory of Machiparo proved every bit as impressive and hostile as billed by Aparia the Great. Given the unremitting hostilities, Orellana and his men had no opportunity to land and explore the country, but they did make some observations about the region. Carvajal noted that for the entire length of Machiparo's domain "it was all of one tongue," the people speaking only the one language. Even more remarkable was the density of the houses and the population; during one 180-mile stretch, both sides of the river were "all inhabited, for there was not from village to village a crossbow shot." One settlement truly impressed the Spaniards, for it extended for nearly fifteen miles "without there intervening any space from house to house, which was a marvelous thing to behold."

Despite not having the opportunity to scout and reconnoiter the interior lands of Machiparo, Orellana saw enough to believe that here might indeed be wealth and riches worth returning to conquer. Aparia the Great's intelligence had been highly accurate, so much so that Orellana was willing to believe that somewhere in this vicinity, lying somewhere deeper in the interior, "there was a very great overlord whose name was Ica, and that this latter possessed very great wealth in gold and silver, and this piece of information we considered to be very reliable and exact." This lure of riches continued to inflame Orellana's imagination, firing his dreams and determination to return, should he make it out of this expedition alive.

After four days and nights of continuous fighting, the explorers reached what appeared to be the far eastern boundary of Machiparo's domain, for the canoes ceased to follow and attack. Ahead they spotted what looked like a garrison or frontier outpost, set up on an elevated bluff overlooking the river. These ramparts and fortifications signaled the beginning of the lands of the Omaguas,* ruled over by a chief named Oniguayal. Orellana assessed the place as they drew near, and he surveyed his men. The place looked promising, but well guarded. Yet if he could possibly take possession of it, it would in turn be defensible. He immediately decided it was worth an attempt; he ordered his oarsmen to steer for it, and his crossbowmen and harquebusiers to the ready.

The Spaniards drew into a calm harbor above the village outpost and noticed that many Indians were gathered there, readying weapons of their own and preparing for a defense. Orellana determined that this was no time to appear timid or hesitant, and in a bold and decisive move he called on his oarsmen to row forward at ramming speed and with full force beach the boats, whereupon his artillery and crossbowmen, as well as swordsmen, would leap over the sides and storm the garrison in an all-out offensive charge. It was a risky, last-ditch, and potentially fatal move, but Orellana had committed to it, and in they flew.

Amazingly, it worked. The Omaguas stationed at the outpost offered resistance, standing firm and hurling spears with their throwers, until the massive Spanish ships came skidding and groaning up onto the beach, guns blazing. As his armored men leaped out shouting, Orellana's daring tactic caused the Indians to flee, abandoning their post and the village beyond, which, to the Spaniards' relief and delight, included a great deal of food.

Orellana planned to remain here for three or four days if he could, finishing the remaining stores of the food and replenishing them with bounty from the village. As he had suspected, the existing fortifications could be used to defend their position, in the very likely event of attacks or incursions from the rightful inhabitants, who even now were massing. Orellana had his men pull the boats into the shallows and tie them off, and he placed sentries on round-the-clock watch.

---

* There is a great deal of confusion surrounding the term "Omagua" and the people it describes. According to historian John Hemming and other sources, the people that Orellana here encountered were probably part of the "Oniguayal tribe, who were later recorded on the north shore near Codajas . . . 155 miles above the confluence with the Rio Negro, whereas the true Omagua were probably Aparia's people, far upriver." See Hemming, *Tree of Rivers*, 30. But for clarity's sake, I will refer to these people as Omagua, as Carvajal and others do.

His concerns were well founded. The next morning the Spaniards awoke to a commotion on the water, and the sentries scanned the water to see numerous canoes headed straight for their position on shore. Some had already arrived at the Spanish boats, and they appeared to be "bent on seizing and unmooring the brigantines which were in the harbor." Orellana reacted instantly, calling on his crossbowmen to quickly board the boats and fire down on the aggressive Omaguas from protected positions. The skilled crossbowmen picked off many Indians with their deadly bolts, doing enough damage to turn the momentum in their favor, and the attack subsided, the Indians retreating and vanishing back across the water into the várzea.

Convinced that the hostiles had fled—at least for the time being—Orellana again posted guards. He put the cooks to work and ordered others to rest, all in shifts. The respite—after days and days of continuous fighting and hundreds of miles of near-constant movement on the water—was well earned. "So we remained resting," reminisced Carvajal, "regaling ourselves with good lodgings, eating all we wanted, and we stayed three days in this village." Orellana spent his spare time scouting the village and its vicinity, during which forays he discovered many well-trodden roads or paths leading off into the interior, so well used and developed that the Spaniards referred to them as "very fine highways." This evidence of a large and vibrant populace confirmed Orellana's suspicion that they were near a wealthy, developed civilization, but the fresh signs of recent use concerned him, too; he feared an organized attack. After three days of rest and no further harassment, he decided that they should press their luck no further and ordered preparations for departure.

Ransacking the fortified garrison and surrounding houses, the Spaniards procured a good deal of "biscuit," or bread, which the Omagua had baked from a combination of maize and yuca into large hard cakes that traveled and stored well. That loaded, and with no other formalities, the men boarded the *San Pedro* and the *Victoria* once more and shoved off, leaving the relative safety and comfort of their protected lodgings and their calm-water "harbor," as they called it. It was impossible for them to know where they were or how far they had traveled, but

Orellana and his captains estimated that they had now gone more than a thousand miles since leaving the village of Imara. Perhaps not knowing was for the better—because had they known their location and their destination, they would have confronted the daunting fact that there remained well more than a thousand miles of hostile and uncharted river ahead of them—many more than that if they factored in the river's diabolical, twisting convolutions.

They were hardly under way—having traveled only five miles or so—when they reached an impressive, powerful river pouring into the Maranon from the south bank. The size of this new river appeared remarkable, even wider—or so it seemed—than the Maranon itself. "So wide was it," Orellana's priest remarked, "that at the place where it emptied in it formed three islands, in view of which fact we gave it the name of Trinity River." They had reached the confluence of the Jurua River, which appeared to flow through an abundant and prosperous land, with numerous houses and buildings dotting the swath of green shoreline. Orellana ordered the men to remain on high alert, but not to provoke any of the local population; he hoped to avoid any fresh confrontations.

They had reached the heart of the dominion of the Omagua, and because Orellana felt that he had plenty of food, he chose to move slowly and quietly downstream without making stops of any kind. They passed thickly populated villages, some of which sent warriors in canoe fleets to attack the Spaniards. "They attacked us so pitilessly," wrote Carvajal, "that they made us go down mid-river." Sometimes the Indians shouted as they approached, moving close enough to attempt to communicate, but they spoke a language that Orellana could not comprehend through the wind and rush of water, so no truce or arrangements could come of their discourse. They moved on, fighting and floating.

At sunset they arrived at a small and intriguing series of well-kept buildings set very high and exposed on a bank, and although the place was inhabited, its diminutive size and apparently limited population convinced Orellana that he should try to land and investigate. As they drew near, Orellana could see that it was very orderly and well maintained, so pristine that he suspected it might be a pleasure palace or place of recreation or leisure for the local overlord, enticing him yet further. The few natives resisted as well as they could for about an hour, but in the end they relinquished the village and retreated into the forest. The Spaniards took control of the perimeter, tied up the boats, and went about investigating, armed and ready.

The bounty of food once again pleased Orellana, and he ordered much of it to be confiscated and prepared for travel. Most interesting, though, was a certain building the Spaniards described as a "villa," a kind of warehouse or storehouse bursting with all manner of pottery of varying quality and sizes, some small but other pieces "very large, with a capacity of more than twenty-five *arrobas*."* Orellana and his men marveled at the workmanship, running their hands over the finely made wares, which included jars and pitchers and also

> Other small pieces such as plates and bowls and candelabra of this porcelain of the best that has ever been seen in the world, for that of Malaga is not its equal, because this porcelain which we found is all glazed and embellished with all colors, and so bright that they astonish, and more than this, the drawings and paintings which they make on them are so accurately worked out that one wonders how with only natural skill they manufacture and decorate all these things like Roman articles.

Orellana had good reason to be impressed by the excellence of the pottery and the skill of the craftsmanship. The sheer volume discovered in the storage rooms suggested that this small village must be the center of a vast pottery manufacturing region, perhaps employed for distribution and trade up and down the river. The immensity further suggested that the region—confirmed by their observations of continuous settlement along both banks—supported a significant population base, perhaps on the order of hundreds of thousands of people. They nicknamed this place China Town, or Pottery Village.

The pottery that the Spaniards found so captivating would come to be known as the Guarita style, part of the so-called Polychrome Horizon

---

* Approximately 100 gallons.

style of works since unearthed by archaeologists along the middle and lower Amazon. The style displays "elaborate geometric patterns executed in painting (usually red, black, and white) and incision, excision, and modeling" depicting human and animal as well as decorative geometric designs.

Orellana was eager to learn even more about these people, and he ordered his men to round up those few who had not fled. These people, through difficult and painstaking sign language, told Orellana that if he thought the pottery was notable, there was an equivalent amount of gold and silver in a village nearby, in the interior. These few friendly locals even offered to take Orellana and his men there if he wished to see it.

Orellana pondered the possibility, his interest in this potential El Dorado clearly piqued. But a foray into the interior would be time-consuming and probably dangerous, and it would take some of his men away from the brigantines, a dividing of his troops he was reluctant to make. Instead, he continued to scout the village, and found further evidence of a complex society, a chapel or house of religious worship, in which

> There were two idols woven out of feathers* of diverse sorts, which frightened one, and they were of the stature of giants, and on their arms, stuck into the fleshy part, they had a pair of disks resembling candlestick sockets, and they also had the same thing on their calves and close to their knees; their ears were bored through and very large, like those of the Indians of Cuzco, and even larger.

The idols terrified the Spaniards and certainly would have conjured connections to the stories that had been brought back from Mexico by Cortés and his men after the conquest of the Aztecs, who also displayed elaborate prayer idols in their temples. Orellana and his men were well aware of the incidents of ritual human sacrifice described by Cortés

---

* Other sources suggest they were woven out of palm leaves. See José Toribio Medina, *The Discovery of the Amazon*, 201n, and J. M. Cohen, *Journeys Down the Amazon*, 62n.

himself in his famous *Letters from Mexico,* letters written to the king detailing his expedition as well as the people and events they encountered. In fact, during one particularly memorable and gruesome episode during the siege of Tenochtitlán, some sixty-five or seventy Spaniards were captured and herded toward the Great Pyramid (the Templo Mayor). Bernal Díaz, who was there, described what happened next as his comrades, stripped naked, were led up to the sacrifice stone:

> When they got to a small square in front of the oratory, where their accursed idols are kept, we saw them place plumes on the heads of many of them and with things like fans in their hands they forced them to dance before [the idol of] Huitzilopochtli, and after they had danced they immediately placed them on their backs . . . and with the stone knives they sawed open their chests and drew out their palpitating hearts and offered them to the idols that were there.

All night long Cortés had watched his captured men at the temples from across a protected causeway, terrified at the foot of these giant idols, illuminated by eerie torchlight coupled with the burning ceremonial copal incense. He cringed at the chants, the incessant drums, the horrific screams of his compatriots as they succumbed to the sharp obsidian blades.

Such thoughts would have raced through the minds of Orellana and his men at the sight of these places of religious worship, the most elaborate such temples they had yet encountered. Their fears were tempered slightly when they also found pieces of gold and silver inside the temples. The local inhabitants, with whom Orellana was learning to communicate, managed to explain to him that these houses of worship, as well as the gold and silver, belonged to those wealthy people who resided inland, "in the heart of the forest," the same people they had spoken of earlier and could lead Orellana to. The idols, which Orellana and his men nicknamed "Orejones" or "Big Ears" because of their large disk ears, presumably represented the tribe's overlords.

Orellana moved away from the temples and the idols, filing the information away for future use. He explained to his men that "our intention was merely to search for something to eat and see to it that we saved our lives and gave an account of such a great accomplishment," and not to plunder for wealth at this time. But he would take this information to heart, noting that here was a complicated, even sophisticated people. Indeed, one chronicler had this to say of the Omagua: "Of all the [people] who inhabit the banks of the Maranon, the Omaguas are the most civilized, notwithstanding their strange custom of flattening their heads." Another report spoke equally highly of the Omagua, saying, "The Omagua are the Phoenicians of the river, for their dexterity in navigating. They are the most noble of all the tribes; their language is the most sweet and copious; and these facts indicate that they are the remains of some great monarchy, which existed in ancient times." Intelligent and industrious, they were also the first known people in the world to harvest rubber from wild rubber trees (*Hevea brasiliensis*) and to make practical items out of rubber. According to firsthand accounts of chroniclers, "the Omagua [used] elastic, waterproof and unbreakable material to make flasks and hollow balls. At their festivals, snuff was puffed from the pear-shaped rubber syringes."*

In their movement about the village, Orellana noted that, just as in the previous village, this one seemed to be a nexus for numerous roads leading into the interior. These interested the captain enough to take Maldonado, Lieutenant Robles, and a handful of other trusted companions to investigate where the roads went. After following one road for a mile or so, Orellana observed that the roads grew wider and better maintained, "more like royal highways." Again, the evidence of so much recent maintenance and use worried Orellana, and he ceased the scouting expedition and turned back for the perceived safety of the brigantines. They arrived just at sunset, and Orellana determined that despite the comfortable and commodious lodgings, it would be a bad idea to

---

* This "snuff," frequently distilled forms of different kinds of hallucinogenic plants, was ingested during ritual religious or spiritual ceremonies. According to anthropologist Robert Carneiro, "the Indians of the upper Amazon seem to have invented the enema syringe. They used to take ayahuasca rectally, as first reported by La Condamine in the mid-1700s."

sleep there, in a place so heavily trafficked. A concerted and well-organized night attack could easily do them in.

So once more Orellana and his intrepid comrades boarded the brigantines, the late sun dying to the west behind them. By the time they embarked it was growing dark, the ghostly silhouettes of bats flitting overhead, the forests filling with the whir and flicker of evening cicadas and the bizarre flashing of the nocturnal lantern bugs, whose outspread wings look like the wide-open eyes of an owl about to swoop down on its prey. Before them the river ran east, a dark and headless black snake slithering into the unknown.

CHAPTER 13

Big Blackwater River

*I*MAGES OF THE IMMENSE, HORRIFIC IDOLS PLAGUED
the discoverers as the sun set and they rowed on through
the blackness, their oars plumbing the water, the eerie
cries of hooting owls echoing across the river. Still,
Orellana pushed his men, urging them on. They kept on
throughout the night, trying to stay in the middle of the
river to avoid any attacks. As the first skeins of light
washed the várzea in a dull haze, Orellana hoped for an
uninhabited stretch where he and his men might relax free
from the fear of attack just for a few moments, but instead,
the farther they went, the more populated the land seemed
to become.

Sometime the next day, having passed finally through
350 miles of the country ruled by the Omagua, Orellana
reached a series of villages along a five-mile stretch of the
river where the people appeared peaceful and greeted the
Spaniards, seeming to welcome them. Once Orellana felt
confident that he was not being tricked or led into a trap,
he agreed to land the *San Pedro* and the *Victoria* and to
learn as much as he could from this new contingent of
natives.

These friendly, docile villagers invited the Spaniards
into their houses and hosted them well, feeding them—
some women made bread for the visitors—and presenting

them with gifts. Orellana managed to communicate, through a few boys that he had gathered up as interpreters, and learned that they were ruled by an overlord named Paguana, "who has many subjects, and quite civilized ones." Just as with the larger Omagua population centers, here again Orellana and Carvajal saw what they described as many roads heading from the village into the interior. The villagers explained to Orellana that the overlord Paguana did not live here in the village along the river, but resided inland, and that the Spaniards should go to visit him, for he would be quite pleased to meet them and learn about them. Orellana came to understand from these boys that Paguana possessed great quantities of silver at this interior capital, and large herds of llamas, and that the land there was "very pleasing and attractive and very plentifully supplied with all kinds of food and fruit, such as pineapples and pears . . . and custard apples and many other kinds of fruit and of very good quality."

As inviting and intriguing as this place sounded, Orellana had already determined that his troop numbers and strength were insufficient for any serious inland assaults, and he had made up his mind not to split up his corps, which such a venture would require. Their safety, he and his captains felt, was best ensured by staying with the brigantines. If he and his men survived this journey, then, God willing, he would return—better armed and better prepared for conquest.

They packed up—some of the men no doubt reluctantly—and entered the river again. As they coursed downstream, Orellana's priest noted that here the Maranon was so wide that from one side they could not see the other. Along this stretch, during the rainy season in late May, at times the swollen river inundates the forest, ascending high into the canopy, rising as much as fifty feet and flooding thousands of square miles of forests. The rise in the river level is so dramatic that one Spaniard later reported that the tribes here built two sets of houses, one on land, often right by the main river and used during the dry season, and the other "built in the trees like magpie nests, with everything they needed to be able to live there while the river is in flood."

The Spaniards traveled for four days without stopping, eating in the boats, trading turns at the oars and on watch, the river overwhelming in its immensity. The first two days they remained in sight of the right or southern shore. The next two they traversed across and could discern the left or northern shore, noting one day as many as twenty villages. On Monday, May 29, they came close to a grand and flourishing village, and Orellana considered many suitable landing sites, but he remained wary about making land despite their diminishing food stores. One village extended a full five miles, with growing hordes of chanting Indians massing as they went, and Orellana tried to steer clear of them without provocation. The largest of these villages, the Spaniards reported, possessed "more than five hundred houses, and there were seen to be many inhabitants along the landing places ready to defend the harbor and the village." Canoes took to the water and attacked the odd-looking Spanish boats, mounting enough of an offensive that, though he had wished to avoid bloodshed, Orellana ordered a reply from his crossbowmen and harquebusiers. Their accuracy and effectiveness drove the canoes away, and the Spaniards continued downstream. They named this hostile place Pueblo Vicioso, or Viciousville.

Later that same day they came to a much smaller village, and Orellana felt confident enough to attempt an aggressive landing to secure the place and seize some food. They described this place as the "end of the province of the . . . overlord Paguana." Here the men noted some changing characteristics of the landscape, significant because for such tremendous distances the river plain is so flat as to be hypnotically similar, such that any difference commands attention. This extraordinary flatness is hard to grasp: from the Peruvian border to the Atlantic, a distance of nearly two thousand miles, the main river descends a total of a mere two hundred feet, and almost a dozen of the main tributaries carry on with similar leisure, flowing more than a thousand miles each and none of them boasting a single waterfall or rapid, giving the impression of an extended, slow-seeping lake.

The feature here that most impressed the Spaniards was the presence of inland savannas, what appeared to be tropical grasslands with scattered trees, and huts with different kinds of thatched roofs:

From there on we saw indications of the existence of savannas, for the huts were roofed over with straw of the kind that grows in savannas. And it was believed that they must bring it there from the inland country, toward which went out many roads which undoubtedly led to the other villages situated away from the river in the interior of the country.

The people of this region—which was the province just beyond that of Paguana—were noteworthy as well, so belligerent that the Spaniards gained no opportunity to parley with them or learn what they were called. Orellana's chroniclers made some observations:

> We entered into another province very much more warlike and one having a large population which forced upon us much fighting. In regard to this province, we did not learn what the name of their overlord was, but they are a people of medium stature, of very highly developed manners and customs, and their shields are made of wood* and they defend their persons in a very manly fashion.

On Saturday, June 3, Orellana ordered his navigators and oarsmen to make port at a small village. The Indians there fought to defend their ground, but the Spaniards managed to expel them from their homes long enough to steal some food—which included, to the delight of the hungry men, some fowl, a delicacy they had gone without for too long. With a few provisions procured, the Spaniards departed, allowing the disgruntled residents to return to their homes, and later in the day, the *San Pedro* and the *Victoria* came to a magnificent confluence, a copious and ferocious tributary pouring in from the north and linking the Orinoco and Amazon basins. It was the greatest tributary they had witnessed thus far, bigger even than the impressive Trinity River (Jurua) they had encountered before. But beyond its size, what captivated Orellana and his men was the extraordinary darkness of the water. The

---

* The reference to shields made of wood is noteworthy, since Orellana and Carvajal point out that the river-based Omagua used shields of manatee hides. Wooden shields might suggest less access to the river, or people living much deeper in the interior.

water they described as being quite literally "black as ink," and it coursed "so abundantly, and with such violence that for more than twenty leagues [almost sixty miles] it formed a streak down through the other water, the one not mixing with the other." They named this river, as a testament to the confounding natural phenomenon, the Rio Negro—the name it still bears today.

Orellana had "discovered" the mouth of the Rio Negro, which is near present-day Manaus, Brazil, and its confluence with the Amazon remains one of the most breathtaking natural wonders of the world. Special tour boats chartered from Manaus today still take spectators to view this wondrous meeting of the turbid coffee-with-cream Amazon with the tea-dark Negro. By most standards the Rio Negro is itself a superlative river—the sixth largest in the world, and the world's largest "blackwater river." Its distinctive character—its blackness—results from the nutrient-poor content of the soils it drains. A useful analogy is that the Rio Negro is a "type of tea brewed in sandy soils. The tea leaves come from the stunted vegetation that grows in sandy soils. The black water works its way from the groundwater to the streams that empty into the Negro."*

Ironically, though dark in color, the Rio Negro is almost distilled—amazingly clear from low angles—because of its extremely low salt content and high acidity. Its appearance captivates and transports all those who witness it, as evidenced by the assessment made by William Lewis Herndon three hundred years after Orellana encountered its then inexplicable magnificence:

> There has been no exaggeration in the description of travelers regarding the blackness of the water. It well deserves the name

---

* The noted field biologist Alfred Russel Wallace, contemporary of Darwin and some would say his superior when it came to actual fieldwork, brought the terms "whitewater" and "blackwater" rivers to international attention when he published his work *A Narrative of Travels on the Amazon and Rio Negro* in 1853. The term "whitewater river," borrowed from the Portuguese *agua branca* (whose Spanish equivalent, *agua blanca,* is used in Bolivia, Colombia, Ecuador, and Peru), described muddy rivers the color of coffee with cream, such as the Amazon, while the term "blackwater river" referred to nutrient-poor, sandy-soil-dominated rivers, deep black in color, such as the Rio Negro.

Rio Negro. When taken up in a tumbler, the water is a light red color like a pale juniper water, and I should think it colored by some such berry. An object immersed in it has the color, though wanting the brilliancy, of red Bohemian glass.

Orellana and his men remained transfixed by the color differences between the waters for some time, but also by the powerful violence of the rivers as they converged, tearing away at the great beds of aquatic grasses lining the shores and carrying these off as detached, floating islands. Giant tree trunks, ripped from the earth by the surging river and yanked into the water, bobbed along like unmanned and rudderless ships, and these floating hazards the brigantine crews had to avoid at all costs, lest they be capsized and drowned.

The next day, June 4, Captain Orellana spotted a smallish village, somewhat inland from the shoreline and elevated, and impressively fortified with a palisade of heavy timbering as if to ward off marauding tribes. Nearer the riverside sat a fisherman's village of huts, canoes, and fishing gear, and Orellana put in here and made for the inland fort, where they came to a single gate protecting the outpost. Warriors behind the gate defended their stockade courageously, but the concerted push of Orellana's armed men proved too much to repel, and the Spaniards crashed through, gaining entry to the village plaza. They fought hand to hand with the defenders, finally scattering them long enough to fall on their food stores, which were plentiful. The Spaniards feasted on an abundance of fish, even celebrating the holiday of Trinity by spending the night there—relieved to have comfortable and defensible lodgings, if only for the one night.

They were still on an expedition of exploration and discovery, but their tactic now had a pattern: they would approach villages only if necessary, and then with great caution, hoping to avoid confrontation but ever wary of the potential for attack. If the natives appeared friendly, they would treat them with respect, explain their need for food, learn and take what they could, and then be on their way. If the people they encountered grew hostile, then the Spaniards would fight for their lives if forced to.

Rested and well fed on fish, they left the military outpost village, whose tribe name they never learned. They rowed warily along, surveying the villages with deep interest, continually amazed by the teeming population all along the way. Late on Monday, June 5, they approached a medium-sized village that appeared less intimidating than the more populous ones, and Orellana ordered a slow but decisive approach. They made port, and were delighted to see that the villagers allowed them to stroll right up to them and through the central square. There, the Spaniards discovered a rather curious structure, one that suggested a different culture than they had thus far encountered. In the center of the plaza was a hewn tree trunk, some ten feet around, on which was carved in relief a walled city, enclosed with a single gate:

> At this gate were two towers, very tall and having windows, and each tower had a door, the two facing each other, and at each door were two columns and this entire structure . . . rested upon two very fierce lions, which turned their glances backwards as though suspicious of each other, holding between their forepaws and claws the entire structure, in the middle of which there was a hole through which they offered and poured out chicha for the Sun, for this is the wine which they drink, and the Sun is the one whom they worship and consider their god.

The Spaniards moved around this worship tree with fascination, noting also that the *chicha* was poured into the hole and then ran out the tree and onto the ground. They found a communicative Indian, and Orellana, trying his luck with the language as best he could, pressed him to explain the wooden structure in the square in greater detail. The Indian responded with a bit of truly compelling information: that

> they were subjects and tributaries of the Amazons and that the only service which they rendered them consisted in supplying them with plumes of parrots and macaws for the linings of the roofs of the buildings which constitute their places of worship, and that all the villages which they had were of that kind, and that

they had that [carved tree] there as a reminder, and that they worshipped it as a thing which was the emblem of their mistress, who
is the one who rules over all the land of the aforesaid women.

After the wanderers had marveled at the sacrificial tree structure and
the story they had just been told, they inquired about another conspicu-
ous structure nearby in the square, a good-sized edifice standing somewhat apart, which they were told was for worship connected to the sun;
it was here, they were given to understand, that the Indians performed
certain ceremonial rites. On closer inspection of the interior, Orellana
and his men found many robes fabricated from feathers of various colors, the reds of the scarlet macaw, the greens of parrots, the feathers fastened to or woven into robes and vests "which the Indians put on to
celebrate their festive occasions and to dance, whenever they came
together there for some holiday affair or rejoicing, in front of their idols."

It was all quite fantastic, and a little unnerving, given what they knew
about the sun sacrifices in the Aztecs' religion and worldview. This was
not the first time they had heard of these Amazons, and their apprehen-
sion now grew—especially on seeing such tangible evidence as sacrificial
idols and prayer houses.*

Orellana had seen enough. It was time to move on. He accepted the
little food offered, then ordered his men back onto the boats. Once more
on the river, they approached another village—this one quite large—
where they spied a similar carved tree trunk and symbolic icon such as
the one that had so captivated them. Orellana determined to check this
village out, too, but here they met unexpectedly strong opposition. For
more than an hour the brigantines maneuvered and yawed for position,
battling canoes and foot soldiers simultaneously trying to access the
beachhead. Finally the Spaniards managed a landing, firing crossbows
and harquebuses as they stormed the banks, but though the Indians fell
back initially, they returned with renewed numbers over the next hours,

---

* While the sun was certainly an important symbol—even a deity in much Amazonian cosmology, often associated with creation mythology as well as fertility rites—there does not appear to
be evidence of human sacrifice associated with the sun as it was practiced, and on a very large
scale, by the Aztecs of Mexico.

each time attacking the Spaniards and then retreating. The ebb and flow of attacks ultimately subsided long enough for Orellana to procure some food, but he did not like the number of Indians he saw, and he ordered his men to fight their way back onto the boats for a hasty departure.

From here they passed village after village where Indians lined the banks, standing there armed and ready to fight should the Spaniards attempt to land. Orellana came to understand that word of his coming traveled downstream—most likely by teams of canoe messengers—much faster than he did. Warriors waved their arms defiantly and called out to the Spaniards, taunting them with their spears and shields held outstretched. Orellana kept the brigantines at a safe distance from shore whenever possible, trying to pass peacefully, but in some villages, warriors congregated so thickly as to form what looked like a solid wall, hurling spears and arrows in such flurries as to prompt a response from Orellana—in the form of crossbow and harquebus fire.

By now, Orellana and his men must have wondered whether the mighty river would ever end. By some estimates—when not stopping often, rotating shifts on the oars, some men resting or eating while the others kept up their momentum, and sleeping for just a few hours at uninhabited islands or midriver—they could make up to a hundred miles a day. But on and on and on rolled the huge river, a seemingly interminable reddish-brown wash cutting its way at a manatee's pace through a green inferno. The men lay sweating in their armor, swatting mosquitoes and black flies through the stifling heat, watching listlessly as flocks of macaws or parrots or toucans darted past overhead or river dolphins played in the brigantines' wakes.

On June 7, 1542, a Wednesday, Captain Orellana spotted a relatively small settlement and gave orders to land—provisions were dwindling once again. They had been reduced to scavengers and raiders, landing only to steal food or fight for it, unless the natives—as they continued to do in some instances—readily offered sustenance. This particular village was small enough and so sparsely populated, or so it appeared at the moment, that the Spaniards managed to land and overwhelm the settlement with no resistance whatsoever. Orellana and Carvajal noted that there were only women moving about the village, and not very many at that. The Spaniards found an abundance of drying fish—enough, they surmised, that they could have filled both brigantines to the gunwales with them. The amount of fish drying on racks suggested that this was a center for fish production and trade, and that from here it was transported into the interior and sold where the commodity was less plentiful. In addition to the drying racks, the fish was also being roasted on spits and barbecues.

After a few hours in this seemingly tranquil village, the comrades got together to ask Orellana whether they might make camp here. Certainly the presence of unattended women influenced this request, although the petitioners added that the next day was Corpus Christi—the first day of celebration after Holy Week—and it would please them to celebrate by staying in comfortable accommodations rather than on the boats or on the soggy banks of some uninhabited island. Initially, Orellana bristled at the suggestion. For one thing, given the treatment they had been receiving just upriver, there was no reason to doubt that—although this place appeared thinly populated—the outlying area held warriors who might this very moment have heard of their arrival and were readying to attack. Orellana, shrewd leader that he was, argued that the best thing to do would be to load up as much fish as they could carry and "go on as we were accustomed to doing, and get to the wilderness to sleep."

But the men were persuasive, as they had been in the past. Tired of the constant raiding and running, they literally begged to stay, asking that the captain grant this wish as a favor to them for all their hardships. Orellana, who some have criticized as being "too kind-hearted a soul by far," consented, against his better judgment. The men dispersed to the nearby houses, enjoying the comfort of shelter from the sun and the elements and perhaps female company, many of them falling fast asleep.

Orellana would soon regret his acquiescence. For just at sunset, the village men began returning from the interior, where they had apparently been busy working crops or trading fish. Shocked, frightened, and angered to find their homes occupied by ironclad aliens, an uproar arose as they shouted at the Spaniards, gesturing for them to leave. Some of them took up arms and massed for a concerted attack. A handful of the Spaniards, responding to the general confusion, banded together and formed a defense line, and not a moment too soon. In poured the angry warriors—but their first experience against slashing steel swords and clanking metal armor was utterly foreign and frightening, and they backed away, for the moment relinquishing their homes to the trespassers.

Night fell, the moon rising and reflecting ominously on the water. Orellana told his men to rest in their armor and be ready for an attack. He doubled the normal number of guards. But despite these preparations, the Indians returned—this time in a fearsome swarm. They funneled in quietly from three sides, their attack so silent and sudden that they seriously wounded three sentinels and then were upon and among the Spaniards. When the alarm pierced the night, mixed with the screams of the attacking warriors, Captain Orellana leaped into the fray, rallying his men. Interloper and Indian fought under the glow of the shadowy moonlight, the warriors darting about with their palmwood clubs. Orellana barked orders to his lieutenants, and the Spaniards repelled the attack, chasing some of the Indians back through the village and into the woods, forcing others to leap into the water as they attempted to flee in canoes.

Orellana took advantage of the pause in the fighting to order the area scoured for timbers and other materials to build a blockade defending the main entrance to the village, where the largest attack was likely to come. He put Friar Carvajal in charge of dressing the wounds of the injured sentinels, and then he moved about posting fresh guards around the periphery. They spent the rest of the long moonlit night fighting subsequent waves of attacks, Orellana directing defense tactics, racing from line to line of their impromptu squadron. When light finally poured over the scene, the Spaniards held a few of the warriors prisoner. As soon as it was bright enough to load safely onto the brigantines, Orellana ordered the bulk of his expeditionary corps onto the ships. He took a few men and rounded up the prisoners, and then he decided to send a message, one that conspicuously contradicted his character and standard behavior.

He hanged the prisoners right there in their own village, in their own homes, in front of their families. Then, as a cruel punctuation to this act, he lit the houses of the village on fire.

Friar Carvajal would explain or justify the act by saying that Orellana hoped to make a point "in order that the Indians from here on might acquire fear of us and not attack us," and there was certainly a good deal of conquistador precedent for such tactics. Cortés famously—at the Massacre of Cholula—slaughtered upward of five thousand unarmed civilians in just two hours, his intention being to strike fear and awe into the population. Orellana knew firsthand of Francisco Pizarro's wholesale annihilation of some seven thousand Incas on the field at Cajamarca, and was of course privy to his own captain Gonzalo Pizarro's torture and assassination approach. But public hangings of this kind were not typical of Orellana; they were not his style. Perhaps he was angry with himself for allowing his mind to be swayed by his men; he had not wanted to stay there, after all—his intuition on that had been right and it had been a bad decision. Perhaps the pressures, the long and seemingly endless journey, had driven him to such barbarity. He certainly knew that word traveled quickly downriver, and he probably hoped the act would give tribes second thoughts about attacking as he and his boats made their way downstream.

In any event, as they rowed resolutely from the place, which they named Corpus Christi Village, they could see people massing on the banks, warriors preparing to follow after them in canoes, women and children wailing and mourning their slain loved ones. Orellana charged his men to make speed, and soon they had outstripped the war canoes chasing them. The village receded into memory behind them, the black plumes of smoke from the burning homes forming dark, angry-looking clouds above the jungle canopy.

CHAPTER 14

Encountering the Amazons

*T*HE NEXT DAY, HAVING NARROWLY SURVIVED THE midnight attack and subsequent night-long fighting, Orellana found an uninhabited anchorage and pulled over to rest his weary men and help the wounded to recover. They slept in a thick bramble of woods a short distance from their boats. The respite was much needed, for the all-night battle, the building of ambuscade barriers by dull moonlight, and the lack of sleep and sustenance had exhausted the men. Orellana finally rousted his haggard oarsmen and set them to toil again. They had traveled only about ten miles when the character of the river changed. They saw what appeared to be a great lake or sea of water downstream and on the right, on the southerly bank. "We saw emptying in on the right side a very great and powerful river, indeed greater than the one which we were following, and, because of its being so wide, we gave it the name of the Rio Grande."*

The river they dubbed the Rio Grande was the present-day Madeira, and their impression of its size and volume were well founded. Its discharge, the power of which they felt beneath the floorboards of the boats,

*The mouth of the Madeira, at its confluence with the Amazon, is more than five hundred miles from the Atlantic Ocean.

exceeded even that of the mighty Rio Negro, and though they only took the time to look up its impressive mouth, the Madeira's headwaters were actually an astonishing two thousand miles upstream, making it the longest of the Amazon's myriad tributaries. The muddy Madeira surges into the main Amazon as thick and dark as chocolate, conveying nearly half of all the sediments carried to the ocean by the main river. At the time, Orellana and his men simply gawked at its sprawling width and power, the currents at the confluence sufficiently strong to force them to cross the main river to its northern bank to avoid its violent whorls.

As they neared the northern shore, Orellana could make out a series of large settlements hewn out of a hillside and descending right down to the river. Wishing for a closer inspection, he ordered the navigators to steer toward the shoreline. What he saw enticed him; here were open roads leading from the forest to the river, and an apparently vacated village. But Orellana's recent debacle with an ostensibly empty village remained fresh in his memory, and he thought better of landing. His instinct turned out to have been prescient, for just as they passed the empty town there materialized more than five thousand warriors from hiding, who poured down the roads shouting and chanting and striking their weapons together in percussive unison. The clamor these warriors made could be felt through the air and on the water, so much so that, according to those present, "beating their weapons together, they made such an uproar that we thought the bottom had dropped out of the river." Orellana's decision not to land probably saved all their lives.

Almost immediately, just a mile or two later, they approached an even larger settlement, and Orellana steered his oarsmen well away, traversing back toward the river's center. They passed out of this hostile territory, noting that the character of what landscape they could see appeared "temperate and one of very great productiveness." They cruised along through similarly developed country unmolested for a few days, until one morning around eight o'clock they advanced on a gorgeous village perched over the river on high ground. Its tidiness and grandeur drew them in, for they described it as "a fine looking settlement, which, from appearances, must have been the capital of some great overlord."*

They rowed hard for the arresting site, but particularly strong currents drew them past the access channel to the wondrous place and prevented them from rowing back upstream. As they passed they gazed back and saw a sight that all remembered in grisly detail: at intervals along the shore stood high wooden posts, onto each of which was nailed the head of a slain victim, probably tribal enemies. "In those villages they have many poles and large sticks of timber stuck up in the ground, and on top of them were placed the heads of Indians, fastened there as trophies or as tokens meaning that the tribe must be respected, or as a souvenir of their victories or as war reminders." The head posts reminded the Spaniards of hanging gallows, and as a result they named this area the Province of the Gibbets. They described seeing seven such displays there, and many more as they continued down the river through this province, which they reported continued for more than 150 miles. But they also spotted evidence of high culture, with "roads made by hand, and on the one side and on the other were planted fruit trees, wherefore it seemed probable to us that it was a great overlord who ruled over this land."†

By the next day they were low enough on food to be forced to make another raid landing. They approached a seemingly silent village with some trepidation, as the image of those ghastly gibbets was still very fresh in their minds. Beaching the boats, they sprang out onto land ready for a fight, which they promptly received. Residents poured from out of hiding and came on with wrath, led by a chieftain of great

* Historian Antonio de Herrera says that this chief's name was Caripuna, and Father Cristóbal de Acuña, who spent nearly two years on the Amazon, mentions a tribe by that name on the Madeira River. They were observed later, in 1852, by Lieutenant Gibbon, U.S.N., near the falls of the Madeira River.

† According to Helaine Silverman and William Isbell, "some advanced Amazonian societies built impressive formal roads, causeways, and canals of monumental scale. Large and small sites in the Tapajos . . . regions [Orellana and Carvajal report] are connected by traces of networks of straight roads with earthen berms suggesting hierarchical socio-political organization at a regional scale." Silverman and Isbell, *Handbook of South American Archaeology*, 172–74.

courage, who ran before them, screaming as he charged into combat. One of Orellana's crossbowmen swung about at the charging leader, leveled his weapon, and dropped the overlord as he came in full stride. This put an immediate halt to the charge. Their leader slain, the Indians dispersed, some fleeing the area, others regrouping to their homes, where they frantically threw up barricades and defense works.

Orellana took stock of his troops. A few of his men had been wounded in the initial fray, and he had no intention of losing men or risking others. From the looks of their fortifications, these warriors planned to fight to the death. As a tactic, with the assistance of the skillful harquebusiers, Orellana ordered the houses set ablaze. The flames crackled up the sides of the wooden and thatched huts, dried leaves and vines exploding in fiery bursts. Men and women and children ran screaming from their homes, allowing the Spaniards their chance to move in and pilfer food. They found many turtles—apparently kept and harvested in ways similar to that of the Omagua—and a large variety of fowl, parrots, turkeys (curassows), and ducks, and much bread and maize.

As the Spaniards scavenged around the burning buildings, they came to one that offered a ghastly revelation: it was filled with a number of burned-alive women and children who had failed to escape. For this reason Orellana named the place Quemados Villa, the Place of the Burned People.

Among the wreckage and ruins they also found a lone girl, who was talkative and clearly highly intelligent. They brought her along with them and rowed across to an uninhabited island where they could rest and eat some of the food they had just stolen. Orellana's intention was to speak with this girl and learn as much as he could, and according to Carvajal, with a little time and practice the captain was indeed able to converse with her—and the story she told fascinated him:

> She said that nearby, in the interior, were many Christians like ourselves, and they were ruled by a chief, who had brought them upriver, and that two of them had Christian wives and the others had married Indians who had borne them children. She told us that these were the people who had been lost out of Diego

Ordaz's party—or so we thought from her indications regarding them, for she pointed to the north.

This story—or some version of it—while seemingly fantastic and improbable, had persisted ever since Diego de Ordaz's ill-fated trip up the Orinoco in search of El Dorado. Ordaz, it will be remembered, was an important conquistador, a knight of Santiago and holder of a good deal of property in Mexico, property won through his exploits conquering the Aztecs under Cortés. In the course of his 1531 expedition to find and explore the Maranon—ironically, the very river Orellana was now on—Ordaz's flagship made land somewhere north of the Amazon's mouth, but the second ship, under Lieutenant-General Juan Cortejo, failed to arrive. Some said it struck rocks and fell to the bottom of the sea, while others said that it ran aground in the Amazon's shallows and that many of its men—some said up to two hundred—survived, went ashore, and were either captured or taken in by various Amazon River tribes.

As unlikely as such scenarios seem, rescues, recoveries, and discoveries of shipwrecked Spaniards living among indigenous populations had in fact occurred, and recently. These, in all likelihood, Orellana would have known about. In 1519, just after Cortés landed on Cozumel off the Yucatán Coast, he heard from locals on the island that across the way, on the mainland, were some white men, Christians like Cortés and his men. Cortés, intrigued by the possibility of Spanish-speaking countrymen who had been living among the mainland Indians, dispatched a ship with two captains—Juan de Escalante and, ironically, Diego de Ordaz himself, with fifty armed men for protection—to look for these Spaniards and deliver a handwritten message from Cortés to them. A week later, Escalante and Ordaz returned saying that they had delivered Cortés's message to a village chieftain, but nothing had come of it.

Then, just as Cortés was set to sail from Cozumel, where they had been repairing their leaky boats, a canoe came paddling up to shore, making land down the beach from where Cortés was hearing mass. Cortés's men ran down the beach to investigate, and they were stunned by what they found. A tall man stood in the prow of the boat, next to a half-dozen naked men holding bows and arrows. The tall man spoke: "Brothers, are you Christians?" he asked.

When the Spaniards nodded that they were, the man knelt in the sand and wept. He was a priest named Jerónimo de Aguilar, and the story he told was miraculous. Back in 1511 the ship Aguilar had been on struck low shoals off the coast of Jamaica, and he and some twenty other survivors escaped in a rowboat. With no food or water, trading turns at their one set of oars, they caught a westerly current and washed up on the shores of the Yucatán, half their number dead and the rest barely hanging on.

Mayan tribesmen found them and took them prisoner, immediately sacrificing their leader—a conquistador named Valdivia—and four other men, then eating those Spaniards during a festival feast. Aguilar and his remaining surviving friends, including a man named Gonzalo Guerrero, were crammed into cages and could only look on in horror at the sacrificial ceremonies, as drums rumbled into the lowland jungle and celebrants blew mournful songs on conch shells. The Spaniards were being fattened for sacrifice. Once they understood their imminent fate, they banded together and broke the cage slats, then escaped into the night.

Aguilar and Guerrero, along with a few others, found refuge in another village but were quickly enslaved, though they were allowed to live. Aguilar acquired the nickname "the white slave," and through hard work, luck, and his deep faith, he survived eight years among his Mayan captors and finally earned his freedom. He had received Cortés's letter from the messengers, and then visited his countryman Guerrero, who by now was living in a nearby village. Guerrero had won his own freedom through feats of strength and hard work, and he was now an accepted member of his tribe, a warrior and a military leader. He had taken a wife, a chief's daughter, and she had borne him a daughter and two sons. His heavily muscled body was covered with tattoos, his ears were pierced, and he wore a hunk of green jadestone as a labret. He had gone native, and he told Aguilar that he had no desire to return.

For his part, Jerónimo de Aguilar had always held out a remote hope that he might someday be rescued, and from the moment of his arrival on mainland Yucatán, he kept his mind sharp and strong by counting the days. Tucked beneath his tattered cloak was a torn old prayer book, which he kept with him at all times. In his eight years marooned, he had learned to speak Chontal Mayan fluently. Cortés could not believe this stroke of providence. Through Aguilar he could learn something of the mainlanders' customs and beliefs and lifeways. But most important, he could now communicate with them. He immediately made Aguilar his translator and interpreter and kept him nearby at all times.

There were other known stories of shipwreck and survival. Orellana might well have heard of the tale of Álvar Núñez Cabeza de Vaca, who was stranded on the coast of Florida in 1527 during an expedition captained by star-crossed Pánfilo de Narváez, known rival of Cortés. Cabeza de Vaca and three other survivors of shipwreck, hurricane, and abandonment walked westward across America for nine years, a journey on foot that took them from present-day Florida through Louisiana and Texas and all the way to California. They were the first Europeans to see buffalo, and they endured enslavement, torture, and near starvation. They lived among various tribes of the American southwest, finally making their way to Cortés's Tenochtitlán by 1536, back among Spaniards after an incredible odyssey in which they became faith healers and something akin to messiahs. Though his written account of the journey, *Chronicle of the Narváez Expedition,* would not be published until the current year, 1542, word of his incredible survival story had certainly spread throughout Spanish-speaking and Spanish-ruled Mesoamerica and throughout the Spanish-controlled lands of the New World, no doubt the subject of many fabulous stories.

So it was with great interest and likely belief that Orellana took in the tale told by the recently captured Indian girl. Because they were temporarily well stocked with food from their last raid, the Spaniards continued downriver without landing at any villages for a number of days, always moving through what appeared to be one continuous province. Finally, at its extreme eastern boundary, they floated toward a substantial village through which, the Indian girl told Orellana, they must pass if they wished to go to the place where his compatriots lived. Orellana considered this option, contemplating his meager forces and their general condition before thinking better of it. Instead, according to

Carvajal, his mind was on a return voyage, one better equipped: "We decided to press forward, for, as to rescuing them from where they were, the time would come for that." As frightening and dangerous as these lands were, Orellana's determination to return only grew with each new demonstration of the magic and wealth potentially to be found.

As Orellana resolved to proceed downriver, two Indians paddled out from the village to investigate. They maneuvered around the brigantines, gazing with amazement at the length and depth and breadth of these boats, the great wooden legs sticking out from them, and their strange grizzled passengers. Orellana attempted to parley with the two, entreating them to come aboard. He tried to entice them with some gifts of cotton blankets and a few of the remaining trinkets and curiosities he had on hand, but the two men remained in their canoe, stolid and resolute. Then they began to gesticulate with their hands, becoming quite animated, pointing to the Spaniards and then running their hands down from their chins, indicating the beards. They pointed back to shore, beyond the village and inland. Orellana and his companions interpreted this to be another reference to the members of the Ordaz party, and they tried to get more information from the two men, who spun about and paddled away. Orellana did not know exactly what to make of this exchange, but for safety, he pulled up near an island facing the village, moored, and anchored. He ordered the men to sleep inside the brigantines—no one was to disembark.

They awoke at dawn to the cries of native warriors and the sight of large battle formations of canoes racing across the water from the village, the Indians shrieking, chanting, and waving their bows and arrows violently. Orellana managed to pull up anchor and retreat before the canoe squadrons could arrive to inflict any damage, and the Spaniards fled down the river. For five days they kept moving almost continuously, sleeping nights hunkered down in the tepid and odoriferous boats, sweating profusely in their armor. On the fifth day, now out of food, they reached a new settlement and came ashore, relieved that the inhabitants chose not to resist.

Moving about this village, the Spaniards pilfered food stores as usual. Most unusual, though, here they found a large storehouse and dispensary for *chicha,* complete with prodigious quantities of maize stored in big basket hampers, for making both bread and, they realized, alcoholic beverages. They also found maize "buried in ashes in order that it might keep and be protected from weevils." Orellana's soldiers were delighted to discover a convenient and working "storehouse filled with liquor, of which our men partook liberally." This would have been their first real festivity since leaving the peaceful Imara and the Aparians, so Orellana was inclined to let them loose to enjoy themselves a little bit.

Orellana took the opportunity to explore this interesting, organized, and well-appointed community. He found stores of high-quality cotton goods here, too, but what really caught his attention and curiosity was another temple, this one containing hanging cotton hammocks for sleeping, perhaps to host travelers coming from great distances away. Also inside the temple they found "many military adornments in the form of cuirasses* and other pieces for all parts of the body; and hanging above all these were two miters, very well made and with natural skill, and in such a way as to be quite like those which bishops and prelates have as a part of their pontifical robes, they were made out of a woven cotton of various colors." The Spaniards named this village, fittingly, the Village of the Miters.

On Tuesday, June 22, winds slashed up and across the river, roiling the surface and taxing the navigators and the oarsmen. As the brigs bobbed along the whitecaps, Orellana noted an extended settlement along the northern shore, observing that "their houses were glimmering white." The captain, transfixed by the gleaming buildings, tried desperately to get his men to coax the brigantines across the river to the other side for a more thorough investigation, but alas, the wind and the waves proved insurmountable: "During the whole day there was no possibility of going over to follow the other shore on account of the excessive choppiness of the rough waves, and these were as broken and as restless as any that could be at sea."

Under calmer conditions, they managed to land and seize a village that sat in a pretty bend of a smaller tributary stream, the landscape there very flat, devoid of undulations or rises for nearly ten miles. As

---

* A defensive protection in the form of a breastplate.

they scouted about, they noted that the village here was orderly and organized, and had a well-designed street plan, with one central street running the length of the village and a village square midway down this main road. Houses flanked both sides of this street, and inside some of these the Spaniards found great quantities of maize and also much cassava bread made of a mixture of maize and yuca. They also helped themselves to a few welcome ducks and parrots. Because it was tucked away on the river bend, and also for its long street, they gave this village two nicknames: Pueblo de la Calle (Village of the Street) and Pueblo Escondido (Hidden Village).

Thursday, June 24, was the feast day of St. John the Baptist. Devoutly religious, Orellana and his men now began to hope they might find a good place to stop and celebrate, though certainly Orellana would have been mindful of how he had let his guard down on Corpus Christi, at the price of injured men and nearly some deaths. He hoped to avoid, at all costs, a repeat of that near disaster, but he knew that for the morale of his men, a break from the routine of the river would do much good.

As they cruised the smooth water, noisy yellow-billed terns—small and streamlined gull-like birds—flitted across the bow, dipping and swooping and soaring for fish or insects. They passed moderate-sized villages that Orellana described as "dwellings of fishermen from the interior of the country." The Spaniards were sailing closer to shore, looking for a safe place to land, when they rounded a large oxbow bend and saw on the shores in the distance numerous villages, these large and impressive, shimmering white in the sunlight. As Friar Carvajal put it succinctly, but with some trepidation: "Here we came suddenly upon the excellent land and dominion of the Amazons."

As the brigantines drew closer to these gleaming villages, Orellana soon realized that the news of his coming had again preceded him, for already many agitated warriors appeared along the banks, some taking to canoes at their approach. They came onto the water, organized and en masse and in a warlike mood, clearly intent on challenging the interlopers. A few courageous leaders paddled directly up to the brigantines, within speaking distance. Orellana made verbal entreaties of peace, even proffering a few trinkets and baubles, but his attempts at civil discourse did nothing to alter the hostile demeanor of the warriors, who threw back chants of mockery, even scornful laughter. There would be no negotiating.

Angered by the standoff and the warriors' arrogance, Captain Orellana made the decision to strike the first blow: "He gave orders to shoot at them with the crossbows and harquebuses, so that they might reflect and become aware that we had wherewith to assail them." Perhaps, as it had done in the past, the shock and surprise of loud, flaming, smoking firearms would cow them. If it did not work, if it was a fight the natives truly wanted, Orellana now resolved to bring it to them. As the smoke lifted from the Spanish boats, Orellana saw that some damage had been inflicted, and the canoes turned and sped for shore to report what they had seen and to rally their tribesmen.

Orellana's vessels were now less than a mile from the villages, and even from this distance the Spaniards could clearly see more droves of Indians massing along the shore at the waterline. Despite this, Orellana gave the order to row at full speed, for they were going to beach the brigantines and storm the place, guns, crossbows, and swords blazing.

But the landing would be more difficult than Orellana anticipated. As he approached he saw numerous well-organized fighting squadrons of Indians, knots of men formed up around the houses and buildings, and the village center teeming with warriors too numerous to count, all animated and well armed. The spectacle was daunting: "At the same moment there came out many armed with bows and arrows from among the trees, along the shore of the river, talking very loud and as if vexed, going through all sorts of contortions with their bodies, indicating thereby that they looked upon [the Spaniards] with scorn."

Nevertheless the brigs closed in, rowing at breakneck speed, but as the Spaniards came within range, the Indians at intervals fired well-aimed and well-timed volleys of arrows into the sky, the darts whistling through the thick tropical air like the wing beats of scarlet macaws. Orellana and his men were in their armor, some still suffering in their metal breastplates, others having adopted the thickly padded cotton variety the Spaniards under Cortés had learned about from the Aztecs. Given the accuracy of the native bowmen, they would need all the protection they had. The arrows fell from the sky in a driving deluge, skewering all about the Spaniards, some thumping and spearing into the wood, some hitting their marks, the men.

Quickly, Orellana countered with his own harquebus and crossbow fire, shooting and reloading and shooting again in rapid succession, dropping many Indians, only to see the fallen stepped over and pulled away and replaced by reinforcements. Those Indians not wielding bows stomped and chanted and danced alongside, encouraging their fellow tribesmen. Cloudbursts of the arrows continued to pour forth with such volume, rapidity, and ferocity that the Spaniards were forced to take cover beneath the thick manatee-skin shields they had captured from Machiparo's territory, to protect their unarmored extremities, and the oarsmen stopped rowing to protect themselves, covering their exposed faces with their hands. As the boats slewed and foundered out of control, native arrows impaled five of the Spaniards, including Friar Carvajal, who caught an arrow between the ribs, surviving only because his densely padded garments slowed the missile. "Had it not been for the thickness of my clothes," he reported, "that would have been the end of me."

Captain Orellana, recognizing their mortal peril, roared at the oarsmen to have courage, for he needed them now more than ever. He ordered them back on the oars and bellowed that they must row with every ounce of their strength and power to beach the brigantines. Sparked by their captain's rallying cries, the oarsmen gripped and pulled in unison, and amid an ongoing patter of arrows and spears, they succeeded in gaining enough speed to ram the beachhead, allowing their companions to leap from the sides of the boats and land chest-deep in the muddy water.

They landed right among fearsome warriors bent on defending their lands.

The Spaniards hacked and parried and thrust with their swords, swinging two-handed in great arcs, mowing down Indians in their path as they struggled through the water to the shore. But the warriors swarmed in from all sides, and they were everywhere, before and behind, a sea of screaming, surging enemies. For more than an hour the Spaniards waged close and hazardous hand-to-hand battle, but no matter how many Indians they slew, more came to replace them, these urging their fellows on with rekindled energies and spirit, leaping wildly over the dead bodies of their friends and relatives as they charged the Spaniards. According to Friar Carvajal, who watched the gruesome battle with an arrow sticking from his side, these Indians had more than just their homes to defend; they were fighting as the subjects, and allies, of the Amazons.

For what Carvajal and the others witnessed next was mystifying. Amid the throng of warriors there appeared ten or twelve extremely tall women warriors, with pale white skin and long hair twisted into braids and wound about their heads. "They are very robust," reported Orellana's priest, "and go about naked, but with their privy parts covered, with their bows and arrows in their hands, doing as much fighting as ten Indian men, and indeed there was one who shot an arrow a span deep into one of the brigantines, and others less deep, so that our brigantines looked like porcupines."

The Spaniards were battling hand to hand with Amazons, live and in the flesh. According to their annals, the women fought at the front line, in the role of leaders or captains spurring on the men, and what the Spaniards witnessed amazed them, for the Amazons "fought so courageously that the Indian men did not dare turn their backs, and anyone who did turn his back they killed with clubs right there before us, and this is the reason why the Indians kept up their defense for so long."

The battle raged at such a pitch that the Spaniards had no time to marvel or reflect on these wondrous women warriors—they were busy trying to stay alive. Finally, after an hour of continuous close, hard fighting, the Spaniards, bulling their way forward behind the thick manatee shields and slashing with their steel blades, managed to slay seven or eight of the warrior women, "for these we actually saw," remarked Friar Carvajal. There they lay, slain and blood-soaked on the beach. The Indian men saw their fallen leaders, too, lost their nerve, and retreated. The momentum had turned in the Spaniards' favor, and they gave chase, hacking at the retreating men and pursuing them back to their village. For a moment it appeared to be a rout, for they had done considerable damage once the Amazons had been felled.

But Captain Orellana could see scores of warriors massing on the outskirts and periphery of the main village, coming in support from nearby settlements with belligerent war cries, and he knew that if he and his men remained here they would be overwhelmed. He barked orders to board the brigantines as soon as they could. But this was no easy feat, for some Indians had already regrouped and fought in support of the few Amazons remaining, and the Spaniards had to retreat with their backs to the brigs, some battling and giving cover while others clambered aboard. Even more pressing, Orellana saw at the same time a wide fleet of canoes racing across the water toward them, trumpets, drums, whistles, and battle chants echoing from shore to shore. As they fought their way back onto the boats, Orellana ordered a seized Indian trumpeter—whose only weapon appeared to be his wooden musical instrument—taken with them as captive, and then they pulled up anchor and set off, the captain urging his oarsmen to row for their lives. Fortunately, the current was strong enough to sweep them downstream without assistance, because despite Orellana's exhortations, his companions were now so spent that they lacked the strength even to hold the oars steady. Instead of coursing at breakneck speed they rather drifted away from this extraordinary place, shifting and slowly turning like the monstrous floating islands they often saw moving lazily down this magical waterway.

Famished, exhausted, and parched with thirst, the Spaniards drifted and tended to their wounds. Mercifully, the canoe fleets did not follow. After a short time they came to a medium-sized village that appeared to be either uninhabited or abandoned—or perhaps the warriors had all gone to aid the village of the Amazons. Whatever the case, Orellana's men were so racked with fatigue and hunger that they begged him to make a landing there to seek needed food and rest. Carvajal remembered well Orellana's initial response: "The Captain told them that he did not want to, and that although to them it looked as if there were no people in the village, it was there [in such circumstances] that we had to be more on our guard than where we could clearly see them."

But his men persisted. At length, he held counsel with his leading compatriots, and all—even Friar Carvajal, who was still suffering from his arrow wound—were inclined to attempt to go ashore, or at least to have a closer look. Once they had already slung past the village, Orellana commanded his men to take up oars and back pull, slowing and cutting an arc nearer the shore. The *Victoria* and the *San Pedro* sat idle for a moment, Orellana scanning the shoreline, when he saw movement among the trees. As usual, his intuition had been right—they should have hurried past.

All at once the woods exploded in frenzied mayhem. Archers ran to the water's edge and fired a fusillade of arrows into the air, the shafts buzzing like swarming wasps and so thick that the Spaniards could hardly see one another inside the boats. Though they were taken by surprise, most reacted quickly, diving once again beneath the Machiparo manatee shields.

Those on the *Victoria* managed to row away from this fresh peril, but not before another round of arrows shrieked from above, and under this barrage Friar Carvajal felt a searing, and he clutched at his face with both hands, writhing there in agony. The arrow had pierced one eye and exited the opposite cheek.

The men on the *San Pedro* responded to the attack by heading for shore, making a bold if foolhardy landing. By the time Orellana reacted and brought the larger *Victoria* about, he saw that a number of men had leapt from the *San Pedro* and were now engaged in vicious hand-to-hand fighting among a press of warriors, who were closing in around the defensive crescent they formed. It was a seething snarl of Spaniards and Indians, and the situation appeared disastrous.

Orellana fired directions at his oarsmen, positioning the *Victoria* so that his crossbowmen and harquebusiers could level fire on the enemies. As he did so, he considered making a run at the shore, but seeing how seriously his priest was hurt, he thought better of it and called out for the men in the *San Pedro* to embark at once, for they must flee. The few men onshore fought their way back and did as their captain bade them, and they managed another hasty retreat, another devilishly close call.

As they drifted away from the ambush site, some of them, including Captain Orellana, took time to survey the landscape there along the southern bank. They saw inland a good distance—perhaps as far as five miles—large cities glistening white as seashells, the land here giving way to more open savanna. Though they had nearly died only moments before, the Spaniards noticed that thick smoke hung over the villages and above the treetops, for here the native farmers burned their fields, making the famous *terra preta* or "Amazonian dark earth,"* which contains low-temperature charcoals in very high levels, creating an extremely fertile soil.

Perhaps it was homesickness prompted by sleep-deprived delirium, but as they rowed away from the area—which they named St. John for the day they had entered it and was near the present-day town of Obidos—for the first time they grew nostalgic and saw in the land resemblances to their mother country of Spain. Perhaps Orellana was even thinking that here would be a good place to colonize, to raise livestock and farm crops similar to those at home, for the earth looked like it would be suitable for growing wheat, and they saw wild grasses and sedges along the shore and on floating meadows, and also uplands and sloped hillsides cleared of trees. The open savannas they imagined filled with game, too.

The left bank remained heavily inhabited, with the shorelines patrolled by flocks of canoes, and Orellana ordered a long pull to the center of the river. Until nightfall, small bands of canoes pursued them downriver, allowing the Spaniards neither rest nor opportunity to land, and forcing them at length to navigate in the darkness. Around ten o'clock that night a large and shadowy form loomed ahead and Orellana called to the steersmen to make for it, and as it happened they reached an uninhabited island where they might finally stop to rest.

---

* Once thought naturally occurring, *terra preta* (and the lighter-in-color *terra mulata*) is now widely accepted as intentionally man-made, improved soil, the culmination of what is referred to as "slash-and-char" agriculture. In slash-and-char, the organic matter is burned incompletely, resulting in charcoal rather than ash. Due to the high charcoal content and other nutrients—imbued into the soil as a result of intentional burning and then turned into the ground along with long-accumulated organic domestic rubbish such as excrement, fish, turtles, and even animal bones—*terra preta* contains much more calcium, nitrogen, phosphorus, and sulfur than typical Amazonian rain forest red earth soils, giving it longer-lasting fertility. *Terra preta* is also characterized by large quantities of potsherds in the soil, signifying human habitation and influence. See Charles C. Mann, *1491: New Revelations of the Americas Before Columbus*, 306–10.

It was pitch-black when they at last eased the brigantines alongshore and moored there, tying them off to stout shoreline trees. Orellana, his voice now a harsh whisper, forbade any man to disembark for any reason, and though the weary men wished to go ashore and sling hammocks or slump on the soft ground, instead they sat cramped and bleeding and wound-stiffened in the soaked and arrow-strewn bottoms of the brigantines. All through the night the floorboards and hull slats groaned against the river's slurry and wash, and the sides of the *San Pedro* and the *Victoria* were so prickled and quill-riddled with enemy arrows that they would have appeared like great nocturnal moonlit hedgehogs or porcupines trying to burrow into the riverbanks in search of a protected dwelling place for a safe night's sleep.

CHAPTER 15

The Trumpeter's Tale

*S*UNRISE POURED OVER THE BASIN IN SMOKE-FILTERED diaphanous light, and the men woke weary and war-sore, blood caking their beards and spattered across their cotton armor. Orellana made haste, ordering his men to pull for the safety of the river's center as they departed the hostile "Province of St. John," home to the Amazons and their fight-to-the-death auxiliaries. But here the river wove through braided channels, a tangle of islands they had no choice but to pass near. No sooner had they shaken themselves awake than they found themselves back in the thick of peril—for the islands appeared densely peopled, the river before them clogged with canoes:

> When they saw us, there came out to meet us on the river over two hundred pirogues, so large that each one carries twenty or thirty Indians and some forty . . . they were quite colorfully decorated with various emblems, and those manning them had with them many trumpets and drums, and pipes on which they play with their mouths, and rebecs, which among these people have three strings: and they came on with so much noise and shouting and in such good order that we were astonished.

The Spaniards were soon surrounded by the fleets, which encircled them in a giant pincer. Orellana responded by directing harquebus and crossbow fire at the closest canoes, which appeared to contain their leaders, and the marksmen felled enough of them to make an impression. The canoe formations parted to allow the brigantines through so that they could continue downstream, albeit escorted by attacking canoes of the "greatest of all riverbank chiefdoms, the Tapajos."

The Spaniards skimmed along with a weird fleet of musical pirogues paddling behind them, some playing their pipes and drums, others firing off arrows, a bizarrely lyrical sort of hostile escort. Along the shore dense formations of warriors stood at the ready, with others designated to play instruments in unison, some dancing about and singing while holding a large and resplendent palm frond in each hand, which they waved back in forth in a kind of mocking farewell. This display continued past very large islands overrun with warriors lining the shore, and dancing and chanting high up on bluffs, at the end of which came forth a warlike reinforcement of battle canoes. Orellana decided to try a token of diplomacy.

Hurriedly, with the canoes pressing down on them, he gave orders to prepare a gourd filled with some of their barter goods—jingle bells and some pearls and other precious stones—and this gourd Orellana tossed into the river as an offering of peace and a demonstration of his friendliness. Some of the lead canoes paddled forth to retrieve the gourd as it bobbed along, but Orellana's hopes of peacemaking were dashed when the Indians merely laughed and mocked the contents, continuing to pester the brigantines all day long, following and stalking them until they had driven the foreigners out of the Province of St. John.

It was the twenty-fifth of June, 1542. By late afternoon that day, Orellana finally managed to locate a landing area he deemed safe enough to stop and sleep, or at least try to rest briefly. They landed and moored beneath a grove of trees, but Orellana saw the faint figures of Indian spies lurking in the woods, so he posted armed and armored sentries on constant guard, taking shifts. This done and the perimeter of the camp secured, Orellana took no time for rest himself. He called for the captive Indian trumpeter and for the next few hours set about creating a lexicon of words and phrases he could use to communicate with the native. Orellana would have cross-referenced these new entries with the growing dictionary he had kept since the very beginning of his journey, way back in Quito in February 1541.

Under the glimmer of a new moon Orellana questioned the trumpeter about where he came from, asking for details about the village from which he had been taken. The Indian replied that the village was his home, and it was ruled by a powerful overlord named Couynco, whose domain and reach were considerable. Orellana wished to know more about the women with whom they had done battle, and the trumpeter relayed a remarkable tale, a story with details so fantastic and incredible that it would become by far the most controversial passage in Carvajal's expedition journal and would raise questions for Orellana to answer and explain, and attempt to comprehend, from that moment on:

> The Indian answered that they lived in the interior seven [in another copy, four or five] days' journey away and that, since Couynco was subject to them, they had come to guard the shore. The Captain asked if they were married, and the Indian said no. The Captain asked how they lived, and the Indian answered in the interior, and that he had been there many times, and seen their customs and way of life, since he had been sent there by his chief to carry the tribute. The Captain asked if they were numerous, and the Indian answered yes, and that he knew seventy of their villages by name. He then named them before those of us who were present, and said that he had been to several of them. The Captain then asked if their houses were made of straw, and the Indian answered no, that they were built of stone, and had proper doors, and that the roads ran between these villages that were walled on both sides, and that they had guards at intervals along them, to collect dues from those who used them. [Another version describes these walls as paneled with silver all around for half a man's height from the floor, and against them were placed silver seats, which they used for their worship and their drunken

feasts. There is the addition, too, of a temple ceiling lined with variegated feathers of parrots and macaws.]

The Captain asked if their villages were large, and the Indian answered that they were. He asked if they bore children, and the Indian answered yes. The Captain asked how they became pregnant, since they were not married and no men lived in their villages. He said that at certain times they felt desire for men and assembled a large army with which they went to make war on a neighboring chief and brought his warriors by force to their villages where they kept them for as long as they wanted. Then, when they were pregnant, they sent their prisoners back unharmed. If when their time came they bore a male, they killed him or sent him to his father. If they are girls they rear them carefully and train them to war. He said their queen was called Conori, and that they had great quantities of gold and silver, and that the principal women are served on gold and silver plate and have gold and silver vessels, while the common women use earthenware, otherwise wood.

He said that in the principal city, where the queen lived, there were five very large buildings used as temples, and sacred to the Sun. He added that they call these temples *caranain,* and that they contain gold and silver idols in female shape, and that from three feet above the floor these temples are lined with heavy wooden paneling painted in various colors. He said that they have many gold and silver vessels used in the divine service, and that the women are clothed in very fine wool. For in that land there are many llamas like those of Peru. Their clothing is a blanket, worn either girded across the breasts or thrown around the neck, or secured at the front with a pair of cords like a cloak. They wear their hair down to the ground and golden crowns on their heads, as wide as two fingers.

The Indian informed us further that no man is permitted to remain in the women's villages after sunset but must depart for home at that time, and that many provinces bordering on these women's lands are subject to them and pay tribute and services to them. But with others they remain at war, and particularly with that tribe from which they seize men that are to get them [with] child. He added that these women are white and of very great stature and numerous.

The trumpeter concluded his amazing story by assuring Orellana and the others listening that he had seen these women many times personally, all his life, and that he often had daily interactions and communications with them. He mentioned specifically two saltwater lakes from which the women harvested salt—a fact that might well have reminded Orellana of stories of the salt lakes and salt manufacture around Lake Texcoco, in Tenochtitlán, Mexico.

Orellana and the others took in all the details, which certainly were similar to and reminiscent of the Inca wealth of Peru, as well as the wonders of Montezuma's Tenochtitlán. Carvajal noted also that it all sounded plausible since he and his compatriots had been hearing tales and reports as early as Quito: the women warriors were so famous that in order to see them, some Indians traveled over 3,500 miles just to behold them, "and anyone who should take it into his head to go down to the country of these women was destined to go a boy and return an old man." The priest also explicitly stated that he found the Indian trustworthy and credible, "because he was an Indian of much intelligence, and very quick to comprehend."

As soon as the priest had heard the story—he may well have been there, albeit not in the best shape, having only the day before lost his eye to an arrow—he began officially referring to these women as Amazons, although as he observed, incorrectly:

Amazon in the Greek language means "having no breasts," in order that they might have nothing to hinder their shooting with the bow. . . . But these women we are dealing with here, although they do use the bow, do not cut off their breasts nor do they burn them off, albeit in other matter, such as in taking men unto themselves for a certain period of time for propagation of their kind and in other respects, it does seem as if they imitate those whom the ancients called Amazons.

Here, too, was born the name of the river, for they henceforth referred to this miraculous waterway as the Rio Amazonas, or River of the Amazons.

The Spaniards had been weaned on just such tales, and given what Cortés had described of Tenochtitlán, which possessed hunchbacks and dwarves and albinos, there was no reason to doubt that such a tribe of warrior women would exist. And, of course, there were the imposing female warriors they themselves had encountered, according to Carvajal's account of the pitched battle. Columbus claimed to have sighted them on Martinique, and one of Cortés's own captains claimed to have seen an island south of Panama peopled only with women. Cortés likely derived the legend—as did Orellana and his literate companions—from the romance *Deeds of Esplandián* (written in 1510), a sequel to the famous and widely read *Amadís of Gaul* (written in 1508). The novel *Deeds of Esplandián* contains a description of the Amazons that locates them definitively, for the first time, in the Americas, or in "the islands of California." Too, there was a very recent Spanish precedent for seeing things and discovering them for the first time. Chronicler Bernal Díaz, who reported with remarkable accuracy and detail the things he witnessed alongside Cortés during the conquest of Mexico, wrote his impressions of seeing the fabled city of Tenochtitlán, the wondrous city on the lake, noting the dreamlike quality:

> When we saw all those cities and villages built in the water, and the other great towns on dry land, and that straight level causeway leading to Mexico, we were astounded. These great towns and temples had buildings rising from the water, all made of stone, and it seemed like an enchanted vision. . . . Indeed, some of our soldiers asked whether this was not all a dream. It is not surprising therefore that I should write in this vein. It was all so wonderful that I do not know how to describe the first glimpse of things never heard of, seen, or dreamed before.

Orellana and his men had understood, from the time that they left Gonzalo Pizarro and determined that there was no turning back, that they were on a voyage of discovery; these women could be their legacy. Despite the fact that the story contained elements of lore and legend, passed down through antiquity, why not believe Carvajal? These connections to known stories or categories, as has been noted by the astute writer Alex Shoumatoff, gave the Spaniards something known or potentially knowable to cling to: "To a large extent people are only capable of perceiving what they already have categories for; however outlandish, the Amazon-women category was one of the few things the Spaniards had to hold on to." And besides, to Orellana and his men, given what they had already seen in Peru and on their amazing river journey, the Amazons would not have seemed outlandish at all. On the contrary, they had fully expected to find them. This leads Shoumatoff—who spent a summer trekking up the Nhamunda River, a tributary of the Amazon where the tribe of women living only with children is said to have lived—to claim: "It is unnecessary and probably unfair to conclude that Carvajal deliberately made up his reports . . . a final possibility, albeit remote, is, of course, that such a tribe of women without men did in fact live on the Lower Nhamunda."

Shoumatoff's journey illustrated, in part, that the people living far up the Nhamunda still speak of and make reference to the warrior women, and they believe they are descendants of a tribe called the Cofiori, which sounds very much like "Conori," Carvajal's rendering of the name of the queen of the Amazons. Shoumatoff transcribes the name as "Coftiori," which is even closer to the Nhamunda tribe's version. Additionally, he points out that "scholars who have tried to reconstruct the journey of the Spaniards from Carvajal's account have placed the engagement with Couynco's tribe on the left bank of the Amazon, before the Trombetas comes in, most likely at the mouth of the Nhamunda."

More tantalizing still, in 1620, Roger North (one of Sir Walter Raleigh's captains) sailed up the Amazon nearly three hundred miles, hoping to settle, colonize, and grow tobacco. One of his hearty men, Bernard O'Brien, took fifty Indians and five of his own men many hundreds of miles upstream, where he claims to have contacted the Amazons, even meeting with their queen.

A few years later, in 1639 (almost exactly a hundred years after

Orellana), an expedition under Portuguese conquistador Pedro Texeira undertook an arduous upstream expedition, chronicled by Father Cristóbal de Acuña, who also heard and recorded many tales about the Amazon women. According to Father Acuña, "The proofs of the existence of the province of the Amazons on this river are so numerous, and so strong, that it would be a want of common faith not to give them credit. . . . There is no saying more common than that these women inhabit a province of the river, and it is not credible that a lie could have been spread throughout so many languages, and so many nations, with such an appearance of truth."

Even the highly respected Alexander von Humboldt, whose Latin American journey in 1799–1804 has been called "the scientific discovery of the New World," leaned toward believing the legends and stories of the Amazons: "Could it have been [he wondered], that a group of women, growing tired of mistreatment by the men of their tribe, had struck out into the forest to live independently, learning the martial arts and, to perpetuate their race, periodically admitting the company of the opposite sex?" The French scientist and naturalist La Condamine, who explored the river basin in 1743 and whose published accounts enthralled and captivated the imaginations of Enlightenment Europe, also accepted the accounts of the Amazon women as plausible and true, and even reported that the Amazons had spread out, migrating up the Rio Negro.

Finally, the noted and deeply respected botanist Richard Spruce makes a strong effort to support the claims made by Orellana and Carvajal and seems to little doubt that they saw, fought with, and even killed women warriors. Spruce spent the years 1849 to 1864 in South America, much of it traveling the Amazon and its tributaries, including the Trombetas and the Rio Negro. He gives a personal example from his own time and experiences in the Amazon, saying, "I myself have seen Indian women that can fight," and speaks of the numerous accounts related by missionaries living on the Amazon during the seventeenth and eighteenth centuries that frequently reiterated tribal stories bearing witness to the Amazons' existence and traditions. Spruce concludes, "Those traditions must have had some foundation in fact, and they appear to me inseparably connected with the traditions of El Dorado."

Captain Orellana knew only what he had witnessed during the recent battle, but he was definitely transfixed by the story this Indian trumpeter told—and there appears in Carvajal's telling no doubt or equivocation of any kind. Particular elements and details—including the women's apparent worship of the sun at temples—the Spaniards had already witnessed firsthand, for in Amazonian cosmology, the sun is among the creators of man, and indeed of all living beings. Orellana noticed that many of the villages he had encountered were laid out in circular design, often positioned in accordance with the sun.

At last, when the sun had gone down and the trumpeter had finished his marvelous tale, Orellana and his comrades slept as best they could, another night spent in the tight and grimy confines of the brigantines, amid the whispery sounds of bat wings flitting past and the discordant croaks of horned frogs and rainfrogs and the ducklike racket of quacking tree frogs. Some of them may even have been exhausted enough to fall asleep and dream, conjuring tall, light-skinned women wielding deadly bows, their long and flowing hair, gilded with crowns, dangling past their breasts until it touched the ground.

Francisco Orellana, first European to descend the Amazon from its headwaters in the Andes to its mouth at the Atlantic Ocean. His voyage in 1541–1542 is considered one of the greatest accomplishments in the history of exploration and discovery, hailed by chronicler Oviedo as "something more than a journey . . . more like a miracle."

EL MARQUEZ DON FRANCISCO PISARRO de Truxillo.

P.E. Bouttats fec.

Francisco Pizarro, eldest of the famous "Brothers of Doom," conqueror of Peru and the Inca Empire.

On the fields of Cajamarca, November 16, 1532, Francisco Pizarro and his 167 men annihilated some seven thousand Incas and took emperor-elect Atahualpa prisoner.

The legendary Gilded One or El Dorado launched many expeditions, including that of Francisco Orellana and Gonzalo Pizarro. Stories told of an Indian king so fabulously wealthy that he charged his subjects with anointing his naked body daily from head to toe with fine gold dust. At the end of each day he bathed in a lake, lining its bottom with gold.

Gonzalo Pizarro started his expedition with nearly two thousand war hounds, trained for battle and intimidation of the Indians.

The Andes Cordillera was so brutally steep and difficult that Gonzalo Pizarro lost most of his ill-clad porters and many of his horses during his initial mountain crossing in late February 1541.

In his dealings with the Amazonian Indian tribes, Francisco Orellana used his considerable language skills and diplomacy much more frequently than force. He found many of the tribes to be generous hosts, some allowing him and his men to remain for over a month at a time in their villages and providing the Spaniards with food and boatbuilding materials.

The conquistadors found the heart of the Andes stunningly beautiful and yet virtually impenetrable. They faced violent flash floods, earthquakes, and volcanic eruptions as they descended to the Amazon Basin.

The fierce and powerful jaguar (Panthera onca) *was the largest cat in the New World. The Spaniards would have observed the great feline's enormous tracks on river beaches along the shores of the Amazon.*

The rain forests that Orellana and his men encountered were filled with large cats like jaguarundi, ocelots, and pumas, and the dark woods echoed with the ominous, lionlike roars of red howler monkeys and the piercing calls of macaws.

During their arduous trek through the Andes foothills, the conquistadors were forced to construct numerous rope bridges similar to this one in order to cross swollen streams and tributaries.

Caripuna Indians with a large tapir near the Madeira River. One such animal sustained Orellana and his men for nearly a week.

Stream crossings over slick fallen trees were frequent and dangerous. Some spans over high ravines were so treacherous that the conquistadors were forced to crawl across, a few plummeting to their deaths below.

Francisco Orellana and his men heard tales of cannibalism and reported seeing evidence of the practice on the lower Amazon. Certain tribes, including the Caribs, were associated with consuming the flesh of opposing warriors to acquire their enemies' powers.

Wie deß Königs Vtina Kriegßleute mit den erlegten Feinden vmbgehen.

15.

SO lang die Frantzofen bey dem groffen König Holata Outina inn Krieg / so er mit feinen Feinden geführet / gewefen / ift nie kein Streit gehalten worden / fo ein Schlacht köndte genannt werden:

The Amazon under moonglow was hauntingly beautiful, but also rife with danger, the river teeming with ferocious caimans and deadly anacondas.

The timeless Amazon

CHAPTER 16

Tides of Change and a Sweetwater Sea

*I*N THE MORNING, STIFF AND SORE BUT FIRED BY THE possibility of further riches to explore and exploit should they ever return, Orellana's men cast off from the scrubby grove, for the first time in days without being harried as they took their leave. They hoped that their greatest difficulties were behind them and that the stretch ahead would be uninhabited and uneventful and offer them an opportunity to rest their wounded men, eat in some semblance of comfort, and recover a bit of their strength.

But their wishes for a proper respite would not be realized quite yet. For very soon they approached some gorgeous country—among the "pleasantest and brightest land that [they] had discovered anywhere along the river"—high bluffs and savannas with hills and valleys. Unfortunately for the Spaniards, the lovely landscape was also quite thoroughly populated, and these people possessed a fighting mien. Still nursing their wounds from the continuous skirmishes, Orellana and his men did not like what they saw. "There came out toward us in midstream a very great number of pirogues to attack us and lead us into a fight." They came from the left bank of the river, in the district of the confluence with the clearwater Tapajos River, a tremendous tributary whose bluish water courses in from the south just above modern-day Santarém, Brazil.

As the warriors came near, Orellana and his brethren could see that these fighters looked different from any they had yet encountered. They were inked soot-black from head to toe, and their hair was cropped tight, very short on their heads. But most noteworthy was their size—they appeared to be extremely tall, even on first encounter in their canoes. The Spaniards quickly assimilated their very large physical proportions, noting, too, their garb: "they came forth very gaily decked out." And then the dyed-black warriors attacked.

Orellana had spotted them early enough to prepare a counter, and with deft maneuvering of the boats and some fast and furious firing of crossbows and harquebuses, the Spaniards did fair damage to them and kept them at bay as they proceeded down the river. Orellana named this region the Provincia de los Negros (the Province of the Black Men), and he later inquired of his captive trumpeter about their origins. The trumpeter explained that all the land that they could see—as well as a large domain that they could not see from the river—was ruled by a powerful overlord named Arripuna. This chieftain "ruled over a great expanse . . . back up the river and across country; he possessed territory so vast as to require eighty days journeying across it, as far as a lake which was off to the north." The interpreter added, to Orellana's great interest and concern, that Arripuna was an exalted warrior and that his subjects, these ink-dyed warriors, ate human flesh.

Orellana also learned that it was in Arripuna's expansive lands, and under his control, that the survivors of Diego de Ordaz's shipwreck remained. Perhaps even more interesting was the mention that Arripuna possessed impressive quantities of silver—yet another enticement for a possible return visit. But right now their primary concerns were avoiding confrontation if possible, and sustaining themselves with food—on which they were running short once again.

For two consecutive days they found no safe or suitable place to land. Finally they happened on a small village that did not appear particularly well defended, and so Orellana ordered a landing. The Indians there offered what resistance they could, but they were soon overwhelmed by the Spaniards, who seized every ounce of food available and then went on. Still needing better stores, Orellana was compelled to raid the next village as well, but this one was larger and the residents fought gamely from the shore, keeping the brigs at bay and denying them landing for half an hour. During this skirmish one of the Spanish compatriots, a man named Antonio de Carranza who hailed from Burgos, was struck in the foot by an arrow and cried out in extreme anguish, exclaiming that he was mortally wounded. He begged for a priest to hear him confess his sins and square his soul with his lord.

Carranza's wishes were granted, but the party was initially puzzled as to how an arrow to the foot was causing him such unbearable pain. An inspection of the wound later in the day revealed that this had been no ordinary arrow, but rather a poisoned one. By the next day,

> the wound turned very black, and the poison gradually made its way up through the leg, like a living thing, without its being possible to head it off, although they [cauterized] it with fire, wherefrom it was plainly evident that the arrow had been dipped in the most noxious poison, and when the poison had mounted to his heart, he died.

Orellana and his men came to the dreadful realization that any arrow wound was potentially fatal, and having watched the horrific and pro-tracted death of their countryman, they carried on in fear of suffering the same demise. They had managed to sack the village where Carranza was initially impaled, taking with them all the maize that they could stuff into the putrid brigantines, because now Orellana determined that they should land only in the most dire necessity, so shaken was he by the gruesome death of his comrade. They would proceed downstream with utmost cau-tion, staying as far from arrow range as they possibly could.

They moved on nervously, eyeing the shores with a newfound fear and respect. By the afternoon of the next day they were exhausted and needed sleep. Orellana spied a wooded grove at the mouth of an incom-ing river tributary that appeared safe. There were no huts in sight, and he thought they might be able to sleep without incident. Here some of the men rested while Orellana put others to work on some protective measures. Badly shaken by the grotesque Carranza death, he instructed a small crew to harvest timbers from the nearby forest to make "railings on the brigantines in the manner of fortifications." These bulwarks or bulkheads extended upward and inward from the brigantines' gunwales "like a rim . . . as high up as a man's chest, and covered with the cotton and woolen blankets which we had brought along," adding, Orellana hoped, a surrounding shield against further poison arrow attack.

The timing of this defensive measure could not have been more opportune, because no sooner were the railings and bulkheads constructed than Orellana noticed great flotillas of canoes spreading out on the river behind and below them, not attacking so much as observing their actions. Orellana regarded these natives carefully, but as they did not attack, he maintained watch only, and they continued to rest for a day and a half, both sides at something of an impasse.

As night of the second day approached, Orellana again looked out over the main river. A multitude of canoes and natives idled on the water and along the shores, and Orellana feared that their position at the river mouth was too vulnerable—he suspected that they would be attacked should they remain there through the night. Some Indians sneaked along the shore, so close to the tied-up brigantines that Orellana and his men could hear them talking among themselves, and the captain told his men to remain absolutely silent and to proceed with a stealthy but hasty departure. With little sound, the Spaniards once again boarded their now reinforced brigs and slipped out onto the glassy waterway to make good their escape.

Orellana, spooked by what had almost befallen them and wanting to make distance, ordered his rowers "tied to the oars" all night long, with no breaks. They rowed rhythmically, backs and arms and legs aching against the pull, until daylight. As the sun rose in their faces, the rowing became even more difficult, the water now exhibiting tidal tendencies. Remembered Carvajal, "The flowing of the tide extended to where we were, whereat we rejoiced not a little in the realization that now we could not fail to reach the sea." They might have been less heartened had they known they were still some three hundred miles from that goal.

Very soon they came to a narrow branch of a river that further cut short any celebration. Two detachments of canoes in full battle cry

poured forth, attacking with spears and arrows the instant the brigantines were within range. Immediately, Orellana's precautionary protective bulwarks paid off:

> With a very great clamor and outcry . . . they began to attack
> us and fight like ravenous dogs; and, if it had not been for the rail-
> ings that had been built farther back, we should have come out of
> this skirmish decidedly decimated; but with this protection and
> with the damage that our crossbowmen and harquebusiers did to
> them, we managed . . . to defend ourselves.

This battle, pitched at midriver, raged on continuously from sunrise
until midmorning, and at no time did the Indians allow the Spaniards
even a moment to rest or cease fighting. With every hour came more and
more reinforcements, until the water was so cluttered with canoes that
the Spaniards could scarcely see the surface between the enemy boats.
Closer and closer they pressed up against the brigantines, until navigating an escape seemed desperate and the two Spanish ships were almost
completely netted by canoes. The canoes impeded even the movement
of the oars, placing the Spaniards in absolute peril, ducking as they now
were beneath the protective railings and listening to the war chants of
the horde, who fought under an overlord named Ichipayo.

Orellana could wait no longer to act, lest they all be slain right there.
He called on Lieutenant Robles to rise to the occasion, and Robles
proved true, standing up in the prow of the brigantine and firing his harquebus with precision, killing two Indians with one shot. The instantaneous deaths of the Indians, coupled with the concussion of the firearm
booming like a violent thunderburst overhead, caused great fear and
panic among the Indians, and they began to spin and wheel their boats
away in terror and confusion. At this exact moment, another brilliant
shot rang out, this one leveled by a loyal harquebusier from Biscayne
named Perucho. His deadly aim felled another leader, and the explosion
caused most of the Indians to leap or fall into the water, affording the
Spaniards easy, slow-moving targets for their swords and crossbows. In
the end, the canoes that were still upright fled for safety, leaving the

natives in the water to drown or be slain by the Spaniards. None of those who fell into the water escaped with their lives.

As the Spaniards rowed away, they saw along the banks thousands of tribesmen, chanting and parading. "The Indian men kept uttering cries, and the women and children kept beating the air with pairs of fans resembling fly-shooers, and kept jumping and dancing, executing many gestures and contortions of their bodies, manifesting great delight and joy, like people who had come out victorious, in that they had driven us out of their country."

The battle had lasted all morning, and now Orellana ordered his oarsmen to hurry to the opposite side of the river so that they might skirt away from the more populated and developed lands they could see coming up fast. As they moved across the river, they noticed that one of their comrades, a mercenary soldier named García de Soria, writhed about in anguish. An arrow had struck him in his thigh, and though the arrow point barely pierced the surface of his skin, actually falling out on its own, the tip of the arrow was glazed with deadly poison—sometimes harvested from the glands of poison dart frogs or, more often, made from toxic tree bark—and he was to suffer the same horrific fate as Carranza before him. In less than twenty-four hours Soria, a native of Logrono, fell dead after suffering unspeakable pain, fevers and convulsions, and finally paralysis. His agonized passing served as yet another terrifying reminder of the fate that awaited anyone so much as grazed by a poison arrow.

The lands the Spaniards were now passing had fortresses and some ramparts heavily garrisoned against attack, and these sat positioned on scrubby, barren hillsides that were some distance to the interior—back quite a span from the river shore. This line of flat-topped hills was likely the Serra de Almeirim, which ascends nearly a thousand feet above the river and runs for nearly a hundred miles along its northern shore. Passing these, they came to a deserted section, and Orellana chose to risk going ashore, for his men sorely needed to walk about and stretch and get out of the boats for a time. The stop was risky, for they were only a few miles downstream from the violent village they had just fought their way through, but the flagging morale of the men seemed to require it.

The land here was savanna, interspersed with thin groves of trees, which reminded the Spaniards of the cork oaks and white oaks of their homeland.* Orellana chose to stay a few days, and while most of the men rested along the vacant shore, he dispatched a small reconnaissance party inland, cautioning them not to stray too far from the main camp. The scouting party discovered a large network of well-used trails leading to and from the water. The tracks, likely made by hunters and fishermen, did not appear fresh, but were well established and deeply fissured and had clearly received much use over a long period of time. They encountered a torched village, apparently raided by rival tribes from the far interior. After two days, when they were well enough rested, Orellana rallied the men to show courage for the remainder of the voyage—whatever it brought—and they put into the river once more to continue their journey, quite literally "come hell or high water."

The fine savanna country soon changed, turning into a wild and nebulous maze of marshes and estuaries and islands, with river channels and arteries so webbed that they could no longer see the mainland shores on either side. Now they threaded their way through narrow channels between islands, forced to row sometimes against the rush of tidal inflow, navigating all the time now on a freshwater sea. "We struck out among islands that are really a part of the river's course," recalled a chronicler, "that are too numerous to count and in some cases very large, navigating among which calls for highly skilled mariners or pilots able to decide where to go in and where to come out, because the islands make the river divide up into many arms." The boats were often in danger of foundering, buffeted by coastal winds hurtling up the channels.

Many of the islands throughout the channels supported villages, some of them quite large. Orellana went ashore at one that appeared abandoned, hoping to make a food raid. But before finding any stores worth taking, Orellana and his men encountered a sight to make them shiver: "flesh roasted on barbecues . . . kept ready to eat, and it was readily recognized as the flesh of a human being, because there were a

* According to botanist Richard Spruce, these trees were *Curatella americana* and *Plumeria phagedaenica;* they are definitely found in the region around Santarém that Orellana and Carvajal describe as having these trees.

number of pieces of it—a few feet and hands that had belonged to a human being." The Spaniards quickly departed this macabre place.

At another village they came across some very intriguing artifacts, suggesting not only that they were now quite near the sea, but that the inhabitants had been in contact with, and been impressed by, other Europeans: two clay representations of sailing ships, hung up on display, possessing both the shape and proportion of brigantines, and very lifelike. These may well have been made to commemorate or illustrate encounters with the ships that Pinzón sent upriver from the mouth, or perhaps even those of Diego de Ordaz. They found, too, a shoemaker's awl, "with the thread and brass sheath that go with it, whence it was understood that the Indians of this country knew of the existence of Christians."

Most remarkable to the Spaniards was the colorful and highly decorative pottery that they found among these islands. So impressive were the illustrations and workmanship that the Spaniards made expressive and elaborate recordings of them, including the following:

> A thing well worth seeing are the pictures which all the Indians along this river put on the vessels which they use for their household service, both clay and wooden ones, and on the gourds out of which they drink, because of the exquisite and beautiful leaves and the carefully drawn figures, and in the excellent skill and organization that is required in making them: they apply colors to them and make them stay on very well, and these colors are very good and very fine, each one being of a special kind and different in shade. They manufacture and fashion large pieces out of clay, with relief designs in the style of Roman workmanship, and so it was that we saw many vessels, such as bowls and cups and other containers for drinking, and jars as tall as a man . . . very beautiful and made out of a very fine quality of clay.

Some of the vessels seem to have been made in daily household contexts, for regular consumption of food, but other more ornate pieces suggested a more ceremonial usage, perhaps during special feasts, and also those associated with tobacco consumption, and the ritual use of hallucinogenic beverages like *yajé*.* Subsequent archaeological digs in and around this area, particularly on Marajó Island, have turned up remarkable gender iconography, with female representation predominating on the funeral vessels and figurines and suggesting elaborate female rites as well as their important (perhaps even dominant) social and political importance and ranking within these elaborate chiefdoms. The Spaniards concluded that the quality of the artisans' work illustrated keen intelligence and high creativity, with style and design of such a level as would "make a very good showing in the eyes of the highly accomplished artisans in that profession in Europe."[†]

Food, however, was scarce, and it soon became obvious to Orellana that, though he wished to avoid it, he was going to need to land at an established and occupied village and either use diplomacy or weaponry to gain fresh sustenance for his flagging company. They navigated up an estuary of a stream, rowing hard and fast at high tide, Orellana piloting the larger brigantine *Victoria* toward the shoreline of an island village situated on an estuary, landing her with a flourish and the companions leaping out, battle-ready.

Following behind, the *San Pedro* attempted the same maneuver, the

---

* *Banisteriopsis,* called *yajé* in Brazil and *ayahuasca* in Peru and Ecuador.

[†] Archaeologist Anna Curtenius Roosevelt's digs at Pedra Pintada (Painted Rock) in Brazil unearthed sherds of the oldest pottery found in the Americas, and other evidence at the site (tortoise shells, animal and fish bone remains, burnt firewood hearths) suggested that the early inhabitants were a culture able to adapt to their environment, contentions that contradicted previously held theory and sparked a long debate known as the Meggers-Roosevelt debate. Excavating in the 1980s at Marajó Island at the Amazon's mouth, Roosevelt used the most modern techniques—ground-penetrating radar, total-station topographic mapping, and others—to construct a picture of the mound builders who had lived there that fundamentally challenged the controversial theories of Betty Meggers in her 1971 book *Amazonia: Man and Culture in a Counterfeit Paradise*. Roosevelt argued that the "Marajoara culture was one of the outstanding nonliterate complex societies of the world," and suggested that at its height, it supported more than a hundred thousand people. She concluded that these complex chiefdoms possessed "territories tens of thousands of square kilometers in size, larger than those of many recognized prehistoric states. Their organization, and ideology of deified chiefs and ancestors, nobles and seers, vassals or commoners, and captive slaves are more similar to those of early states and complex chiefdoms elsewhere in the world than to the present Indian societies of Amazonia." Her theories and findings offered paradigm shifts in thinking and sparked debates that continue to this day; many of her theories—including early human arrival, and the existence of tribal societies and their pre-agriculture pottery—are now widely accepted.

oarsmen bringing her up to beaching speed on the surging wash of tide, when they felt a sickening impact and came lurching to a halt. The *San Pedro* had impaled itself on a submerged timber. The pole stove in a plank, rupturing a great hole in the bottom of the boat. It listed now over to one side, water rushing in and swamping the vessel until she lay imperiled, "until there remained only four finger widths of the gunwales uncovered."

Up ahead on the beach, Orellana and his crew had scattered the inhabitants they encountered and were scouring the village for food. But only moments later, crowds of Indians began to return, armed and dangerous, and they drove the Spaniards back to the *Victoria,* which to their dismay had now been left aground by the receding tide. Carvajal reported that "Here we saw ourselves in a very trying situation, one more trying than any into which we had fallen along the whole course of the river, and we thought we should all perish."

With one boat swamped, one beached, and hostile Indians pouring down the creek, Orellana belted out orders, dividing his crew into squads: one would remain engaged with the Indians, fending them off as best they could, while the other group had dual duty, trying simultaneously to heave the large *Victoria* into the water where it might float freely again, and to repair the leaking *San Pedro* enough to sail it away. Orellana and the two priests stayed aboard the *Victoria,* guarding the exposed water to their rear against canoe attack.

For three terrifying hours the Spanish fighters managed to fend off the island-dwelling Indians while the rest of the crew worked tirelessly to repair the *San Pedro,* stuffing blankets and bedding and clothing into the rupture and hammering spare planks inside and out, furiously bailing water to make the vessel at least temporarily seaworthy. At almost the same moment, the *San Pedro* was repaired and the *Victoria* finally floated on the water once more. The Spaniards loaded what foodstuffs they had originally found, boarded the brigs, and hurriedly departed, limping away from this hostile harbor and thanking their God for deliverance.

Floating aimlessly through the marshlands, that night the crews slept aboard the brigantines. At sunrise Orellana began looking for a suitable place to land. Although the men were seriously malnourished, his most immediate concern was the repair of the *San Pedro,* which was unfit for navigating the flat tidal waters they were on, much less the open ocean, which they now seemed destined to reach. They came later that morning to a protected wooded area that looked to Orellana defensible and sheltered, and he ordered the boats moored there and tied off to trees along the shore. His plan was to repair the *San Pedro* first, and also to begin preparations for serious retrofitting of both boats to make them seaworthy oceangoing vessels. To do this, they were again going to need more nails.

At this island encampment Orellana set up another forge and nail-making factory. While volunteer carpenters pulled the *San Pedro* out of the water, dried its hull, and began patching its damaged bottom, others set to felling trees, drying them, and manufacturing charcoal in order to melt, form, and forge nails from ferreted-away pieces of metal. It was the first time they had done such work since leaving the village of Aparia the Lesser, and the break in monotony did the men good, a respite from fighting and foraging for food.

But the work was slow and laborious, in part because the men were weak from undernourishment, and also because hard rains made it difficult to keep the forge going and timbers dry. Food ran so low here that Orellana ordered the strictest of rations: "We ate maize in rations counted out by grains." During one of these toilsome evenings, Orellana stood peering out at the river's swirl when he saw an odd shape floating along, a bobbing quadruped that appeared to be the size of a mule. As it floated near, he saw that it was a dead tapir, and he quickly ordered a few men to take a dugout canoe and go after it—perhaps the carcass would be in good enough shape to consume. The men returned soon with the providential animal that "had been dead for only a short time, because it was still warm and had no wound whatsoever on it."

Orellana and his men could offer no explanation for the tapir's demise, but they were too hungry to care. They considered it a divine gift or intervention that saved their lives, for the very large animal (tapirs are the largest terrestrial animals in Brazil, some weighing as much as 650 pounds) sustained the crew of fifty Spaniards for nearly a week. They consumed every ounce of it, entrails and all. By the time the *San Pedro*'s hull was fully repaired and Orellana decided that enough nails had been fabricated for the work that remained, eighteen days had passed—most of the month of July—during which they had all "toiled with no little amount of endeavor." But Orellana needed a bigger, flatter, more open beach where both boats could be brought ashore and fitted out for sea, and so on about July 25, he continued in search of such a place.

Downstream among the many islands and beaches they found a suitable island, uninhabited and well positioned for scouts and guards to survey the water above and below them for attackers. Most important, there was enough room on the beach to haul both boats ashore and set to the serious labor of making them oceanworthy. Using makeshift rollers of felled trees and spare (though rotting) ropes, the weak, gaunt men hoisted the boats up onto the beach and began the difficult retrofitting work.

By now, they were fairly practiced at the craft, having already built the two vessels from scratch along the way. Some wove rigging and cordage for lines and halyards out of vines gathered nearby, while others set to sewing together sails out of the Peruvian blankets they had carried with them, as well as any spare woolen clothing they had brought along. Blacksmiths hammered away at the oar fittings and mast stays, while other crewmen found strong, tall palms for proper masts, shaping other cut timber into rudders and spars. Anticipating the very high likelihood of taking on water from sea spray and open ocean waves, the famished crews even built two bilge pumps—one for each craft—with plungers sealed with grease made from "rancid turtle fat" and the remaining leather parts they could find.

While the smiths and carpenters worked, others scoured the beaches of the island for food. The starving and disoriented men plodded about, grim and despondent, "for we did not eat anything but what could be picked up on the strand at the water's edge, which was a few small snails and a few crabs of reddish color the size of frogs." They were reduced to roasting these on spits along the beach, along with a few maize kernels, and sharing all among the crew, making sure that the shipbuilders received more than a fair share to sustain them. Given the condition of these men, their achievement on this island was nothing short of miraculous.

The effects of serious undernourishment include devastating lethargy, not only physical but psychological as well. With little to look forward to but more fighting with Indians, the specter of poisonous darts or arrows, and who knew how many terrible days of want—including vicious thirst and hunger—at sea, Orellana and his men might well have been at an all-time low. People who are starving—or severely undernourished—experience blackouts from standing up suddenly, swollen hands and feet, and abject irascibility. Concentrating on even the simplest task becomes nearly impossible. Couple all this with the very real fact of seeing their bodies weaken and emaciate, atrophying and losing muscle and fat, and there was the perfect recipe at this island—which the Spaniards named, appropriately, Starvation Island—for giving up. But it is a true testament to both their tenacity and Orellana's leadership that in just two weeks, they had made both the *San Pedro* and the *Victoria* seaworthy.

On August 8, 1542, Orellana urged his men aboard the ships and they departed Starvation Island now under sail, dizzy with hunger but bolstered by their accomplishment with the boats. They would continue toward the mouth of the Amazon, come what might.

Through the intricate and convoluted maze of waterways they sailed, using the winds to tack from one side to the other of the widest sections of the river. The sailing was tricky, the shifting winds challenging the pilots, who, in any event, were not experienced sailors but mercenary fighters for hire who had either volunteered or been chosen for the arduous task of keeping the brigantines from shipwreck or running aground. The surging tides added to the difficulty, as did the fact that neither ship had a proper weighted anchor, an extremely useful tool for waiting out tides. According to Carvajal,

> What grieved us most was having no anchors for either one of the brigantines in order to be able to lie at anchor, waiting, as it was necessary to wait, for the tides, for the time when the water should fall; and, as we anchored to buckets made of stone and sticks, it happened many times that the brigantines would drag these crude anchors along the bottom, with the risk of being smashed to pieces.

As they zigzagged their way through this tortuous and twisted patchwork of islands and streams, shorebirds rode the wind across the bows, terns and sandpipers flitting and swooping, and the men saw snowy egrets and huge jabiru storks wading the marshes, their tall white bodies bright flecks against the dark water. Sometimes they temporarily ran aground on sandbars created by the surging tides, but Orellana refused to allow the men to panic, instead ordering them to leap from the boats and lift them back into deeper water, or choosing to wait it out until the incoming tide would right them again. The want of food they had suffered on Starvation Island gripped them still, and the men moved with the sloth and despondency of the walking dead. Orellana understood that none of them could last much longer without food.

When it finally became clear to Orellana that they simply must land and obtain food or perish, he risked going ashore in one of the estuaries, and with tremendous good fortune found the inhabitants mostly docile and hospitable. Still haunted by fear of being attacked with poisonous arrows, however, in this place he took aside a young woman and decided to test one of the arrows that had been pulled from the protective railing of the *Victoria* to see what happened. He scratched this girl on the arm with the arrow tip, then waited to see what fate befell her. When nothing happened to her, he decided that the village was safe, and they obtained what food they could, but it was scarce, or possibly hidden from them. But to the Spaniards' great relief, the coastal Indians throughout the remainder of their estuary journey greeted them unarmed, and generally provided at least some food—mostly in the form of roots or tubers they referred to as *inanes*—a kind of yam—and some maize.

So they pushed on through this coastal morass, the winds and tides so strong here that they sometimes lost an entire day's forward progress in a single hour, and all they could do was pull up oars and take in sails and watch the boats move backward up the shoreline. It was disheartening, but at least during these weeks the men were learning—to the degree that they could in such extreme circumstances—how to sail. At some of these coastal villages the inhabitants approached Orellana and his men and pulled or pointed to their beards, ran their hands over their Spanish clothes, their padded linen brigandines and jerkins, then indicated, through animated sign language and speech, that "not far away from there were some lost or colonizing Spaniards." Orellana and his men could not know whether this was true, but they took it as a good sign that they might soon again be among Christians.

At the last of these docile villages, near the end of the Amazon, Orellana exchanged the remaining barter goods he had on hand for a few fish, and here he told his men that they must make final preparations for the sea, which they would soon enter. There was much to do. They needed to stock up on strong ropes and hawsers for the rigging, which they made from bush-rope vines and other lianas or vines dangling from trees in the mangrove forest; here also they constructed proper rudders for the ships, made final adjustments to the bilge pumps, and sewed together spare sails for the voyage, in the event that the ones they were using, pieced together as they were, should become torn or tattered in a squall.

Orellana told each man to carry his own provisions for the voyage, which included very scant stores: a small jarful of freshwater each, and a small satchel of roasted maize or some yams—meager fare at best. Orellana divided the most experienced seamen between the two brigantines, so that each ship might have at least some crew members with nautical backgrounds, but they lacked trained navigators or pilots, and the men were apprehensive about the next part of their journey, knowing that despite all they had survived and fought through on their epic odyssey, they might easily die in the next day or two on the open sea:

> In this manner we got ready to navigate by sea wherever fortune might guide us and cast us, because we had no pilot, nor compass, nor navigator's chart of any sort, and we did not even know in what direction or toward what point we ought to head.

But this aspect of the unknown had never stopped Orellana before, nor would it now. Nearly the entire expedition, from its origins in Quito in early 1541, had been predicated on the unknown. Still, some of his men were terrified of the impending sea journey, and it took a good bit of diplomacy and leadership on Orellana's part to calm their nerves and bolster their spirits. There was palpable tension among the men, and

Carvajal remembered it very well indeed: "I am telling the truth when I say that there were among us a few so weary of this kind of life and of the long journey that, if their consciences had not kept them from so doing, they would not have failed to remain behind among the Indians." But Orellana's control, guidance, natural leadership, and skilled captaincy kept even a single man from deserting, and they loaded the ships, each man with his water and food kit, and prepared to set sail.

Captain Orellana and his trusted priest Gaspar de Carvajal boarded the *Victoria*. It was Saturday, August 26, 1542, and they had taken nearly three weeks to navigate the saline marshes and islands and tributaries, the coiling river braids that comprise the region inside the great mouth of the Amazon. Even more remarkable, it had been more than eight months—and seemed like a lifetime to some of the men—since that fateful day after Christmas 1541 when they had split from Gonzalo Pizarro's force and struck out down the river in search of food. Now they finally sailed to the north of the big island of Marajó, a massive, country-sized landform in the Amazon's maw, the world's largest river island. Orellana and his compatriots felt the curious freshwater sea breeze in their faces, tasted the sweet seawater wash on their lips as they passed from the mighty Amazon, the greatest river in the world, and out onto the ocean. For here, the Amazon's freshwater discharge is so voluminous as to prevent salt water from inundating the main channel of the river, the water remaining fresh for more than one hundred miles out to sea. And while they did not yet know exactly what they had achieved, they were awed by what they saw heading out to the open ocean: the mouth of the river channel they passed through, "from cape to cape," was more than fifteen miles wide, and as they sailed along they could see other mouths even larger and more impressive.

Captain Francisco Orellana had successfully navigated and descended the world's largest river, from its source in the Andes to its nearly two-hundred-mile-wide mouth at the Atlantic Ocean, but his journey was far from over. Though he did not know precisely where he was, Orellana did know that there were Spanish-occupied settlements to the north, on the pearl-fishing islands of Cubagua and Margarita, lying just off the northern coast of what is today Venezuela. What Orellana would not have known, nor perhaps would have wanted to, given all he and his men had endured, was that those islands were more than 1,400 miles away.

During their first few days at sea, Orellana was blessed with the same brand of good luck that had helped him get this far already. The weather held, for one thing, and they were not buffeted by the summer squalls that can characterize the mouth of the great river. Most fortunate, though, they were almost immediately caught up in and rode the Southern Equatorial Current, a massive current deflected northward along the coast that pushes straight up past the Guianas toward the top of the South American landmass, which is exactly the direction they needed to go.

For three days the *San Pedro* and the *Victoria* sailed in tandem up the coast, tacking as best they could so as to maintain sight of the mainland shore. Sometimes they drew far enough away to lose sight of land, and this concerned Orellana greatly, given that they were traveling in small handmade brigs with no navigation systems, and not proper caravels built for ocean crossings. Also, each man had so little water that losing sight of land meant losing sight of freshwater rivers, and this to the men spelled potential death from thirst at sea, something none wished to think about but certainly all did.

On the third night moving northward in unison, a storm set in and separated the two boats. At sunset on August 29, the men aboard the *Victoria*—including Captain Orellana and Friar Carvajal—worried that their compatriots aboard the smaller and frailer *San Pedro* were forever lost at sea, or had smashed into the rocky coastline, because they perceived they "had been navigating along the most dangerous and roughest coast that there is around this whole vast ocean." Scanning the ocean horizon, Orellana could see nothing but whitecaps and an endless expanse of blue water, with no sign of the scrappy little *San Pedro,* the boat he had built with Gonzalo Pizarro and in which he and his followers had gone off in search of food those many months ago.

By the ninth day at sea, Captain Orellana had problems of his own. After passing by the mouth of the mighty Orinoco (which Ordaz had ascended a decade before), Orellana skirted the devilish and narrow Boca de la Sierpa (Serpent's Mouth) and managed to navigate around the island of Trinidad, between Trinidad* and Tobago, but found him-self drawn into the northern entrance to the Gulf of Paria, the dangerous Boca del Dragon (Dragon's Mouth) named by Christopher Columbus on his third voyage. Here treacherous rocks and small islands extend from the anvil-shaped point of northwestern Trinidad, jutting out toward the Paria Peninsula, and even today this narrow entrance pre-sents extreme hazards to small craft. The *Victoria,* narrowly escaping di-saster entering the Mouth of the Dragon, followed too far into the gulf thinking this was their best route, and spent the next week trying to sail and row free from its jaws. Deep inside the Gulf of Paria, the freshwater pouring out from the Rio Grande and San Juan River of mainland Venezuela mixes with the salt water, creating an angry turmoil difficult to maneuver in. Remembered Carvajal of that perilous time, "When we found ourselves within it we tried to go out to sea again; getting out was so difficult that it took us seven days to do so, during all of which time our companions never dropped the oars from their hands, and during all these seven days we ate nothing but some fruit resembling plums, which are called *hogos."*

After a week of constant struggle the winds abated long enough to allow them to row themselves from the Dragon's Mouth—which they described as a "prison"—and out to safety. Two more days of sailing, without really knowing where they were or where they were heading, and they spotted land over the bow, the low-lying outline of an island just ahead. The oarsmen lay slumped, their hands destroyed. Others clenched their water jars, which they had been holding aloft to catch rainwater whenever there was a squall or even a drizzle. Their lips were cracked and bleeding.

The navigator bellowed out "Land ho!" and the men woke and peered excitedly over the gunwales, hardly able to contain their elation when they saw a small port, the Spanish outpost town of Nueva Cádiz. They had reached Cubagua, the tiny eight-square-mile "Pearl Island,"

---

* Although Columbus discovered Trinidad in 1498, it was not colonized by Spain until much later, in 1588, and thus there were no landing ports or populations there as Orellana sailed past in 1542.

lying just south of the much larger Margarita Island and the site of the first Spanish outpost in the Americas. With incredible circumstantial irony that Orellana would learn of only later, the entire city of Nueva Cádiz had been leveled by earthquake and tidal waves on Christmas Day 1541, just before Orellana and his small crew embarked on their ordeal down the Amazon.

Now, on September 11, 1542, at around three in the afternoon, they had arrived at the partially rebuilt township, joyful to see a few proper sailing vessels in the small harbor and the outlines of recognizable dwellings—and even a Spanish flag—coming into focus in the distance. They made port, dropped planks, and disembarked, wobbling weakly ashore and standing on this tiny island, Captain Francisco Orellana and his crew having completed one of the most remarkable, daring, and improbable journeys in the history of navigation and discovery. Orellana's achievement would later be called one of the world's greatest explorations, "something more than a journey, and more like a miraculous event."

News of Orellana's arrival spread quickly about the town, and soon, to Orellana's immeasurable relief and euphoria, some members of the *San Pedro* came down to the beach. Astonishingly, they had arrived on the island two days before, somehow having managed to avoid the savage jaws of the Mouth of the Dragon. Remarked Father Carvajal, "So great was the joy which we felt, the ones at the sight of the others, that I shall not be able to express it, because they considered us to be lost, and so we considered them."

After a meeting of men that included tears and embraces, Orellana took a muster roll: 43 of his original 57-man expedition had survived the ordeal. Only three had been killed in battle; the other eleven had succumbed to disease or starvation or consumption of poisonous food. As Captain Orellana strode up the path from the port leading into town, the one-eyed hidalgo from Trujillo had no way of knowing exactly what he had accomplished, but the briny smell of the fishing town would have reminded him and the others of what they had all been dreaming and fantasizing about for a very long time—sitting down at a big table for a lavish and sumptuous Spanish meal, one with plenty of wine.

The Homeward Reach

*T*HE MIRACLE OF FRANCISCO ORELLANA'S DISCOV-
ery of and his successful journey down and to the mouth
of the Amazon was perhaps nearly equaled by the safe
arrival of both the *San Pedro* and the *Victoria* on the
tiny island of Cubagua. Using only the stars and a few
Spaniards' innate navigational abilities, and the good fortune of the Equatorial Current, the two retrofitted brigantines had sailed nearly 1,400 miles of ocean seas, and
Orellana and his crews had much to be thankful for and
proud of as they ate and rested and nursed their ill health
and battle wounds. There would be time in the coming
weeks and months for many among them to contemplate
where to go next, but for Orellana there seems never to
have been any question: he was destined to return to his
river, it was only a matter of how and when.

However, there remained plenty to do and account for,
not the least of which was the nagging question of Gonzalo
Pizarro and where things stood with him. Soon after their
arrival, the Spaniards learned of the death of Francisco
Pizarro, which had occurred more than a year before.
Father Carvajal also discovered, to his great sadness, that
his dear friend and fellow prelate, the Dominican bishop
Valverde of Cuzco, had been slain by Indians while fleeing
from the Almagro faction. Orellana did not yet know of his

former captain Gonzalo Pizarro's fate, but all he could control at the moment was his own, and to that end he endeavored, with the dutiful assistance of his priest Gaspar de Carvajal, to chronicle and record the events as accurately and with as much detail as possible.

Captain Orellana and his friar, now with just two good eyes between them, worked from the notes Carvajal had been compiling along the way, ever since the expedition's split at Christmas Camp. While Orellana made plans to secure ships and stores for his next move, Carvajal worked tirelessly on his narrative, making at least two copies, one for Orellana to take with him, and another that he would keep himself and carry back to Peru, where he had determined to return to fulfill his obligations and service to the Order of the Dominicans, which was his calling. When he had finished transcribing and copying the documents, he signed off with words underscoring the truth and accuracy of his tale, words that would subsequently be difficult to contest given that he went on to serve the crown for more than three more decades, ultimately ascending to the high office of archbishop of Lima:

> I, Brother Gasper de Carvajal, the least of the friars of the order of Saint Dominic, have chosen to take upon myself this little task and recount the progress and outcome of our journey and navigation, not only in order to tell about it and make known the truth in the whole matter, but also in order to remove the temptation from many persons who may wish to relate this peregrination of ours or publish just the opposite of what we have experienced and seen; and what I have written and related is the truth throughout; and because profuseness engenders distaste, so I have related sketchily and summarily all that has happened to Francisco de Orellana and to the hidalgos of his company and to us companions who went off with him [after separating] from the expeditionary corps of Gonzalo Pizarro, brother of Don Francisco Pizarro, the Marquis and Governor of Peru. God be praised. Amen.

Carvajal's account, in addition to detailing Orellana's discoveries, was at least in part intended to justify Orellana's actions and protect him, to the extent that it was able, from any accusations of treason or desertion which might be levied upon him. Orellana was thorough in this regard, for though he did not know it, Gonzalo Pizarro had only days before recorded his own version of the events, which he sent to King Charles V on September 3, 1542. It would be up to the king's court, and the very powerful Council of the Indies, to pore over the different versions and make their judgments concerning them.

Most of the companions who survived the Amazon journey were determined to return to Peru, despite the uncertainties and the factious political situation there. Since they had failed to garner any wealth or lands during their journey, no doubt most were motivated to return to Peru to regroup and access what possessions and assets they had left behind when they had begun their journey. Nearly all of these men eventually sailed from Cubagua to Panama and then back to mainland Peru, where they spent the remainder of their lives, most becoming embroiled in the civil strife that would dominate the next few years, now fighting under the royal banners of the Spanish crown and against their old leader Gonzalo Pizarro, who would soon be in open rebellion against his mother country.

For his part, Francisco Orellana's course was clear in his mind. The wonders he had witnessed along the river, the good and peaceful tribes of Aparia, the thriving chiefdoms on the lower reaches of the Amazon, the mysterious women warriors rumored to possess untold wealth, all had an irresistible hold on him, and he vowed to himself to return, properly outfitted, on another expedition, this one bent not only on discovery but on conquest. In order to achieve this goal, Orellana knew that he must have the backing, support, and approval of his crown and government, and in order to garner this support, he would need to return to Spain to make his case and justify all his previous actions to date.

Of all the surviving comrades and hidalgos, only four chose to sail with Orellana to Santo Domingo, an important seat of Spanish power in the region. These men were Comendador Enríquez, Alonso Gutierrez, Hernán Gutierrez de Celis (one of the more accurate and skillful harquebusiers), and, most notably, the thirty-year veteran Cristóbal de Segovia—Maldonado—who had agreed to serve as Orellana's lieutenant should they manage to mount a return expedition. Maldonado, a driven and ambitious conquistador, was politically important, for he had been with Sebastián Benalcázar during the taking and founding of Quito in 1534 and was established as one of the city's first settlers and prominent citizens. He had distinguished himself in the conquest of Popayán (also with Benalcázar), and he had been among Gonzalo Pizarro's soldiers when they rode out on the expedition to La Canela. Under Orellana, Maldonado had fought courageously on numerous occasions, proving a trusted leader and fearless soldier.

Maldonado possessed enough savvy and experience to understand the legal workings of the Indies and his native Spain, and so while agreeing in principle to travel with Orellana, he took steps to explain and justify his own exploits as well. While Orellana arranged for transport from Cubagua to Trinidad, where he hoped to buy or deal for a ship to Santo Domingo, then to Spain, Maldonado called on magistrates from the island of Margarita to draw up papers outlining and detailing his services: signed legal affidavits and testimonies that he could present and have housed at the Council of the Indies and later, if needed, in Spain. Most of the documents attested to his early and long-standing record in Nicaragua and New Granada, but the last few questions addressed his service under Orellana on their recent journey of discovery. The most important of these protected Cristóbal de Segovia and his captain, Francisco Orellana, from charges of desertion and treason:

> Item, whether they knew that, desirous though they were of returning to the main expedition, where the Governor [Gonzalo Pizarro] had remained behind, it was impossible to do so since the currents were so strong, and they were thus in a desperate situation, and that Captain Francisco de Orellana therefore ordered a boat to be built despite the fact that there was no shipmaster to build it, and in this and another small boat, they continued down the river until they reached the Marañón, down which they went to the sea, coming to port in the island of Cubagua, nearly dead from hunger and thirst, where God saw fit to bring them, and where they found salvation of their lives and consciences.

Before an assemblage of magistrates, Orellana's companions swore and signed to the veracity of this statement, and the entire document was filed and deposited in October 1542.

It took another month for Orellana, Maldonado, and their three compatriots to work some kind of deal and purchase a ship in Trinidad. By the end of November they were ready to share embraces and bid farewell to Friar Carvajal and the rest of their brethren, men with whom they had toiled, built ships along hostile shores, and witnessed wonders no one else in Christendom had yet seen. Father Carvajal opted to return to Peru immediately, hoping to find out all he could about the death of his mentor, Bishop Valverde, and to provide his own clerical expertise and assistance in the region.

Orellana, Maldonado, and the others set off from the tiny Venezuelan Pearl Islands and headed northwest, through the Caribbean Sea, past the Lesser Antilles and Puerto Rico to Santo Domingo—Hispaniola— the administrative headquarters of the Indies. Here Orellana would need to make his first real case for what he had accomplished, discovered, and encountered before a Royal Audiencia, a representative appellate court overseeing issues related to the Spanish Empire both at home and abroad.

As it happened, the man that Orellana was charged with meeting was none other than Gonzalo Fernández de Oviedo, the noted Spanish historian, chronicler of the Indies, and, at the time, governor of the Hispaniola fortress. Oviedo was respected and deeply trusted by the crown, and by 1523 he had already written his famous *Natural History of the West Indies* and much of his even larger *General and Natural History of the Indies*. During his illustrious lifetime and more than half a century of service to the crown, he would cross the Atlantic twelve times, explore many of the jungles of the New World, and contribute thousands of pages in a variety of genres. His responsibilities in Hispaniola included reporting to the crown the political and economic situation in the American colonies, as well as chronicling and transcribing reports of expeditions such as the one that Orellana had just concluded.

Oviedo would have been particularly interested in Orellana's story, since it appears that by now he was in possession of at least some of

Gonzalo Pizarro's version, for Oviedo had certain "letters written in August, 1542, received in Santo Domingo from Popayán, giving the first news of the return to the region of Quito of the remnants of Gonzalo Pizarro's expedition to the Land of Cinnamon."

During Orellana's visit to Santo Domingo, the captain relayed verbally to Oviedo the details of his itinerary, which even to the well-traveled scholar and historian seemed exotic, astounding, extraordinary. The court historian was particularly fascinated by the various chiefs who were said to be subjects or vassals of these curious and perplexing Amazons, and he recorded these names dutifully in lists. Captain Orellana supplemented his own personal verbal narrative of the expedition with a copy of the account that had been penned on the river and in Cubagua by Friar Carvajal, and this journal Oviedo pored over, transcribing his own version while remaining true to the original. Further supplementation and corroboration of Orellana's story were provided by a handful of Orellana's crew who traveled as far as Santo Domingo. These men Oviedo referred to as "other hidalgos and commoners," and they testified to the events as described by Orellana and Carvajal. Oviedo was so struck by the story, and especially so impressed by its importance in the history of the region's geography, that he claimed the expedition to be "one of the greatest things that have happened to men."

Oviedo deemed the discovery of the world's largest river sufficiently important to immediately write a lengthy letter to the powerful Cardinal Pietro Bembo in Italy, in which Oviedo announced Orellana's achievement and asked that the discovery be made known across Europe at once. Bembo, a Venetian scholar, poet, and literary theorist, was at the time in a love affair with the controversial Lucrezia Borgia, daughter of the mighty Rodrigo Borgia (Pope Alexander VI). Bembo's reach and influence were wide, and the letter sent to him by Oviedo was eventually published in a volume concerning significant world navigations.

Orellana concluded these depositions with Oviedo and prepared to return to Spain, where he knew he would need to produce equal documentation and then gain audience with the king, before whom he would need to give his account once more. By early 1543 he and Maldonado boarded ships bound for their homeland, no doubt hoping for a hero's welcome, celebration, fanfare, and—if everything went well—a governor-ship and license to return to the Amazon.

During the arduous Atlantic crossing their ship sustained some damage, necessitating an unexpected stop in Portugal. Word of Orellana's exploits had preceded him, for shortly after anchoring there, Orellana was visited by emissaries of the king of Portugal, who requested he remain for a time as the king's "guest," though it is not altogether clear just how convivial this guest-host relationship was. The king of Portugal, John III (John the Pious), had clear and important interests in Orellana's expedition, especially in trying to locate precisely the mouths of the Amazon, which might well lie in Portuguese territory as set forth in 1494 by the Treaty of Tordesillas. This line of demarcation, accepted in principle by the rulers of both Spain and Portugal, fell 370 leagues (1,250 miles) west of the Cape Verde Islands and gave all discoveries to the west to the rulership of Spain, and those to the east to Portugal. The line of demarcation, rather imperfectly mapped and measured longitudinally at the time, fell somewhere near the mouth of the Amazon, so just whose territory this uncharted resource was located in remained in serious question and the subject of further debate and exploration.

The Portuguese king, then, took great interest in what Orellana had to say, and to that end he detained the Spanish captain in Portugal for nearly three weeks, during which time, according to Orellana's subsequent report to the Council of the Indies, the king was busy "acquainting himself in very great detail with the facts in connection with this voyage of discovery and making advantageous offers to him [Orellana] in an effort to get him to stay there, it being his intention to make use of him in the matter." At the same time, perhaps under the aegis of and direction from John III, Orellana was approached by a wealthy Portuguese official who clandestinely offered the discoverer of the Amazon considerable financial assistance and backing should he agree to make a return expedition to the region under Portuguese banner and sail.

As tempting as this offer may have sounded to the cash-strapped Captain Orellana, he graciously declined, aware that his patriotic obligation (and personal political plan) was to return to Spain to make his case to his own sovereign. He managed, through his skillful diplomacy and appeals, to extricate himself from this somewhat awkward situation in Portugal, though he now understood that the Portuguese had their own vested interest in his discovery of the region, and he suspected that with or without him, they would be immediately planning an expedition of their own to the Amazon. King John III, after all, had listened with rapt attention to every tale and detail of the miraculous journey, though Orellana took care to be intentionally obfuscating and circumspect about the precise location of the mouth of the Amazon.

With the ship repaired and his dealings there concluded, Francisco Orellana departed Portugal around the first of May and sailed for Spain on his homeward reach. He arrived at the Spanish court at Valladolid on May 11, 1543, his first homecoming since departing for the Indies and the New World sixteen years before and, for the intrepid conquistador and discoverer of the Amazon River, what must have felt like a few lifetimes ago.

CHAPTER 18

The Last Stand of the Last Pizarro

*A*LTHOUGH FRANCISCO ORELLANA DID NOT KNOW
it at the time, and would only learn the details by degrees,
back in Peru, Gonzalo Pizarro, his captain turned nemesis,
was now embroiled in full-scale civil strife that had become
his full-time occupation. The young Pizarro's struggle
through the jungle, his arrival in Quito at the head of
eighty men in rags, and his stoic refusal to mount a horse
for his final few miles into the city had made him something of a legend in the country, celebrated for his tough-
ness, his stubborn and steadfast will; he was a survivor,
and his actions garnered him a significant personal following, one he would very soon require. Events surrounding
the timing of Pizarro's return also dramatically helped
Orellana, because political exigencies there in Quito and
throughout Peru put dealing with Orellana well down on
Gonzalo's list of priorities.

The situation in Peru on Gonzalo's return had trans-
formed since his departure for La Canela. He learned, of
course, that his rich and powerful brother El Señor
Gubernador Francisco Pizarro had fallen, mercilessly
murdered at the hands of Almagro's henchmen. Now, he
discovered, Licenciado Cristóbal Vaca de Castro, the man
originally sent to adjudicate the constant Pizarro-Almagro
disputes, had been granted the governorship—one that

Gonzalo Pizarro felt was rightfully his own. Had not he and his brothers, through battle and toil and tenacity, won the empire for the crown? As he fumed and pondered his next move, Gonzalo stole some time to deal hastily with the case of Francisco Orellana, which he did in his concise September 3, 1542, letter to the king.

In addition to summarizing the details of his journey into the land of La Canela, Gonzalo Pizarro reported on the building of El Barco, the expedition's separation at Christmas Camp, and Francisco Orellana's failure to return upriver after the agreed-upon twelve days. This failure Pizarro viewed as an act of outright mutiny, saying that in abandoning them, Orellana thus "[displayed] toward the whole expeditionary force the greatest cruelty that ever faithless men have shown, aware that it was left so unprovided with food and caught in such a vast uninhabited region and among such great rivers." Gonzalo added, in no uncertain terms, that he believed "Orellana had gone off and become a rebel."

Unfortunately for Gonzalo Pizarro, Orellana was now the least of his problems. Two coincidental factors complicated Gonzalo's immediate situation. The first was that, with Vaca de Castro now installed as governor of New Castile, Gonzalo had lost his political (and, he thought, legal) hold on the Quito region. Francisco Pizarro had in fact bequeathed to Gonzalo the governorship by "previous royal concession," but this was now a contentious matter for the courts and *audiencias* to decide, should the impetuous young Pizarro choose to wait for legal proceedings to run their course. He decided to meet with Vaca de Castro at Cuzco, where the new governor had made his headquarters and was charged with eradicating the remnant Almagro faction; Gonzalo even offered his services to Vaca as a kind of political concession. Vaca tactfully, though conclusively, declined, for the Pizarro brothers were now persona non grata in the eyes of the crown, despite all they had won in its name.

Vaca did listen attentively to Gonzalo's story of his jungle and river adventures, and assured the now rebuked and ruffled conquistador that his efforts and exploits would be dutifully reported to the king. He then suggested that Pizarro ought to "return to his estates and there enjoy the leisure to which his valiant services entitled him."

Gonzalo Pizarro had been dismissed, brushed off and sent away, so he did the only thing he could at the time, which was to retreat to La Plata, in the Potosi region, to tend to his *encomienda,* which included significant silver deposits and other mining concerns.

The second of the coincidental factors that kept Gonzalo busy—and by extension kept him from further pursuit of Orellana—was the imposition, begun on November 20, 1542 (just a few months after Gonzalo's resurrection from the jungles), of the so-called New Laws, signed by Charles I of Spain as the revised code of colonial government. These New Laws, spurred by the writings of Fray Bartolomé de Las Casas, would have a direct impact on all *encomienda* holders in the New World, including Gonzalo Pizarro.

Las Casas, who arrived in Hispaniola in 1502 and would come to be referred to as "the Apostle of the Indians," was a Spanish priest (the first, in fact, to be ordained in the New World) and writer who lived and traveled throughout the West Indies during its initial conquest. Witnessing the atrocities perpetrated on the indigenous people and believing that they could be converted by more peaceful and humanitarian means, he became an ardent defender of their rights and improved treatment. By 1542 he had been back to Spain a half-dozen times, reporting to the crown on the situation in the Indies, and because of his standing and reputation, he had garnered a great deal of respect from and influence on the king.

The New Laws that Las Casas urged were drastic, even radical, and among those holding *encomiendas* (like Gonzalo Pizarro), the laws were as unpopular as they were initially unenforceable. The laws called for no further exploitation of native peoples, the release of slaves, and no "branding of Indians under any pretext, as prisoners of war or otherwise."* The Indians—on the islands as well as the mainland—were declared subjects rather than vassals of the king, guaranteeing them the same rights (on paper, anyway) as those held by their previous owners. And they went further: they outlawed the granting of any new *encomien-*

---

* The branding of prisoners of war, signified as slaves by searing the symbol *g* (for *guerra,* Spanish for "war") into the cheek, had been a common practice of Cortés during the conquest of Mexico, as well as in the Indies.

das under any circumstances, and perhaps most important and progressive was the provision that settlers who could establish legal title to their *encomiendas* could retain them, but not transmit them by inheritance—the title would revert to the crown upon the death of the original grantee, potentially leaving a landholder's family homeless, penniless, and without a workforce. The implications for colonists like Gonzalo Pizarro and many of his companions were profound. If carried out, the New Laws would completely eradicate the entire *encomienda* system and eliminate the Indian as a source of nearly free labor—the very system on which much of the colonists' wealth relied.

To attempt to enforce these New Laws, the king needed emissaries in Peru, and to spearhead this cause he settled on Viceroy Don Blasco Núñez Vela, a haughty, well-bred cavalier whose egocentric overzealousness would soon precipitate more years of bloody civil strife. He, along with four judges, sailed for Peru. Núñez Vela arrived in early March 1544, charged with enforcing the controversial New Laws to the letter.

But by now, opposition among the Peruvian colonists had galvanized and become widespread, and it was Gonzalo Pizarro who came out of forced retirement at his mining properties near La Plata and assumed the mantle of leadership in the rebellion against these New Laws. He took the position, urged by some of his faithful men and other *encomenderos,* with proud defiance. He had, after all, more than a decade before won this land for Spain with his brothers on the fields of Cajamarca. He would not relinquish his spoils without a fight, and he would gather arms and men in their defense. He wrote to fellow military commanders who had agreed to take his side, reminding them "[Spain wishes] to enjoy what we sweated for, and with clean hands benefit from what we [have given] our blood to obtain. But now that they have revealed their intentions, I promise to show them . . . that we are men who can defend their own."

Viceroy Vela, however, was equally headstrong, and no sooner had he arrived than he burst into bold, if rash, action. He immediately imprisoned Governor Vaca, whom he felt was not doing enough to quell resistance, placing him on a ship to await a formal *residencia*. With the de facto ruler of Peru temporarily out of the way, he then issued a formal proclamation that Gonzalo Pizarro was to surrender and disband his army. Gonzalo simply scoffed at this demand, despite its implications, and he was from that moment branded a rebel. Vela announced, "Anyone who spoke favorably of Gonzalo Pizarro or against the New Laws . . . would be given a hundred lashes at the pillory in the Plaza de Armas." This was a punishment nearly worse than death, for the man who managed to survive one hundred lashes was a disfigured, scarred, and humiliated man indeed, publicly bearing the marks of his rebellion to the end of his life.

Vela added in a last proclamation that all of the properties previously awarded by Francisco Pizarro would be confiscated, their slaves freed, and that any who opposed these actions would be hanged as traitors, up to seventy at a time if necessary. It was, in effect, a declaration of war against Gonzalo Pizarro.

Impudent, brash, but acutely aware of politics, power, and Spain's legal protocols, the defiant Gonzalo now wrote to his king, an appeal that spoke for all the *encomenderos* and Spanish citizens in cities like Quito, La Plata, and Cuzco. It was something of a last-ditch effort, at once a request that the unreasonable New Laws be either rescinded or amended and a reminder of his previous services to the crown, underlying his belief in the inherent truth, justice, and righteousness of his own cause. Written from Cuzco and from his military camps, the letters were sent to Spain, though the impetuous, ambitious last Pizarro knew full well that blood would be spilled long before the missives reached their destination in the mother country.

That political business taken care of, Pizarro then saddled up and rode, leaving Cuzco in a bold and calculated march on Lima. It was he and he alone who should govern Peru. Viceroy Vela, now clinging tenuously to his own support and power, saw the youngest Pizarro gaining strength, and he dispatched an emissary to try to reason with Gonzalo, if not quell the march. But Gonzalo's mind was now bent on supremacy: "See here," he railed, "I am to be Governor because we would trust no one else . . . I don't care a jot for . . . my nephews or nieces or the eight thousand pesos I have in Spain . . . I must die governing! I give this as my reply and there is nothing more to be said about it."

Pizarro cut a violent swath across the land, leaving no room for equivocation: you were either with him or against him. In his black-and-white worldview, there was no such thing as neutral, so that any Spaniards in Peru who chose not to support him he considered enemies, and he dealt as harshly with them as he had dealt with Indians on his trek over the Andes back in 1541, when he displayed his signature tactics. Even wealthy *encomenderos* who had fought alongside his brother Francisco Pizarro slept fitfully, if at all, knowing what awaited them should they be considered deserters from his cause—savage torture, hanging, burning alive. In Lima, the three most prominent citizens were "set astride mules, taken to the outskirts of the city, and hanged." Using such tactics, Gonzalo ultimately executed more than three hundred of his fellow Spaniards, annihilating all who stood in his way.

Under the circumstances, the judges the king had sent to oversee the situation were themselves terrorized into capitulation, and essentially under the sharp edge of a sword blade, they appointed Gonzalo Pizarro as governor and captain-general of Peru. That same day, October 28, 1544, Gonzalo rode into Lima at the head of his 1,200-strong army, the horses neighing and stamping amid thunderous cannon booms and the clanging of church bells. Clearly Gonzalo had no scruples about publicly ignoring the New Laws, for his munitions, cannons, and 22 pieces of field artillery were hauled into the city by some six thousand Indian porters. Once in power, Gonzalo extended his rule all the way to Panama, sending captains and forces there to buttress his position, holdings, and presence.

In response, Viceroy Vela, who had long since fled to Quito to avoid Gonzalo's headlong wrath, now enlisted experienced conquistador Sebastián Benalcázar, one of the vaunted Men of Cajamarca and onetime commander of Quito. He had fought alongside Francisco Pizarro but now rather reluctantly sided with Vela. What followed were many months of guerrilla fighting, with Pizarro's larger and more experienced armies dogging the smaller Vela-Benalcázar force all across the land, spanning bone-dry deserts and jagged mountains and the swampy Peruvian coastline, with the viceroy always in retreat. These feint-and-parry skirmishes culminated in a final meeting of the two armies on the field of Añaquito, just five or six miles from the high mountain city of Quito.

Nearly a year of running left the Vela-Benalcázar army weakened and sparse and short of gunpowder. At Añaquito, Pizarro held a distinct advantage numerically, at 700 soldiers to just 400, and Pizarro's troops proved better armed and prepared as well, "because they were skilled from long practice and had plenty of good powder." Gonzalo rode in at the head of a hundred horsemen, confusing the opposition, and though Viceroy Vela fought bravely along with his own cavalry, in very short order he found himself overwhelmed on a low knoll, where one of Pizarro's soldiers struck him a blow with a two-handled battle-axe, knocking him to the muddy ground. A Negro slave moved in to finish Viceroy Vela, striking off his head, "which was stuck on a pike and paraded among the victors, some of whom tore the hairs from the beard as the grisly trophy passed them."

The viceroy's head was summarily and ingloriously ridden into Quito and for a time displayed on a gibbet, but when Gonzalo Pizarro learned of this disrespectful act he ordered the head removed and buried along with the body, and he marched as chief mourner, showing his respect for a fallen compatriot, albeit a rival and thus an enemy. Almost immediately, illustrating reverence for past service and an uncharacteristic clemency, Gonzalo pardoned Benalcázar, allowing him to return to his own jurisdiction with part of the surviving army, under the provision that he swear to obey and serve the Pizarro name. By late January 1546, Gonzalo Pizarro was now effectively the supreme ruler— some would even say *king*—of Peru.

Had he actually become king of Peru, as some of his closest confidants and *encomendero* allies suggested he do—breaking free from the tethers of the Spanish throne altogether and declaring Peru an independent monarchy—his rule over the land would no doubt have lasted much longer. In a drunken and raucous postvictory celebration, Pizarro's cronies rallied around their new master and conceived a kingdom and dynasty, wherein Pizarro himself would handpick (presumably from among his friends) dukes, duchesses, marquises, and counts, assuring his rule into perpetuity. These fanciful notions seemed forgotten the next day, or perhaps Gonzalo, whose origins were humble, his education primarily in the martial arts, thought of himself as more soldierly than kingly.

But chivalrous victory in battle begets some degree of pomp and ceremony, and Gonzalo was certainly not against accepting a glorious hero's welcome on his return to Lima. There was even a suggestion by some of the local clergy and citizenry that a number of the city's buildings be razed for the construction of a large avenue entering the city that would thereafter bear the name of the victor Gonzalo Pizarro, but he declined such a tribute. Still, his entry into Lima in September 1546 included plenty of pageantry, for he rode in gleaming armor, wearing a red velvet cap, with the crimson and gold banner of Spain snapping as he came:

> A procession was formed of the citizens, the soldiers and the clergy, and Pizarro made his entry into the capital with two of his principal captains on foot, holding the reins of his charger, while the archbishop of Lima, and the bishops of Cuzco, Quito, and Bogata . . . rode by his side. The streets were strewn with boughs, the walls of the houses hung with showy tapestries, and triumphal arches were thrown over the way in honor of the victor. Every balcony, veranda, and housetop was crowded with spectators. The bells rang out their joyous peals, as on his former entrance into the capital; and amidst strains of enlivening music, and the blithe sounds of jubilee, Gonzalo held on his way to the palace of his brother. Peru was once more placed under the dynasty of the Pizarros.

The newly self-appointed governor and captain-general of Peru now possessed an empire that stretched from Panama to Chile, a stunning swath of southwestern America that he controlled with a nautical fleet and a powerful coastal and interior army and cavalry. Then, in a stroke of gratuitous fortune, immense wealth was assured Pizarro when workers at the Potosi mine, on his *encomienda* at La Plata, unearthed a massive vein of silver. The vein was so rich, in fact, that all the other mines in the region were abandoned to work only this one, which guaranteed a richer haul than any yet (or since) mined in Peru, or even in Mexico under Cortes.* In one of history's greatest ironies, the man who went looking for El Dorado, and very nearly died searching vainly for it, quite accidentally struck silver under his own feet—and it made him fabulously wealthy.

For a time, as would be natural for a young and impetuous man of only thirty-four years who had lived as hard and adventurous a life as he had, and who had achieved so much, Gonzalo let the wealth and fame and power go to his head. He chose to dine in public at elaborate gatherings attended by no fewer than one hundred guests, and—probably to avoid the fate of his brother Francisco—always attended by 80 to 100 well-armed guards. But despite all his newly won comforts, there remained a nagging unease, for Gonzalo Pizarro must surely have known that, as popular and seemingly untouchable as he was in Peru, hailed as a savior and conqueror, he was no doubt equally reviled in Spain, for he had audaciously ignored the king's laws and, worse, he had been responsible for the death and beheading of the king's own appointed viceroy. These actions, he well understood, would eventually bring consequences. Someone, at some time, would arrive in Vela's place. It was only a matter of when.

As it turned out, Vela's replacement and Gonzalo's new nemesis was already near, in Panama.

Back in Spain, while Charles did not know the full extent of the ongoing rebellion and the shameful Spaniard-on-Spaniard battle at Añaquito, he had enough information already to have seen the error in his appointment of Vela, and he made a backup plan, overseen by his son, Prince Philip. Charles and his council nominated and elected a judicious, politically savvy, and highly educated ecclesiastic, a man with a master of theology degree and a proven war record, named Pedro de la

---

* Potosi, the greatest source of silver in the Americas, became a thriving city of more than 200,000 people (at 13,352 feet above sea level, called the highest city in the world), and it still produces silver today, though under world criticism for the poor treatment of indigenous workers and dangerous work conditions.

Gasca. Gasca, devoutly loyal to the throne, readily accepted the perilous Peruvian mission, an appointment confirmed in a letter handwritten by Charles, and took on his title of President of the Royal Audience of Lima with tremendous pride and responsibility and humility. Nothing less than the fate of the Spanish Empire rested in his able hands, and the king and court reasoned that if Gasca's judiciousness and shrewd political dexterity could not bring Gonzalo Pizarro to some semblance of obedience, then the cause might well be lost.

But what only King Charles, Prince Philip, their closest court officials, and Pedro de la Gasca knew at the time (and this Gasca would keep quite to himself until the information proved essential or efficacious) was that his title of President of the Royal Audience of Lima carried with it unprecedented powers, powers never previously bestowed on any man in Spain's history save a king. As head of every major department in the colony of Peru—judicial, military, and civil—he and he alone had the power to declare war, levy troops, appoint or dissolve offices or military positions, punish or pardon whomever and however he saw fit, granting amnesty to rebels if it made political sense; and he could, at his discretion, repeal or annul any of the New Laws. He carried on his person a stack of royal writs, blank but bearing the royal signature or seal. He and he alone was empowered to write above that seal or signature in any way he chose. Gasca wielded awesome power, but even more important, he possessed the shrewd and learned diplomacy to wield it wisely.

As soon as he arrived in the New World—landing first in the port of Santa Marta, Colombia, and then traveling on to Nombre de Díos in Panama—Gasca learned of the unfortunate battle at Añaquito and of Gonzalo Pizarro's absolute rule across the land. He determined to act quickly and resolutely, but he also showed notable restraint and stealth, arriving not with a gaudy show of regal display or military force, but landing instead under the guise of an interested and passionate man of the cloth—in spare and humble clerical attire, with a small retinue of followers. Nothing about Gasca's appearance or arrival suggested anything of the unparalleled powers he bore beneath his modest tunic. Indeed, on learning of his arrival, one of Pizarro's soldiers charged with guarding the Panamanian coastline remarked lightly, "If this is the sort of governor His Majesty sends over to us, Pizarro need not trouble his head much about it." It was precisely the reception that Gasca had conspired and orchestrated. Now, he was safely and inconspicuously landed, and he was free to begin his machinations, which were swift and effective.

Very soon, using his austere bearing, a sensible, persuasive diplomacy, and a desire for peaceful resolution, Gasca had met with the governor of Panama as well as Pizarro's naval captains there, and after quietly and by slow degrees revealing to them the scope and breadth of his authority, he had effectively seized control of Pizarro's significant twenty-two-ship naval fleet. Next, wishing to communicate directly with Gonzalo Pizarro, he asked that a ship be dispatched immediately bearing two letters to Pizarro, one from King Charles and the other from Gasca himself. This request met, Gasca waited and plotted and wrote—sending literally hundreds of letters to the most important and powerful followers of Gonzalo Pizarro all across Peru, declaring the New Laws revoked and encouraging them now to acquiesce to the royalist side.

The letters to Pizarro were lengthy but straightforward in content. They neither threatened nor warned nor admonished Pizarro for his actions against Vela or his outright snubbing of the New Laws. Instead, the king's letter suggested that Pizarro's conduct had been commensurate to the circumstances, and implied that he would be pardoned and receive amnesty (and his followers would as well) should they simply lay down their arms and allow Gasca to proceed with his work. The letter signed by the king asked, mainly, that Pizarro cooperate with President Gasca in every way so that there might be a peaceful resolution.

Gasca's personal letter went even further. In it, he told Pizarro that the New Laws had been revoked, so that the very conditions that had prompted Pizarro's rebellion no longer existed. The dissolution of the New Laws had been conceded; the viceroy Vela who had imposed them so strictly was dead, so now there remained nothing for Pizarro to rebel against. All that remained was for Pizarro and his supporters to formally relinquish rule and display their loyalty and obedience to the crown, and all would be forgiven. He and his followers would even be given the opportunity for "new conquests . . . and future discoveries and [thereby] gain wealth and honor." But if Pizarro opted to remain in opposition and rebellion, that rebellion would now clearly be against his sovereign. Gasca deftly reminded Pizarro that few colonists wished to be in open rebellion against the crown, and that most would surely abandon him should he persist. He ended by appealing to Pizarro's honor as a soldier and a subject, suggesting at last that Pizarro's failure to comply would prove that he was motivated not by patriotism but by personal ambition.

Gonzalo Pizarro considered the letters, met with his councils, and then made the most fateful decision of his short life. He declared outright rebellion against his king. He opted for war, and he soon got it.

Gasca's manipulations from Panama had been effective, his letters delivered into the right hands, and by summer of 1547, when Gasca himself finally arrived on mainland Peru, already most of the northern cities, including Quito, had crumbled and acquiesced to the king's side and now flew the royal banner. By the end of the summer, desertions among Gonzalo's highest officers made it clear to him that he must abandon Lima, for his own army had now dwindled to a mere five hundred men, while Gasca's force included Sebastián Benalcázar (whom Gonzalo now must have wished he had hanged rather than pardoned) and Alonso de Alvarado, who had long commanded under Francisco Pizarro. Desertions and defections by such long-trusted brethren were difficult for Gonzalo to bear, but he hardly had time to consider them as his power and rule collapsed all around him and he drove south for the coastal area of Arequipa, where he vowed to hold out no matter who abandoned him, declaring, "If but ten only remain true to me, fear not but I will again be master of Peru!"

These were the wishful and boastful words of a stubborn conquistador clinging to a lost dream and a lost cause. For now Pizarro learned that his own navy, appropriated by Gasca and sailing under the royal banner, was headed to various Peruvian ports. Knowing he must flee, he mounted up and rode his army east over the Andes to Lake Titicaca (which, at some 12,500 feet, is the highest lake in the world navigable to large vessels). There, on the southeastern shore, Pizarro's smaller but well-armed force met Gasca's on the high plains of Huarina. God fought that day, according to one chronicler, "on the side of the heaviest artillery," for though he was outnumbered two to one, Pizarro's army possessed an impressive 350 harquebuses, and many of his harquebusiers charged into battle bearing two loaded weapons, one in each hand.

Pizarro commanded the cavalry and he rode at the vanguard, now a proud and defiant rebel and outright traitor. The two sides charged into action, the horses' hooves pounding across the high alpine plain, the harquebus fire deafening and percussive against the clear cobalt skies. The swordsmen and pikemen gasped for air as they hacked and speared at one another in desperate hand-to-hand combat. By the end of the day, October 26, 1547, when the smoke from the guns finally cleared, miraculously—and owing unquestionably to his superior artillery—Gonzalo Pizarro and his smaller army had won the Battle of Huarina, killing 350 of Gasca's men while losing only 80 of his own. Another one hundred of Gasca's severely wounded men perished that night, unable to move or retreat and freezing to death in that high, biting-cold, and inhospitable place.

The victory, such as it was, proved fateful for Pizarro, for it bolstered his spirits and determined his next course of action. He had originally planned to retreat to the south, to Chile, to escape Gasca's growing royalist armies. But the victory convinced the egomaniacal Pizarro that he might still hold on to his power. Instead of retreating south, he struck northeast for Cuzco, where he decided that the fabled Holy City of the Incas would be his headquarters. He would make one last stand there.

For his part, President Gasca, though disheartened by his side's loss at the Battle of Huarina, remained steely, steadfast, and politically astute. He even gave Gonzalo Pizarro one last chance to submit to royal authority. He penned a letter near the end of the year, 1547, stating unequivocally the following ultimatum:

> Insignificant as I am, your Excellency would have little to fear from me if I had not on my side God and the King, justice and fidelity, and all the good vassals who serve His Majesty; but fighting against these things, Your Excellency has good reason to

quail; and if you do not repent and return to the service of both Majesties, Divine and human, you will lose both body and soul as you will shortly see.

More prophetic words have scarcely been written, for cling as he might to his tenuous power, Pizarro's reign in Peru was near its end. The brash and newly emboldened Pizarro, now comfortably ensconced at his headquarters and feeling invincible since his one-sided victory at Huarina, flatly ignored this offer and chose to remain at Cuzco. He would hold out and fight to the very end. In his mind, he had good reason to be confident, even arrogant, for in his sixteen years in Peru, he had yet to lose a battle.

Gonzalo felt that his position at Cuzco offered him strength, protected as he was by the strategically important Apurimac bridge, an impressive fiber cable spanning some 250 feet and dangling 150 feet above the ravine, blocking direct approach to the city, with white water raging below. Pizarro ordered the bridge destroyed to cut off Gasca's only entrance, but he underestimated the military skills and tactics of the clergyman Gasca, who simply moved his troops upriver, built another bridge at a more passable place, and got his troops across.

The die had been cast; the fates were now poised for a final battle between the Pizarrists and the loyalist force. On April 9, 1548, Pizarro rode out onto the high, barren, wind-scoured plain of Jaquijahuana, "an exquisite place . . . enclosed by mountains and traversed by causeways and ancient aqueducts," and there assembled his 1,500 or so heavily armed troops. He formed his squadrons just as he had at the victory at Huarina, although now he possessed significantly more cavalry, allowing him to support and cover all flanks of his infantry. Then, with inspiring bravado and aplomb, Gonzalo Pizarro, big and bold, his black beard long and flowing, mounted his chestnut charger and, wearing a "coat of mail and a rich breast guard with a surtunic of crushed velvet and a golden casque on his head with a gold chin guard," spurred his mount up and down the ranks in a display of breathtaking horsemanship. His captains and officers gathered around him for final plans and preparations.

Almost instantly, the famed Battle of Jaquijahuana devolved into a farce, something of a general desertion. Gasca fired heavy cannon—which Pizarro had assured his men the president did not possess—directly into Pizarro's ranks, instantly killing Gonzalo's personal squire, charged with keeping him armed. Then one of Gonzalo's most trusted officers, Diego Cepeda, wheeled his horse as if to charge into battle, but instead galloped off to the other side, joining Gasca's similarly sized force. Many other officers and men—secretly bought off, it turned out, with promises of pardons—then defected, too, scrambling to the safe haven of loyalty. Pikemen and swordsmen alike laid down their weapons and sprinted across the lines, leaving Gonzalo embittered, dismayed, and devoid of a worthy fighting force.

Daunted, despondent, but undeterred, the courageous Pizarro barked out orders for trumpets to sound the attack, but at that order nearly all of the harquebusiers marched in slow and orderly fashion across the plain to Gasca, their loaded guns cradled in their arms. Gonzalo could only lift the visor of his helmet from his eyes and stare in disbelief across the plain, then look around him to see that at last he stood with less than a dozen followers ready to die for him. He turned to friend and compatriot Juan de Acosta and asked, "What shall we do, my brother?" Acosta, committed to the end, replied, "Let us charge, and die like Romans."

But Gonzalo saw that all was lost. "Better to die like Christians," he replied, and he wheeled his chestnut and rode toward Gasca with his handful of hidalgos at his side. Then he offered up his sword in surrender, and the battle, and Gonzalo's rule, were over.

The next day Gasca quickly tried Gonzalo Pizarro, took his confession, and sentenced him to be beheaded. The sentence included that all of Gonzalo's goods and worldly possessions be confiscated, and his houses in Cuzco and elsewhere be destroyed and razed to the ground, which was then to be sown with salt. Pizarro could do nothing but stoically accept the terms.

Walking calmly up to the executioner's block, Gonzalo Pizarro is said to have given his fine clothes, "a military cloak of yellow velvet, almost entirely covered with gold embroidery, and a hat to match," to the executioner. Then he set his notorious head on the block and listened to priests quietly chanting prayers for the dying. Gonzalo, who had refused a blindfold, looked up after a few moments of silence and asked that the headsman "do his duty with a steady hand."

At that, the executioner brought down the steel axe and in a single, brutal blow severed Gonzalo Pizarro's head from his body. The head rolled into a basket poised to catch it. Shortly afterward, as part of the terms of his execution sentence, Gonzalo Pizarro's head was displayed in a special frame made for just this purpose.

> [It was] hung on the royal pillory of the city of Los Reyes. It was covered with an iron mesh and above it was placed the notice: "This is the head of the traitor Gonzalo Pizarro who rebelled in this country against His Majesty, and fought against the royal standard in the Valley of Jaquijahuana."

Such was the inglorious end of forty-two-year-old Gonzalo Pizarro, the last of the Pizarro brothers remaining in Peru. In his sixteen-year career as a conquistador in Peru, he had seen the toppling of perhaps the greatest empire in the world, had achieved riches and power that most men hardly dared dream of, and had faced privation and struggle that few possess the courage and tenacity to survive, his fabled march up the Aguarico River referred to as "the worst march ever in the Indies." But in the end, Gonzalo Pizarro, who had called his second-in-command Francisco Orellana "the worst traitor that ever lived," died shamed as one himself, with large signs posted on stone pillars at all his destroyed houses bearing this inscription: "Here dwelled the traitor and rebel Gonzalo Pizarro."

CHAPTER 19

The Expedition to New Andalusia—
Return to the Amazon

*U*PON HIS ARRIVAL IN HIS NATIVE SPAIN IN MAY
1543, Francisco Orellana could now rightfully call himself
"Discoverer of the Amazon," and given what he had
accomplished, he should well have been heralded as a
national hero. But unlike Gonzalo Pizarro, who staggered
into Quito after his disastrous march to a street-lined
hero's welcome, Orellana—the first European to successfully descend the world's largest river—sailed into port in
Spain and disembarked in relative anonymity.

Despite this apparent snubbing, Orellana wasted no
time with his ambitious plans. He had long before
determined—perhaps even before the battle with the
Amazons—that he must be the one to return to this mythical region of unimaginably giant rivers, his memories
fueled by images of albino Indians casting spells in great
plumes of ashes blown from wooden pipes, of black-
painted warriors two heads taller than the tallest Spaniard,
of great highways leading from chiefdoms into the interior,
where powerful overlords possessed untold riches waiting
there to be plundered. Perhaps he had even convinced
himself that somewhere out there among those endless
rivers dwelled El Dorado himself, the vaunted Gilded
Man.

But there was much for Orellana to do before he could return to see all of this for himself once again. First, he needed to give a personal account of his expedition to the king and his council, both verbally and in writing, and in so doing also persuade the crown to grant him the title of El Gobernador that he believed he had earned. If his account was well received and his title granted, he would be in position to request permission—and financial and material support—to mount a return expedition to officially conquer and claim the Amazon regions for Spain and secure immortality for himself.

And of course there was the important matter of Gonzalo Pizarro's written accusations of Orellana's treason to contend with. Fortunately for Orellana, he had less to worry about than he had feared. Gonzalo's letter, written in September 1542 from Peru, had indeed arrived and been read by the court by the time Orellana landed safely back home and sought audience at Valladolid in May of the following year, but its contents and accusations of treason, mutiny, and desertion were not particularly convincing or persuasive to the Council of the Indies. As luck and empire building would have it, the council, the court, and the crown were much more interested in the possibility of acquiring new and rich realms than they were in the squabbles between two rival conquistadors, even if one happened to be a Pizarro. Further aiding Orellana, Gonzalo Pizarro was far away in Peru, his mind and labors at that time still occupied with avenging the death of his brother. He had not yet pressed, and, destined soon to embark on another fateful path, never would.

This freed Orellana to proceed with his personal case, which he did immediately, submitting to the royal court an oral testimony of his entire journey from the time he split with Pizarro's main expedition up to his arrival at the Pearl Island of Cubagua. Along with this, Orellana presented one version of Carvajal's written account, as well as the two legal documents penned by the scrivener Isásaga and signed by all the men under Orellana, documents that fundamentally supported Orellana and Carvajal's version of all that had taken place. His tale, his descriptions of the people he had encountered, their lifeways, the animals never before witnessed, the jaw-dropping descriptions of the river's immensity, and of course his battle with the Amazons, all aroused tremendous excitement in Valladolid, in Seville, in his native Trujillo, indeed all across Spain as people told and retold Orellana's story of discovery.

But the initial official governmental response, delivered almost instantly by Charles's secretary Juan de Sámano, practically devastated Orellana. Sámano ruled that because the great river's mouth might well be within Portugal's jurisdiction, as designated by the most current mariners' charts, its further exploration might not be to Spain's advantage. Still, Orellana was urged to submit formally his written account and appeal, in which he might clarify the location of the river and assuage any doubts about a return expedition. This he did immediately.

Orellana's written appeal and petition included a summary of his considerable services in Nicaragua and Peru prior to the expedition, "performing many services for the King in the various honorable commissions with which he had been interested, not only as captain, but as lieutenant-governor." Orellana went on to outline and summarize the personal expenses he had laid out and lost in the expedition to La Canela and down the Amazon, focusing at length on the importance of his recent discoveries, the immense size and wealth of the country and its provinces, and their potential benefit to Spain. He closed with a formal request to return to and colonize the Amazon region:

> I beseech Your Majesty to see fit to give it to me as a territory
> to be held by me as governor in order that I may explore it and
> colonize it on behalf of Your Majesty, and in case Your Majesty
> grants me the favors . . . I offer myself for undertaking what fol-
> lows, for the sake of serving God and Your Majesty.

In his recounting of past services, Orellana conveniently and shrewdly left out his participation in the Battle of Las Salinas during the War of Chupas, during which time he had sided with the Pizarros in open civil strife against the rival Almagristas, for he well understood that open participation in Spanish civil strife was looked upon quite unfavorably by the crown.

His story, documents, and petition presented, now all the one-eyed

Orellana could do was await the decision of the council and court. Orellana's petition had been convincing in its own right, but two other factors contributed to the court's final decision, both with global political significance. The council was well aware of Orellana's recent stopover and extended visit with the king of Portugal, and as well, they knew that "some three or four years earlier the king of Portugal . . . had built a fleet to go up the Amazon from the coast; that in the House of Trade in Seville it was rumored that as a consequence of Orellana's voyage another fleet was being fitted out for the purpose of penetrating up the river." If this competition for the region were not enough, the council had also heard rumors of a possible French fleet: "It also seems quite likely to us," they added, "that, as far as may be judged from the indications that have been given out on the part of the King of France of a desire to look into matters connected with the Indies, if this thing should come to notice he might have covetous designs in connection with it."

For Orellana, bent on titles and fired by dreams of a return to the New World, the wait for a decision must have seemed interminable. Finally, after careful deliberation, the Council of the Indies concluded the following:

> According to the said account and judged from the location in which this river with the lands that he says he has discovered is, it might be a rich country and one by the occupation of which Your Majesty might be rendered a service and the Royal Crown of these realms enhanced. . . . And for this reason, it is the opinion of the greater part of the Council that it is advantageous . . . that the banks of this river be explored and settled and taken posses-sion of by Your Majesty, and that this be done within the shortest time and with the greatest amount of diligence as possible . . . and that this expedition of exploration and colonization be car-ried out, and that it be entrusted to this man Orellana on account of his having discovered [the river].

With a few strokes of a quill pen, his future appeared ensured. Orellana would return to his river. But that return would not be as soon as the anxious conquistador hoped, and there would be stipulations and provisions attached to his expedition.

First of all, the opinions of the Council of the Indies suggesting actions by the crown in no way guaranteed them, and Orellana still needed Prince Philip, handling things in his father's absence (for the king was away from court on other royal business), to accept these opinions and formally grant them. At long last, after a nine-month period in which Orellana visited family and attempted to get his personal business and finances in order, Prince Philip on February 14, 1544, signed into law the council's recommendations and granted Orellana the title of Adelantado—or governor—of this outpost frontier and its Amazonian regions, authorizing him to conquer, settle, and colonize "New Andalusia." It was a well-earned vindication, final attainment of the titles and power that he sought and dreamed of and toiled for. Now, Orellana must have lustily fantasized, he could become the third marquis of the New World, after only Cortés and Pizarro.

Francisco Orellana needed to consider carefully the expedition's numerous stipulations before he formally signed his response—called "articles of agreement." Of the central expectations, first and foremost was that Orellana, on reaching the Amazon again, build and garrison two towns, one as near as possible to the river mouth and the other farther upstream and inland, both of them at locations chosen by Orellana and approved by the royal officials and friars who would be going with him. The region granted him was rather vague—he could conquer and settle "the regions that stretched towards the south from the river that he had discovered, for a distance of two hundred leagues as the crow flies."

He was obliged to take on the expedition at least three hundred Spaniards, one hundred of whom would be cavalry and two hundred infantrymen, a total that the crown considered to be "a sufficiently large number and force for colonizing progressively and defending yourself and your men." After building the two towns, he could proceed upriver, in boats either built there or brought along in parts in the ships' holds, accompanied by eight friars (to be hand-selected by the council), whose mission would be to convert the native populations to Christianity.

Heading upriver, Orellana could then attempt to settle what domains, chiefdoms, and lands he wished, provided that under the New Laws he enlist no Indian slaves for the purpose, other than the occasional interpreter. Last, he must take great care to respect the Treaty of Tordesillas and its line of demarcation, attempting to ensure that these newfound lands fell within Spanish jurisdiction, and he must refrain from altercations with any Spanish captains who happened to already be in the area, "so that there may be avoided those disturbances which have hitherto arisen out of such situations, both in Peru and in other parts." This last was a direct reference to the unseemly and ongoing Pizarro-Almagro situation, but the crown had dealt with similar problems in Mexico with Cortés.

As compensation, Orellana was to receive a salary of five thousand ducats from the date that the armada set sail, this figure capping at one million *maravedis* per year,* which would pass on to Orellana's heirs into perpetuity. Should everything go as planned, this payout would certainly make Francisco Orellana an extremely wealthy man.

But there was one significant problem with the terms, though they were quite common for such expeditions. Orellana must undertake the entire expedition—the purchasing of materials, arms and powder, men and weaponry, equipment, horses, boats and rigging, food—at his own expense. The crown was thorough and deliberate in its contractual language, stating that Orellana would be responsible for all the preparations "at your own expense and on your own responsibility, without there being on the part of His Majesty or of the kings who shall come after him any obligation to pay you back or to settle for the expenses which you shall have incurred in it, beyond what is going to be credited to you by the terms of this agreement."

Looking over the documents, Francisco Orellana felt badly snubbed. He had hoped that his discoveries would have put him in a more advantageous and powerful position, and that the crown would at the very least subsidize his venture. Now he realized that if he were to ever see the magnificent braided streams again, the banks teeming with manatees and turtles, the rivers the size of whole seas, he would have to finance the

* A ducat was a gold coin of 23¾ carats fine and equaled 375 *maravedis*.

journey on his own, essentially a speculative investment in his own personal dream.

Orellana went away disappointed but undaunted, and he appears never to have considered abandoning the enterprise, not for an instant. Just five days later he signed the articles of agreement in the presence of a notary, making sure that the language of the first paragraph absolved him of any treachery or wrongdoing in his previous expedition under Gonzalo Pizarro, to which the prince consented. The papers signed, Orellana set to work frenziedly organizing his own return to the Amazon.

By May 1544, the industrious and indefatigable Captain-General Orellana had managed to raise enough money, either through relatives he still had in Trujillo or loans from investors, to procure two caravels and two galleons, all of which he claimed were ready and waiting in the waters of the Guadalquivir River, navigable as far as Seville. The two smaller vessels, which would be used for ascending the Amazon after the towns had been constructed, were apparently also being built, so initial preparations seemed to be progressing well. At this time Orellana tried to appeal to the king's good nature and requested arms and guns for the ships—he would, after all, be sailing under the royal banner and was quite likely to be attacked by pirates—but this request was flatly refused.

To hamper matters further, Orellana deeply desired to employ a Portuguese pilot for the journey, for no Spaniards knew the Brazilian coastline well enough; but this request, too, was denied, for under the agreements of the time, no foreigners could be hired for journeys of exploration and discovery. As a concession, Prince Philip did suggest the Spanish pilot Francisco Rodriquez (whom he attempted to lure with promises of lucrative financial gains), but on interviewing the man, Orellana found him ill suited for the job, saying "this man talks less intelligently about the coast than any other" he had interviewed.

During this time Orellana made some progress, hiring on Cristóbal de Segovia—Maldonado—as chief constable for the journey, responsible for recruiting, hiring, and equipping the cavalry and infantry for the voyage. Maldonado, it turned out, was the only compatriot of the original expedition down the Amazon to enlist for the return. Orellana also found a suitable treasurer, an accountant and revenue collector named Vicencio de Monte, whom Orellana hired to help raise money and agreed to install as magistrate of one of the two towns they would found and build at the Amazon. Shortly afterward, however, there arrived in Seville a man named Friar Pablo de Torres, the king's inspector-general for the expedition, and it was through him that all details had to pass before Orellana might set sail. He had the power of final oversight, and in fact came carrying a secret envelope to be opened in the event of Orellana's death, inside which was the name of the person who should succeed him.

Problems plagued Orellana's great venture from the beginning. A number of arguments broke out between the crew members, most notably between Maldonado and de Monte, the fund-raiser, who Maldonado felt had too much influence over Orellana. Orellana began to distrust those around him, going so far as to suggest that there might be someone on the inside trying to thwart his journey. He wrote a letter to the king, saying that there was without question "a worm within our midst." Orellana's concerns seemed well founded, for things went afoul at every turn. A promise of financial backing and support would come, only to be withdrawn, sometimes shortly after the original offer. Merchants selling gear and rigging demanded cash payment when before they had agreed to credit. Soldiers of fortune signed on to the expedition, then instantly backed out.

Then, rather mysteriously and ominously, Maldonado—one of Orellana's most trusted companions—disappeared. This must have pained Orellana greatly; they had fought and survived together down the entire span of the Amazon Basin. Now, it turned out, he might well be a spy for Portugal, where he resurfaced. This development intrigued and worried Orellana, for of course Maldonado had been with him during their lengthy visit with the Portuguese king, and there was the distinct possibility that he had formed some kind of alliance either with the king or with the wealthy businessman there who had originally offered to finance Orellana on an expedition. After his departure, Orellana learned that Maldonado, referred to now as part of "secret and sly factions," had been involved in the slaying of a man in Seville.

In October 1544, Orellana benefited from a visit by his stepfather, Cosmo de Chaves, who came in from Trujillo offering to assist with financing. He had some property in Trujillo to sell, but when no Seville buyers stepped forward in time, he raised the money in other ways and pledged this—some eleven thousand ducats—to the venture. This cash helped pay for some of the boats, but Orellana remained short, and much was still needed before he could convince the inspector-general, and by extension the crown, that he was ready and fully equipped to sail.

With Maldonado gone, the Genoese backer-financier Monte became even more involved in the expedition, not only offering to help personally finance it, but also stepping forward to offer Orellana a wife. Orellana had decided that he did not wish to return to the Amazon unmarried, no doubt desiring to produce an heir, but also because there was no telling when, if ever, he would return to Spain. It also made fiscal sense, especially should the proposed wife come with a suitable dowry.

In November 1544, Francisco Orellana indeed married, much to the surprise and consternation of Inspector-General Torres, who had encouraged what he believed was a more lucrative match. "The Adelantado has married," wrote Torres to the king, "despite my attempts to persuade him not to, which were many and well founded, because they did not give him any dowry whatsoever, I mean not a single ducat, and he wants to take a wife over there, and even one or two sisters-in-law also: he alleged on his side that he could not go off without a woman, and in order to have a female consort he wanted to marry." The wife in question was Ana de Ayala, a very young girl of perhaps only fourteen, arranged by Monte and presented with jewels and silks, so perhaps there was some secret dowry after all to which Torres was not privy.

Just then came news that the Portuguese were indeed preparing an expedition of their own to the contested region, equipping four large ships with cannons, horses, powder, stores, and men—and worst of all, it appeared that they had employed Maldonado as their guide for his intimate knowledge of the Amazon. The Portuguese expedition would be financed by a wealthy Castilian recently arrived from Peru. The threat of competition from the Portuguese heightened the need for immediate departure, which Orellana most desired—for despite his hardships there, he longed to be back on the savannas of the lower Amazon, the river calling him like the sirens to Odysseus.

By late March 1545, with the combined support from Monte and Orellana's stepfather Chaves, the four ships finally sailed down the Guadalquivir River to the port at Sanlúcar (some 55 miles below Seville) for final preparations. For Orellana, it had been a lengthy, painful, and frustrating process, one fraught with political and bureaucratic complexities he had grown unaccustomed to during the harsh simplicity of sailing down a river for more than a year. But he could almost taste the odd sweet tang of the Sweetwater Sea again, and he pressed forward with all of his resources and attentions.

But first he had to pass inspection, and given the stringent royal requirements, this would be difficult. When Inspector-General Torres and the other appointed royal officers boarded the ships at Sanlúcar, they found them in substandard condition for a journey to conquer and colonize New Andalusia. First of all, not all of the required three hundred soldiers were on board, nor were the two hundred horses. Orellana pointed out that the horses remained grazing ashore, fattening for the Atlantic crossing, and as to the men, many were saying good-bye to their families and were on their way—he assured the inspectors of this. The inspectors noted the lack of rigging for the upriver launches, to which Orellana replied that such rigging was easily fabricated using timber and vines from the river mouth region—he had done so twice before, and at any rate, this was where he intended to build those craft.

Because of tensions about the possibility of a rival Portuguese fleet landing first, many of these perceived insufficiencies were overlooked, though when the royal officers and inspector-general returned on May 5 for a final inspection, the assessment they gave Orellana's armada could not have been less glowing. According to Father Torres, Orellana was attempting to conquer New Andalusia in four vessels that appeared "as thoroughly dismantled as if they had just been plundered by the French or the Turks"—hardly the endorsement that Orellana had hoped for. He was flatly instructed that under no circumstances should he even consider leaving port until personally ordered to do so by the king, under penalty of ten thousand ducats and the revoking of those commissions and favors that had been bestowed upon him. But by now he had decided to depart, inspector-general's blessing or no, with or without the approval of the crown.

Orellana understood that greatness was achieved through action and boldness, not slow deliberation. Cortés famously scuttled his ships and became a rogue, a fugitive from justice, then conqueror of Mexico and a Spanish national hero—wealthy beyond imagination and revered as the Grand Conquistador. Francisco Pizarro and his brothers freelanced, too, operating essentially under their own set of rules and laws, and this had won them the empire of Peru, untold riches, and glory. Orellana had seen his empire from inside the *San Pedro* and the *Victoria,* and he resolved now that nothing—including the censure of a king—would keep him from that quest.

On May 11, 1545, two years to the day after his return to Spain and without formal approval from Inspector-General Torres—indeed, without Father Torres at all, for Orellana abandoned him on shore, along with another of the assigned clerics—the thirty-five-year-old conquistador Francisco Orellana pulled up anchor and sailed his four ships fast for the open sea, illegally and in direct defiance of the king. In the end he was embittered by the lack of support from his own country, and he feared that if he did not leave now he might never see his Amazon again. On board with him were his young bride Ana de Ayala, her sister-in-law, and many other Spanish women ensconced in the poop of the flagship. Serving as master of the flagship—also against the terms of his contract—was an unheralded pilot from Sicily. Orellana did by now have more than the three hundred required men on board, and most of the horses as well. Also on hand were many freshly slaughtered cattle, sheep, and chickens, which they cured and salted as they sailed, having only just stolen them the night before departure in a last-ditch farm raid that left some of the poor and defenseless shepherds seriously wounded. Apparently the pilfer-plunder-and-depart tactic learned by Orellana on his journey down the Amazon died hard in him.

Francisco Orellana was now effectively a rogue, a pirate, a renegade, even a traitor. But he reasoned that the risk was worth it. He had sadly learned that it was not enough to discover an empire; one must conquer it to achieve everlasting glory. Perhaps if he could win for Spain one of these wealthy and exotic dominions in the mode of Cortés or Pizarro, all would be forgiven.

No sooner had Orellana's convoy found its way to open sea than he encountered a large caravel, which he waylaid, boarded, and plundered like a pirate for whatever supplies he could find, mostly food and water and jars for catching rainwater, for he was short on both should the trip take longer than a few weeks.

Despite being ill equipped, Orellana's fleet managed to reach Tenerife, in the Canary Islands, just off the coast of western Africa, near the end of May. Here Orellana made port and, free from the constraints of inspectors and officials, set to putting his ships into better repair, which took nearly three months. When he felt the ships and gear were in good enough order, he sailed on to the Cape Verde Islands, the last stopover before the nearly two-thousand-mile Atlantic crossing that would bring him to mainland South America.

His stop at the Cape Verde Islands included procuring some much-needed supplies that he had arranged for. Unfortunately, Orellana spent too much idle time there, for during this interval an epidemic broke out aboard his ships and nearly everyone on the voyage fell dangerously ill, with ninety-eight dying. This number constituted nearly a third of Orellana's entire force, and he had to abandon one of his ships. He salvaged its rigging, anchors, navigational equipment, and anything else useful and installed the gear on the other ships. Then he prepared to set sail for the coast of Brazil.

But a number of his men had now lost their nerve, or considered themselves unfit to embark on a journey that promised even greater hardships. Fifty or sixty soldiers deserted, including three captains. But Orellana, nearly mad in his obsession, would not give up. In the middle of November, he ordered what remained of his sorry crew onto the three remaining ships and hoisted sail for New Andalusia, which he still believed he could win and govern.

The men who abandoned the mission at Cape Verde escaped a hellish ocean voyage, for foul weather beset Orellana immediately, slowing progress enough to see his ships run dangerously low on water. Men and women and horses alike slumped wan and parched on the blistering decks, the edges of their mouths cracked and salt-stained. It appeared that they would all perish before ever seeing land again. Mercifully, a tropical deluge filled their water jars, and this alone saved them. Just when matters seemed to be improving, one of the ships, this one carrying "seventy-seven colonists, eleven horses, and a brigantine that was to go up the river," inexplicably disappeared, never to be seen or heard from again. There is no explanation for its loss—presumably the thirst-crazed and delirious crew lost their way or even died of thirst, or the ship ran aground somewhere along the coast. The only report concerning this misfortune, left by Francisco de Guzmán, who survived the journey, concluded, "And amidst this hardship and struggling one ship put in toward land, the persons on board saying that they had no water. Regarding [this] ship, up to the present time nothing more has ever been heard."

The two remaining ships managed to catch the north wind and regain a proper course. Finally, after believing they would certainly die at sea, Orellana and some of his men spotted land, and they sailed close to inspect, though Orellana knew to remain wary of the jagged and dangerous coastline: "We went and reconnoitered the shoals," remembered Guzmán, "and taking our bearings from the shore we went in close, on the lookout for the Maranon." Remaining in sight of the coastline, they sailed on until, some thirty miles out to sea, they found the vaunted freshwater, the Mar Dulce, the Sweetwater Sea. Orellana had long remembered the curious water's distinctive taste and smell, of sea salt sweetened with the freshest water, and rejoiced: despite everything that he had endured, he had returned to the Amazon.

But grave danger lay on the shoals extending from the coast; because the ships had lost some of their anchors en route, the pilots struggled to control the craft, and both nearly wrecked on the rocks. Somehow they plowed safely through, now using a few of their cannons as anchors, and on December 20, 1545, Orellana's two sorry ships lurched into port at a village situated between two islands. More than three years since his first heroic arrival there, Francisco Orellana disembarked on the sandy banks. He was, in a way, home.

Upon landing, however, there was little to celebrate. Counting the nearly one hundred dead in the Canaries, the fifty or so defectors, and the ship with seventy-seven lost at sea, Captain-General Orellana had already lost two of his ships and more than two-thirds of his original crew. The only good news was that there did not seem to be any sign of Portuguese or French presence, and the first village they came to appeared peaceful. But these were small consolations.

For a few days Orellana and his weakened force rested at this village among the floodplain islands, the soldiers and women delighted by the hospitality of the locals, who in exchange for their barter goods brought forth plenty of fish, maize, yuca, and succulent local fruits. But almost immediately Orellana grew impatient, wanting to continue farther upriver to find the main branch of the Amazon. He certainly would have been mindful of the crucial role of the tides here, and the many confusing channels braiding and coiling, and he wished to start upriver straightaway, anxious to return to those exotic people and kingdoms that so captivated his dreams and fantasies.

A number of his men, however, disagreed. Much better, they said, to regroup here, where they were guaranteed food, kind treatment, and what looked to be a suitable place for construction of a worthy upriver brigantine, parts of which they had brought over in their ships, that needed only to be assembled. The men also pointed out that the eleven horses that had survived the trip were in poor condition, lank and dehydrated, for on the ocean crossing they had suffered terrible want and they, too, needed to recover in order to be useful in explorations or battle.

Although the crew's entreaties were reasonable and prudent, Orellana still felt inclined to move. He argued that he knew from first-hand experience that the lower reaches of the river were well inhabited, and that there would be numerous landing places even better than this one. So, on Christmas Day 1545, almost exactly four years from that fateful day he took the *San Pedro* and split from Gonzalo Pizarro at Christmas Camp, Francisco Orellana made another momentous decision. Overruling his crew, he ordered the ships loaded and started upriver in search of the primary channel.

Though remaining there to recover and construct a boat made sense, it is not difficult to see Orellana's rationale, either. Fatigued though he and his men were, Orellana must have felt that with the armor, men, horses, weapons, and gunpowder that he possessed, they certainly presented a sufficiently strong force to begin the complicated navigation upriver, and he felt that he knew what to expect, having been there before. Cortés had, after all, landed in mainland Mexico with just sixteen horses, and within a year he held the great Montezuma captive and in chains, the emperor's golden treasure at his disposal. Perhaps Orellana, seizing the initiative with equal celerity, could capture a wealthy overlord like Machiparo, or Ica, or even Queen Conori of the Amazons, and begin sending his own treasure ships of gold back to King Charles.

The two ships sailed up the giant entwining braids, swallowed in the river's great mouth. Under sail and using the tides to their advantage, they passed through flooded forests and rough woodland savanna, Orellana always on the lookout for landmarks he might recognize. What he failed to realize was that the channel he had entered was foreign and different and unrecognizable—certainly not the broader main channel through which he had earlier escaped with his life in the *Victoria*. To make matters worse, this circuitous and marshy limb of the river was virtually uninhabited. The tribes and villages he had counted on visiting, trading with, and conquering were nowhere to be found on this stretch of the river. After sailing up this branch of the Amazon for over three hundred miles, they at last came upon a half-dozen Indian huts, hardly the chiefdom of the Omagua or the Aparians. Still, Orellana stopped, figuring they must now build a brigantine for more efficient maneuvering up the braids in search of the main channel.

It was a wretched and inhospitable place to survive and build, but the dogged Orellana had overseen the building of two brigantines under such conditions already, so he pressed his men on in their work, though in this instance without the support of villagers daily bringing them food. Here, the only Indians they encountered were hostile, arriving in small and stealthy attack parties, some of them wielding the dreaded and deadly poison arrows. For three long months—through January, February, and March of 1546—Orellana's expedition encamped here, some of the men scouring about for food while most worked, but it was a "country so poor that little food was to be had in it," and they were forced to eat all of the horses and dogs they had brought.

By the end of three months' time, resorting to dismantling the smaller of the two ships and salvaging from it planking and nails, Orellana had succeeded in building a rivergoing brigantine, but this had come at devastating cost, for during that nightmarish time another fifty-seven of his men had perished through starvation, lingering disease, or violent Indian attack.

Once the brigantine was completed, rigged with oars, and ready, Orellana sent a small crew away in it to find food, but this search yielded only more tragedy: "Their efforts were fruitless, and, after many of the crew had died also of hunger or from wounds received in the encounters which they had with Indians, the survivors returned to camp." There was now disaster everywhere Orellana looked or turned, and both he and what few remained of his corps clung tenuously to their lives and their faculties.

Orellana decided that they must make an attempt for the central channel of the Amazon, though in truth by now he had no idea where it might be. Taking the last of his ships and the newly constructed brigantine, Orellana went in tandem, navigating on a southeasterly course, hoping for some miracle. But it seems that all of Orellana's miracles were used up, for they had not gone seventy-five miles when, as they lay idle at anchor, a sudden and violent river tide surged and spun the ship he was in, snapping its only hawser, spinning them out of control, and dashing the vessel into the shore, wrecking it.

The crew and remaining women, including Orellana's young and no doubt terrified wife, Ana, clambered from the shipwreck and sought safety on a small island a short distance away, where in a stroke of rare good fortune they found a tiny band of peaceful Indians who sheltered them and gave them food.

At this point, when all seemed fairly lost, Captain Orellana might well have turned back, but his steadfast confidence in finding the main source of the river compelled him to take the remaining brigantine, a small crew, and his wife and search once more for the mighty river that had brought him fame. He left behind at the island camp twenty-eight or thirty soldiers, telling them that he would soon return with information, but by now they could see that they were essentially on their own, and after Orellana had been gone a few days the soldiers started building another boat, gathering wood and making shuttle forays to the shipwreck for beams, planking, and futtocks.

Orellana was gone twenty-seven days in the brigantine, his skeleton crew including a pilot and shipmaster named Juan Griego. Up and across the wide waters they coursed, casting toward a promising-looking branch here, then another miles upriver, every twist and turn in the coiling labyrinth a mirage, a phantom, a cipher as numinous yet unattainable as El Dorado himself. At last, after nearly a month of aimless wanderings, Orellana returned to the shipwreck. Juan Griego told the others that they had sailed nearly five hundred miles and still failed to rediscover Orellana's river.

The men at the shipwreck had meanwhile busied themselves in their boatbuilding project, and they were now clearly bent on escaping the Amazon's grip and sailing, if they possibly could, back to safety. Orellana, now feeble, feverish, and perhaps clinging to the last threads of his sanity, seemed in some sort of dream state. He did not remain at the shipwreck long, but told the men that he intended to continue his search. Francisco de Guzmán recalled Orellana's final words before he left:

> He went off again saying that he was ill and would not be able to wait for us, and that, by way of saving time, inasmuch as he did not have enough men to set up a colony, he wanted to go back again to look for the branch of the river and go up as far as the point of San Juan to barter for a certain amount of gold or silver to send to His Majesty, and that if we felt like following him after our boat should be built, we should find him somewhere around there.

To the last, Francisco Orellana conjured gold and silver and images of the Amazons, for San Juan, where he believed in his mind he was heading, was the place they had named St. John, near the Trombetas River, in the heart of Queen Conori's fabulous domain: the realm of the Amazon warriors.

As they watched their delirious captain, his wife, and half the remaining crew sail away, the shipwrecked soldiers turned resolutely back to their boat, now their only hope for salvation, quite doubtful that they would ever see the one-eyed, single-visioned Orellana again. After two more months of continuous construction, they had indeed built a boat, but the fresh-cut lumber rendered it porous and leak-prone. Still, it floated. So they persuaded some Indians with canoes to guide them, and, rather nobly, went looking for their captain, the Adelantado of New Andalusia.

The Indian guides led them well upriver, to a place where the Amazon splits into three large arms—quite close, it turned out, to the very place that Orellana sought.* But they could find no sign of him, nor of his boat, and given their shortage of provisions they chose finally to turn back and make for the sea, their God willing. On their escape from the rivers Amazon, at a point still some two hundred miles from the Atlantic, they came across a small and prosperous village, and six of the Spaniards, perhaps themselves now crazed by this endless maze, ran off into the trees, choosing to remain there rather than submit to the horrors of the ocean in such a small and unseaworthy craft. Shortly afterward, four other soldiers also leaped from the boat onto shore and went native, "because they considered the country to be a good one." Now there would be tales of Orellana's men in the region to go along with the stories of Diego de Ordaz's shipwrecked survivors living among the river tribes.

Those still on the boat prepared for the worst, and they got it. Once on the open sea a violent tide dashed them back toward shore, battering them through a tree-choked mangrove swamp, where they stayed marooned for three days on the tepid banks, tormented by mosquito swarms. But eventually the seas and the undertows calmed and they managed to push and pole the craft onto open water again, where they caught—as the *San Pedro* and *Victoria* had done some years before—the

* Francisco de Guzmán reports ascending to a wide branch of the river that divides into three large arms. Here, for three days, as many as a hundred Indian canoes accompanied them. Guzmán and the searchers appear to have reached the Amazon, though Orellana did not.

strong Southern Equatorial Current. Staying as close as they could to shore and bailing constantly in shifts both night and day, on one of the final days of November 1546, these eighteen survivors, incredibly, landed on the island of Margarita. There, to their utter disbelief, were twenty-five of their compatriots as well as Ana de Ayala. They, too, no doubt captained by Juan Griego, had managed to escape the dark and impenetrable river.

But where, the men asked, was Captain Orellana?

Francisco de Guzmán listened silently to Ana de Ayala, who was with Orellana at the last, and he related her story:

> [She] told us that her husband had not succeeded in getting into the main branch which he was looking for and consequently, on account of his being ill, he had made up his mind to come to a land of Christians: and during this time, when he was out looking for food for the journey, the Indians shot seventeen of his men with arrows.

These last indignities—his sickness, and the deaths of his men and his dream—finally proved too much even for Orellana. He died, she said in a whisper, "from grief."

For the conquistador the El Dorado adventure ended in kidnap, solitude, and lunacy. His province—the dream of the third Spanish marquisate in the New World, after Mexico and Peru—became the ghost province of the Spanish Empire.

—V. S. NAIPAUL, *The Loss of El Dorado*

Epilogue

$\mathcal{T}$HE SPANISH SAYING THAT HAD BEEN ASSOCIATED
with Diego de Ordaz, that "he who goes to the Orinoco
either dies or comes back mad," could now be rewritten
and hung on Francisco Orellana: "He who goes to the
Amazon goes mad and dies."

For those who measure an expedition's success or failure in ledger-book fashion, Orellana's ill-fated attempt to
return to the river kingdoms becomes an accumulated sum
of numerical disaster: of the nearly 350 men and handful of
women that departed with him, only 44 survived—43 of
the men and Ana de Ayala, Orellana's wife.* Lost were the
lives of more than 300 men and women and 200 horses.
Gone were all four ocean ships, tons of powder, ammunition, and Spanish firearms and cannons.

But ironically, despite all this, the myths of El Dorado
and the Amazons still lived.

For a short time after his journey, for a decade or so, the
stupendous river system he and his men pioneered and
explored bore his name: the Orellana River. And it is likely

---

*Ana de Ayala subsequently became involved with another of the survivors, a
man named Juan de Panalosa, though they did not marry. She traveled to
Nombre de Díos and later Panama, perhaps intending to claim land in
Guayaquil left to her by Orellana. She lived until at least 1572. See José
Toribio Medina, *The Discovery of the Amazon*, 137–38.

that had Orellana lived to rediscover it instead of perishing on its banks, the great waterway would bear his name still. But in a short time the river—a singular misnomer given its thousand tributaries—came to be called the River of the Amazons, truncated today to the Amazon.

Orellana's discovery engendered in his native Spain excitement, speculation, and desire for continued exploration, although any follow-up expeditions would have to wait, at least for a while. The influential Las Casas had continued to preach his anticolonial message in the mother country, railing against the injustices and immoralities of torturing, enslaving, and killing native Americans in the New World. He went so far as to warn King Charles about Spain's reckoning at the Day of Judgment, and of the jeopardy of his very soul should such atrocities persist: "Because of these impious and ignominious deeds, so unjust, tyrannical and barbarously done in the Indies and against the Indians, God must certainly envelop Spain with his fury and anger."

Such persuasive rhetoric had a profound impact on the devout monarch-emperor, and from 1550 to 1560 he suspended all expeditions of conquest in the New World until the issues regarding his own soul and salvation, and that of Spain's, could be resolved through a debate between the clergyman Las Casas and the humanist philosopher Juan Ginés de Sepúlveda. The eloquent Las Casas won the debate, but in the end, power, politics, and empire expansion outranked moral indignation, however well-meaning, and Charles V lifted the ban. The plundering could continue, eternal damnation or not.

In the wake of Orellana's discoveries, over the next fifty years, two significant follow-up expeditions in search of El Dorado took place, one in 1560 under Spaniard Pedro de Ursúa aimed at finding and colonizing the rich lands of the Machiparo and Omagua that Orellana had found, and the other in 1595, by Sir Walter Raleigh himself. Raleigh's voyage later officially heralded the death of the El Dorado myth.

The Pedro de Ursúa venture, coming virtually as the ink dried on the parchment lifting the king's ban, was fueled by Orellana's story, then fully ignited when Spanish colonists in Chachapoyas, an Amazon headwater river settlement in the northeast of Peru, witnessed the arrival of 200 to 300 Indians who had traveled more than 1,500 miles to reach the outpost—on foot at first, and afterward in their canoes, paddling upstream on the Amazon, the Maranon, and finally the Huallaga. They said they had fled to escape the Portuguese now encroaching on their lands from the Atlantic coast of the Amazon. Their journey of migration had consumed ten years. The Indians, probably Tupinambas, described in similar terms the very lands that Orellana had so recently passed through: "They emphasized the variety and multitude of the tribes they had encountered, and particularly the wealth of the province called Omagua." The Spanish reports added that the arriving nomadic Tupinambas spoke of "the inestimable value of the [Omagua's] riches, and the vastness of their trading."

Those enticing descriptions, echoing as they did Orellana's and Carvajal's narratives, were all the king needed to sanction yet another assault on El Dorado, though now he began referring to it as a place, a province of "Omagua and Dorado." The Gilded One, a person, had morphed into a golden place.

It did not take long for Pedro de Ursúa, the man chosen to lead this foray, to recruit and assemble 370 Spanish mercenaries to go along, ruffians and vagabonds and civil war veterans who had sat idle for the decade when expeditions had been banned. With thirty horses, this motley crew, and a few thousand conscripted Andean bearers (so much for the New Laws, apparently), the Ursúa-Aguirre expedition, as it came to be known, would be almost equal in size to that of Pizarro-Orellana. From its very beginning, it would be an unequivocal, unmitigated catastrophe that would ultimately devolve into utter pathos and horror, the darkest of the Amazonian annals.

The untested Ursúa turned out to be a tragically incompetent leader prone to disastrous decisions. His two biggest blunders were bringing along his mestizo mistress, Inés de Atienza (plus a dozen other women guaranteed to cause fighting among the men), and the inclusion of a paranoid, maniacal Basque named Lope de Aguirre who believed he would one day soon conquer and rule all of Peru. In fairness to Ursúa, neither he nor anyone else could have known or predicted the insane behavior of Aguirre, who turned out to be a full-scale psychopath, a man who began his Amazonian voyage insane and deteriorated from there. About forty-five years of age, Aguirre had been in Peru for more than twenty years and had participated in the civil wars, fighting against Gonzalo Pizarro's rebellion, but for all his efforts receiving nothing but a missing hand and two bullet wounds in his leg that left him lame. Aguirre took with him his beloved and desirable sixteen-year-old daughter, Elvira, over whom he doted and kept armed guards.

In September 1560, after trekking through dense mountains and cloud forest, the expedition embarked in three large transport boats and a flotilla of canoes, first down the Huallaga, which farther downstream becomes the Maranon. Ursúa's personal transport barge was built with a cover, like a houseboat, to comfort and accommodate his stunningly beautiful Inés—said by all accounts to be among the most beautiful women ever seen in Peru. But the bulky construction made this boat awkward, heavy, and prone to running aground, and all the transport craft leaked and ultimately failed.

For seven weeks and 750 miles they worked downriver, passing the mouth of the Ucayali, the headwaters of which constitute the origin of the Amazon in official calculations of its length. They sailed past the confluence of the Napo, where Orellana had met the main Amazon, and arrived eventually in Machiparo's domain, which, just as Orellana had said, was organized and well populated and rich with resources such as turtle farms. But the long-sought El Dorado was nowhere to be found. By now, half-crazed by salt deficiency, the incessant rains, and swarms of black flies and mosquitoes, Aguirre had planned a coup and enlisted a dozen other mutinous soldiers.

On New Year's Day 1561, at a small Machiparan village called Mocomoco, Aguirre and his murderous band silently attacked Royal Governor Pedro Ursúa in his hammock, running him through with daggers and killing also a brave officer who tried to save him. The conspirators then formed their own sort of river government, installing a man named Fernando Guzmán as the expedition's general and giving Aguirre the title of Camp Master. The next day, when they officially signed their new governmental papers—which they eventually presented and which survive in the Archives of the Indies in Seville—Aguirre defiantly inscribed "Lope de Aguirre: TRAITOR" on the formal *información* explaining his actions, which he fully intended to be read by his king.

From here on, Aguirre led a bloodstained retracing of Orellana's journey. Reduced to one boat, much as the Pizarro-Orellana expedition had done with the original *San Pedro,* Aguirre and Guzmán moved downriver—some hacking overland along the tangled shores, the others in the leaking craft—dragging a sorry train of weakened bearers and useless horses with them. Just as Pizarro and Orellana had discovered, horses were ill suited to dense jungle travel, and Aguirre slaughtered them all, consuming the meat and using the hides for clothing. There remained now some two hundred people on the expedition, who would never make it out on foot with only one vessel; the decision was made to build two more. The search for El Dorado had once again devolved into a struggle for survival.

Deep in the Amazon, as the group labored on the new boats, Aguirre's delusional fantasy of ruling Peru reached fever pitch. Before witnesses, he and Guzmán drew up yet another bizarre paper, this one naming Fernando Guzmán "Prince of Peru," which Aguirre celebrated by kissing the hand of his new prince as he lay in a hammock attended by mock pages, who cooled him with feather fans. The new Prince Fernando also took to sleeping with the gorgeous Doña Inés, causing jealousy throughout the camp.

The goal of settling "Omagua and Dorado" having been abandoned, the insane plan was now to finish the boats, sail the remaining length of the Amazon, march overland across Venezuela, then cross the Andes to claim Peru.

By early April 1561, the two new and larger boats were completed, so they continued slowly descending the mighty river. But soon Aguirre snapped completely, deciding that he must lead. He persuaded a corps of forty trusted infantrymen to rally behind him, convincing himself and them that they must kill all "gentlemen or persons of quality." Over the next few months Aguirre and his armed henchmen went on a killing spree, stealthily and in cold blood murdering more than a hundred people, strangling them in their hammocks, slitting their throats, or stabbing them repeatedly as they pleaded for mercy and forgiveness. It was a macabre and gruesome bloodletting.

Among the first to be slain was the lovely Inés, who was stripped of her jewelry and fine clothes, no doubt raped, then impaled with more than twenty sword thrusts. Shortly afterward, Aguirre fell upon Prince Fernando in his own quarters, shooting him with a harquebus and finishing the deed with a sword. Aguirre now proclaimed his blood-slaked crew of forty "Men of the Amazon," and himself "the Wrath of God."*

Aguirre and the remainder of his select ghastly crew continued downriver, stopping only for food raids and rest. Unlike Orellana and Carvajal, they made no notes or observations about the river and its inhabitants, focusing only on trying to get out—which they just managed. In early July 1561 they reached the mouth of the Amazon and the Sweetwater Sea and, precisely as Orellana had done, caught the strong coastal current that drove them along the shores of Guiana. By July 21, nearly a year after the expedition for El Dorado and Omagua had departed, Aguirre and his horsehide-covered crews arrived on the island of Margarita, where the rogue tyrants promptly murdered its governor and took over the island.

The Wrath of God was short-lived. Aguirre and his rebels sailed to mainland Venezuela and commenced their overland march. By now, however, many of his own men, back in Christian civilization, in fear of the megalomaniac Aguirre and perhaps realizing the sinful error of their ways, deserted whenever they could, stealing off into the night. And, apprised now of the bloody takeover on Margarita, a royal army had been dispatched to overtake and capture or kill the self-proclaimed traitor Aguirre and his rebels. When he realized that the end was near, in October 1561, Lope de Aguirre wrote a letter to King Philip (who had been Prince Philip during Orellana's journey), a now-famous, seething missive in which he boasted about the people he had murdered, then closed with dire warnings about the fool's errand that attempts to settle the Amazon had become:

> This river has a course of over two thousand leagues of fresh water . . . And God only knows how we ever escaped out of that

---

*The Ursúa-Aguirre expedition is immortalized, in its weird way, in the dark and obsessive Werner Herzog film *Aguirre: The Wrath of God*.

fearful lake. I advise thee not to send any Spanish fleet up this ill-omened river, for, on the faith of a Christian, I swear to thee, O king and lord, that if a hundred thousand men should go up, not one would escape, and there is nothing else to expect, especially for the adventurers from Spain.

Shortly after writing this letter, Aguirre prepared to continue his overland flight across Venezuela, but the royalist force had hemmed him in, and most of his men had by now deserted. Alone in his tent now with only his daughter Elvira, he heard the arrival of the authorities. Convinced that they would rape her, and exclaiming that he wished to spare her the shame of being called the daughter of a traitor, Aguirre palmed a crucifix into the unfortunate girl's hand and stabbed her to death with his sword. A few moments later, the royalists stormed in and fired two fatal harquebus shots into Aguirre's chest. They beheaded the traitor, quartered his corpse, and carried back his tyrannical head on display in an iron cage.

So the second complete transcontinental navigation of the Amazon Basin—this one mostly retracing precisely Orellana's original voyage, though starting at a place farther south in the Andes—had been accomplished. Aguirre's horrific trip, which has been called the "most appalling in the annals of Spanish enterprise," confirmed much of what Orellana witnessed and reported, especially concerning the prosperity and complexity of the Omagua peoples, though the shocking nature of the Aguirre journey and his despicable actions offered Spain nothing to celebrate or even make public. For a time this psychotragic chapter of Spain's conquest history remained little known.

But sensational sagas such as El Dorado die hard, and eventually Elizabethan courtier, philosopher-poet, and captain of Queen Elizabeth's guard Sir Walter Raleigh heard about it. By 1595, using his significant powers of rhetoric and persuasion, he had managed to convince Queen Elizabeth that there was indeed much gold to be found beyond the Orinoco hills, and he succeeded in obtaining from her a commission of colonization, discovery, and exploitation of *The Empire of Guiana and the Golden City of Manoa, Which the Spaniards Call El Dorado.*

An educated and well-read man who thrived on adventure, Raleigh was aware of all the Spanish stories and legends connected to El Dorado, from Ordaz, Orellana, and Aguirre (he mentions each in turn in his book). In the mid-1590s, Raleigh had discovered that a Spaniard named Antonio de Berrio, an elderly conquistador who had spent more than a decade up the Orinoco River, claimed to have located the mythical place at last, near a Lake Manoa, a great salt lake so huge that it took three days to cross in canoes. According to Berrio, "They say that once this lake is crossed, the great provinces of Guiana stretch to the Maranon."

Raleigh wasted little time. In early April 1595, he sailed to Trinidad, landed, sacked a town, and captured the seventy-five-year-old Berrio, with his intimate knowledge of this Lake Manoa and the Guiana highlands. He took Berrio as his prisoner-informant-guide, crossed to mainland Venezuela, and planned an ascent of the Orinoco, just as Diego de Ordaz had done sixty-five years earlier. Raleigh pried as much information as he could from Berrio, but the Spaniard—who clung still to his own dream of winning the rich region—tried his best to dissuade the Englishman by exaggerating distances and emphasizing the real hardships they would encounter. The tough conquistador saw clearly that Raleigh was a pampered court dandy, his skin soft and white. Raleigh bore out this assessment of his character when he wrote of the crossing to the mainland, which is a very short journey, exclaiming that he had been forced "to lie in the rain and weather, in the open air, in the burning sun, and upon the hard boards, and to dress our meat . . . there never was any prison in England that could be found more unsavory and loathsome."

Once across, on the boggy mudflats at the Orinoco's mouth, Raleigh retrofitted five boats of his large sailing vessels into serviceable upriver galleys that could be rowed or sailed, and off he and a hundred men went on an exploration aimed at ascending the Orinoco to the mouth of the Caroni, and then continuing up the Caroni until he reached the magnificent salt lake Manoa. On the way upriver, Raleigh grew confounded, much as Orellana had been on his return journey, by the endless twists and snaking of the river: "I know all the earth doth not yield the like confluence of streams and branches, the one crossing the other so many times, and all so fair and large, and so like one to the another, as no man can tell which to take. . . . We might have wandered a whole year in that labyrinth of rivers. . . ."

Orellana had known exactly how this felt, and just as Orellana had been, very soon Raleigh himself was lost, frequently running aground despite having an Arawak Indian guide along. They toiled in the brackish tidewaters for weeks, arriving at May's end on the main Orinoco. The landscapes here enchanted Raleigh, and he described the savannas in glowing phrases:

> We passed the most beautiful country that ever mine eyes beheld . . . plains of twenty miles in length, the grass short and green, and . . . groves of trees by themselves, as if they had been by all the art and labour in the world so made of purpose: and still as we rowed, the deer came down feeding by the water's side, as if they had been used to a keeper's call.

But there were also dangers lurking in the dark and frightening waters. Raleigh reported seeing thousands of alligators—*largatos*—lolling like logs along the banks.

When he encountered Indian tribes, Raleigh took great care to treat them well, much as Orellana had, whenever possible. He forbade his men to treat the Indians roughly, and particularly outlawed the rape of their women, for which the Spaniards were notorious. He always paid or bartered for food.

En route upstream to the Caroni River, Raleigh observed much about the Indians' lifeways and customs, including their weaponry and warfare. The alchemy of poisoned arrows fascinated him, as did finding out what plant mixture constituted a remedy. He surely knew of Orellana's graphic reports of soldiers dying daylong, excruciating deaths, and referred to such encounters:

> There was nothing whereof I was more curious, than to find out the true remedies of these poisoned arrows, for besides the mortality of the wound they make, the party shot endures the

most insufferable torment in the world, and . . . a most ugly and lamentable death, sometimes dying stark mad, sometimes their bowels breaking out of their bellies, and are presently discolored, as black as pitch.

Raleigh's reconnaissance reached as far as the mouth of the Caroni River, eventually arriving at a village called Morequito where their chief, a man named Topiawari, hosted the Englishmen elaborately. The curious villagers laid out a feast, bringing venison, fish, fowl, various tropical fruits including pineapples, manioc wine, and delicately cooked parakeets. The impression on Raleigh was of an idyllic Eden, and he later waxed poetic about its beauty, especially at the hour of sunset: "The birds towards the evening singing on every tree with a thousand several tunes, cranes and herons of white, crimson, and carnation perching on the river's side, the air fresh with a gentle easterly wind, and every stone that we stooped to take up, promising either gold or silver by its complexion." This last was exaggerated, for they had as yet to find great stores of gold.

Well fed, they pushed up the Caroni in search of Lake Manoa, but the powerful river precluded their rowing upstream. Forced to go on foot, Raleigh and his men pressed overland upriver until they saw great plumes of mist that appeared like smoke in the distance. On closer inspection, Raleigh realized they were great waterfalls, a dozen or so, as high as church steeples and sending spray into the air like rain. These would prove impassable, much as the Atures rapids had been for Ordaz on the Meta, and Raleigh turned back.

Preparing to leave Morequito, Raleigh gathered some alluring information from chief Topiawari concerning Lake Manoa and its gold operations and smelting. Topiawari explained to the engaged Englishman that

most of the gold which they made in plates and images was not severed from stone, but that on the lake of Manoa, and in a multitude of other rivers they gathered it in grains of perfect gold and in pieces as big as small stones, and that they put in it a part of copper, otherwise they could not work it, and that they used a great earthen pot with holes round about it, and when they had mingled the gold and copper together, they fastened canes to the hoes, and so with the breath of men they increased the fire till the metal ran, and then they cast it into moulds of stone and clay, and so make those plates and images.

Raleigh mentally filed away these elaborate images and vowed to return.

Within a month, Raleigh had navigated back downstream, reached the mouth of the Orinoco, and boarded his ships. By the middle of June 1595, his "discovery" of Guiana—as he soon called it—was complete. As evidence of the region's great wealth, he brought back many ore samples—some that appeared to hold veins of gold and silver, and others that resembled sapphires. On his way home, he released Antonio de Berrio on the mainland, figuring he had served his purpose.

Sir Walter Raleigh's journey, compared to that of Orellana, was something of a lark. Still, it was historically the first English pioneering quest into Spanish-held South America, and it prompted the literary Raleigh to write a book about his travails. Almost immediately on his return, driven in part by naysayers who doubted the veracity of his journey and in part to persuade Queen Elizabeth, with whom he had fallen out of favor, to back a return venture, he penned the magically narrative and lyrical (and, in places, imaginatively fanciful and fictional) *Discoverie of the Large, Rich, and Bewtiful Empyre of Guiana, with a Relation of the Great and Golden City of Manoa (Which the Spaniards call El Dorado).* Published in at least four different editions in 1596, the sensational narrative became an immediate best seller in England and was subsequently published in numerous languages, including Latin, German, French, and Dutch. Though he had failed to find a golden man, lake, or city, that did not stop Sir Walter Raleigh from making the legend of El Dorado a commercially viable, mass media, almost pop culture event.

Raleigh's effort was the last great hope for the golden dream, but his failure to mount a full-scale return signaled the beginning of the end of the El Dorado myth.

The remainder of Raleigh's star-crossed life was a web of legal and political complexities, and his world disintegrated around him. After the death of his patron Queen Elizabeth in 1603, the new king (James VI of Scotland) tried Raleigh for high treason and tossed him into the Tower of London, where he would remain for the next twelve years (now with plenty of time to contemplate whether this London prison was indeed "more unsavory and loathsome" than the exposed deck of a sailing ship). Raleigh became an even more celebrated national hero and the Tower of London's most popular tourist attraction of the day.

Raleigh was temporarily released in 1616, just long enough to launch a disastrous return to his "discoverie" of Guiana. Raleigh was by now too old and decrepit to make it all the way, and during the voyage, his own son Wat was killed in a skirmish with the Spaniards.

Raleigh was later thrown back into the Tower of London by King James, this time after a closed and secret trial on counts of high treason, and sentenced to beheading. On October 29, 1618, Sir Walter Raleigh placed his head on the block and bravely told the executioner to "fear not, but strike home."

These were the last words of the last of the men who would go in search of El Dorado.

FRANCISCO ORELLANA'S EPIC JOURNEY ultimately fueled the imaginations of a wave of followers who struck out for the exotic, measureless region on their own expeditions of adventure, discovery, and colonization. In 1542, Orellana opened a last frontier, a river portal to an uncharted new world. His transcontinental voyage was a seminal, watershed moment, at once climactic and cataclysmic, for it also foretold the beginning of the end of many of the tribes Orellana encountered.

Amid the undeniable catastrophic failure of Orellana's tragic return voyage, one must consider him and his journey in light of what he did accomplish rather than what he did not, and the implications of what those accomplishments engendered and ignited. Whatever else one can say about him, Francisco Orellana was the audacious but judicious leader who first navigated the most sprawling, complex, grand, and voluminous river in the world. He discovered peoples and places no

European had ever seen or even imagined, great chiefdoms with mystical customs and perhaps even magical powers. He discovered previously inconceivable plants and animals, rodents the size of small horses, and freshwater fish the size of small whales.

And the river itself, nonpareil, an inland freshwater sea beyond scope or comprehension. All this Orellana saw and lived.

Orellana's first expedition down the Amazon indeed taught us a great deal, much of which bears directly on the thinking of modern anthropologists and archaeologists. The large, relatively complex, and densely populated "chiefdoms" he encountered showed that—contrary to popular scientific thought as recent as the mid- to late twentieth century—the Amazon River Basin once sustained tremendous numbers of people, somewhere on the order of four to five million. Those populations were decimated by the diseases brought by the flood of Europeans and are much smaller today than they were when Orellana traversed the continent.

As a result of Francisco Orellana's incredible voyage, what followed in the succeeding decades and centuries was a mass invasion of this wild and untamable basin, this extraordinary, inscrutable river that sinks its teeth like a vampire bat into all who go there and will not relinquish them. First the missionaries, then the slavers, then the naturalists, then the rubber barons, then the timbermen and the oilmen, and finally the biotech companies and the New Age gurus and the ecotourists—all came and come still, drawn inexorably toward the river's mysteries, bounties, and riches, whether these be in the form of people, plant and animal products—or ideas. Orellana's Amazon remains a final frontier, to this day one of only two places on earth (the other is Papua New Guinea) to support tribes of people who have never been contacted by the outside world.

Francisco Orellana's dream of El Dorado and its wonders lives on in the river itself—the Amazon—the siren that lured him over the Andes, through the Land of Cinnamon, and down her sinuous but deadly waterways. The Amazon—that dark and hypnotic enchantress that became his muse, his mistress, his maker, and that, for a brief breath in history, bore his name.

Chronology

1519–21—Hernán Cortés seizes emperor Montezuma and conquers the Aztec Empire of Mexico.

1524—Francisco Pizarro, Diego de Almagro, and Hernando de Luque form the Company of the Levant, a partnership dedicated to conquests.

1531—Diego de Ordaz's failed attempt up the Amazon, then expedition up the Orinoco River.

1532—Francisco Pizarro and the "Men of Cajamarca" capture Atahuala Inca, begin the conquest of Peru.

1541—In February, Gonzalo Pizarro and Francisco Orellana depart over the Andes on the expedition looking for La Canela and El Dorado.

1541—Francisco Pizarro is murdered on June 26, killed in his home by supporters of Diego de Almagro.

1542—In late June, Gonzalo Pizarro returns in rags to Quito after his failed expedition to La Canela.

1542—On August 26, Francisco Orellana successfully reaches the Atlantic Ocean, becoming the first European to navigate and descend the Amazon River.

1543—Francisco Orellana arrives back in Spain on May 11 and begins planning his return to the Amazon.

1545—Francisco Orellana departs from Spain on May 11, taking 4 ships, 300 men, and 200 horses on the expedition to New Andalusia.

1546—Francisco Orellana dies on the banks of the Amazon in early November.

1548—Battle of Jaquijahuana. Gonzalo Pizarro is executed.

1561—Pedro Ursúa and Lope de Aguirre's disastrous descent of the Amazon.

1595—Sir Walter Raleigh's expedition to Guiana and ascent of the Orinoco in search of El Dorado and Lake Manoa.

A Note on the Text and Sources

River of Darkness deals not only with Francisco Orellana's historic descent of the Amazon and his return, but also in ancillary ways with the conquest of Peru, the historical search for El Dorado, and the history of the Amazon River Basin. The source material for *River of Darkness* is correspondingly rich, varied, and worthy of a few comments and observations, especially useful for those wishing to further explore specific areas of interest. For those desiring such inquiry, numerous works are listed below and in the extensive bibliography that follows, works that have been cited, quoted directly, or used as reference in *River of Darkness*.

The primary source material for Orellana's journeys (his initial one of 1541–42, which began with Gonzalo Pizarro and continued after they separated, and his return in 1545–46) comes principally from firsthand participants who were on the voyages, and also from a handful of contemporary historians who recorded the events based on interviews with the participants either directly following, or some years after, the expeditions. Central among these is the most famous of them all, *Carvajal's Account,* which is published in English in two main sources. The first written version of this account, as mentioned in the text in chapter 17, was given by court historian Gonzalo Fernández de Oviedo y Valdes (often shortened to Oviedo), chronicler of the Indies and, at the time, 1542, governor of the fortress in Santo Domingo. Oviedo was respected and deeply trusted by the crown, and by 1523 he had already written his famous *Natural History of the West Indies* and much of his even larger *General and Natural History of the Indies*. Oviedo then incorporated a version of Carvajal's account into an amended version of his *General and Natural History of the Indies* (*Historia general y natural de las Indias*).

Next to chronicle and comment on Carvajal's account of Orellana's journey were the historians Francisco López de Gómara, in his *Historia General,* and Antonio de Herrera, in his *General History of the Vast Continent and Islands of America, Commonly Call'd the West Indies, From the First Discovery Thereof: With the Best Accounts the People Could Give of Their Antiquities.* Gómara gained recognition and considerable skill as Hernán Cortés's chaplain, secretary, and biographer, writing Cortés's account of the conquest of Mexico.

Fortunately for modern readers (and especially readers of English), all of these accounts—as well as court documents, proceedings, petitions, and letters from participants and survivors of the various journeys (including letters from Francisco Orellana and Gonzalo Pizarro)— have been compiled and published in the outstanding, scrupulously researched, and very lengthily titled *Discovery of the Amazon River According to the Account Hitherto Unpublished of Friar Gaspar de Carvajal with Other Documents Relating to Francisco de Orellana and His Companions, Put into Print at the Expense of the Duke of T'Serclaes de Tilly, with an Historical Introduction and Illustrations by José Toribio Medina* (Seville, 1894). The book was later published by the American Geographical Society as Special Publication no. 17 under the title *The Discovery of the Amazon,* translated from the Spanish by Bertram T. Lee and edited by H. C. Heaton (New York, 1934). In *River of Darkness,* I have quoted and sourced extensively from a handy complete and unabridged paperback version of this book by Dover Publications: José Toribio Medina, *The Discovery of the Amazon* (New York, 1988).

José Toribio Medina was a prolific Chilean scholar, and his *Discovery of the Amazon* painstakingly and conveniently compiles under one cover nearly every existing source relevant to the Pizarro-Orellana voyage, Pizarro's trek back to Quito, Orellana's voyage down the Amazon, and finally Orellana's return to New Andalusia. *The Discovery of the Amazon* includes biographies of the central figures (Pizarro, Orellana, and Carvajal), analytical chapters relative to Orellana's supposed treason, and exhaustive appendices and notes that include everything written and published by Oviedo, Herrera, and Gómara and all testimonies from judicial inquiries, royal audiences, and the Council of the Indies. Medina's *Discovery of the Amazon,* in short, proved indispensable in the writing of *River of Darkness.* The fact that all these sources are collected in one text also explains the heavy leaning on Medina in the notes. When the source is other than Medina himself, I indicate by citing the name of the author first, e.g., Oviedo, in Medina; Carvajal, in Medina.

Aspects of the Pizarro-Orellana expedition to La Canela, of Pizarro's march back to Quito, and of Orellana's continuation down the river were chronicled by three main sources, all firsthand observers and significant historians of the conquest of Peru. These are Pedro de Cieza de León, Garcilaso de la Vega (El Inca), and Agustín de Zárate (though Zárate did not arrive in Peru until 1544, quite late in the events).

Cieza de León, who arrived in the Indies as a boy (with his father) in 1535, has been called the "prince of Peruvian chroniclers," and his writings reveal a fiery, intuitive, and curious intellect, as well as a degree of formal education, for he makes reference to Caesar's *Commentaries,* Plutarch's *Lives,* and Hannibal's crossing of the Alps. He was known to be a diligent note taker, and the details, names of places and people, and specifics of personal anecdote and episodes in his writing are remarkable. Relied on in *River of Darkness* is the following important Cieza de León text: *The Discovery and Conquest of Peru: Chronicles of the New World Encounter,* edited and translated by Alexandra Parma Cook and Noble David Cook (Durham, North Carolina, and London, 1998). This excellent work includes an informative introduction and biographical sketch. Also instrumental were the exceptional texts Cieza de León wrote about the wars and civil wars in Peru as produced by the Hakluyt Society, translated, edited, and introduced by Sir Clements Markham. These are *The War of Quito* (1913), *Civil Wars in Peru: The War of Chupas* (1917), and *Civil Wars in Peru: The War of Las Salinas* (1923).

Important, too, in illuminating the episodes of the discovery and conquest of Peru is the monumental work of romantic historian Garcilaso de la Vega, "El Inca." He was the illegitimate son of a Spanish conquistador (of the same name) and an Inca princess. While he tends toward hyperbole and overdramatization, his sources are dutifully cited.

Most useful is his *Royal Commentaries of the Incas and General History of Peru,* 2 vols., translated and with an introduction by Harold V. Livemore (Austin and London, 1966).

Last of the notable firsthand Peru historians is Agustín de Zárate, a treasury official in Peru during the conquest period who interviewed many of Francisco Pizarro's companions and wrote with great drama about the wars. He also provided detailed and revealing personal portraits of conquistadors Francisco and Gonzalo Pizarro. A convenient and streamlined version of his work is *The Discovery and Conquest of Peru,* translated and with an introduction by J. M. Cohen (Baltimore, 1968).

Useful and entertaining—as he always is—for an overview of the entire conquest period is William H. Prescott, *History of the Conquest of Peru* (New York, 2005, originally published 1847). Especially interesting and contextually useful is Prescott's thorough treatment of the Inca history, royal families, political and social organization, and general conditions on the eve of the Spanish conquest.

An excellent companion to Prescott, and a book that, in the best vein of new histories, provides education while also offering a page-turning read, is *The Last Days of the Incas* (New York, 2007), by Kim Mac-Quarrie. Focusing on the Incas' rebellions and holdouts over the period of the conquest, MacQuarrie does a fine job of modernizing the tale and transporting the reader nearly five hundred years back in history while making the participants seem real and authentic and especially by fleshing out the important native Inca personalities.

Volumes have been written on the Amazon River Basin and environs, but one scholar-historian-writer deserves special mention, and that is John Hemming. Dr. Hemming, who served as director and secretary of the Royal Geographical Society in London between 1975 and 1996, has produced a tremendous list of books about the Amazon based on his personal research projects, explorations, and observations. His prize-winning *Conquest of the Incas* (San Diego, New York, and London, 1970) betters Prescott in style and scope (no mean feat), but it is on the subject of the Amazon River that Hemming really flourishes, and his contributions to the literature are unprecedented. Vital to *River of*

Darkness have been the following: *The Search for El Dorado* (New York, 1978); *Red Gold: The Conquest of the Brazilian Indians* (New York, 1978); and *Amazon Frontier: The Defeat of the Brazilian Indians* (Cambridge, 1987). Most necessary, even essential, for anyone desiring a complete (and exquisitely readable) history of the Amazon River from the arrival of the explorers-conquerors to the present day is Hemming's *Tree of Rivers: The Story of the Amazon* (New York, 2008). This stunning work is like a desk reference that reads like a good novel, and is highly recommended.

Finally, the decades of scholarly work and numerous books of two key academics deserve mention here, for their writings and contributions have greatly deepened our understanding of the peoples whom Orellana encountered along his journey. First among these is Robert Carneiro, curator and professor of anthropology at the Richard Gilder Graduate School at the American Museum of Natural History. With research and scholarly writing spanning six decades, Dr. Carneiro's expertise and wisdom are far-reaching and diverse, touching as they do areas of history, ethnology, archaeology, and cultural anthropology (especially cultural evolution). His "Circumscription Theory," put forth in "A Theory of the Origin of the State" (*Science,* August 21, 1970), aroused tremendous worldwide academic interest; his theory (insufficiently summarized here) explained how warfare played a vital role in state creation and how kingdoms and empires evolved as a result of geographically bounded or "circumscribed" areas. Carneiro performed ethnographic fieldwork in central Brazil in 1953–54 and again in 1975 and also did fieldwork in Peru during the early 1960s and in southern Venezuela in 1975, and he is still producing vital articles and books today. A few of his many important works include *Evolutionism in Cultural Anthropology: A Critical History* (Boulder, Colorado, 2003); *The Muse of History and the Science of Culture* (New York, 2000); and *Anthropological Investigations in Amazonia: Selected Papers* (Greeley, Colorado, 1985).

Last, but of great importance to *River of Darkness,* has been the work and guidance of archaeologist and anthropologist Anna Curtenius Roosevelt. Curator of archaeology at the Field Museum of Natural

History from 1991 to 2002, Roosevelt researches human prehistory and land use sustainability in tropical forest Amazonia. The essential Roosevelt works are *Amazonian Indians from Prehistory to the Present: Anthropological Perspectives,* edited by Anna Roosevelt (Tucson and London, 1994); *Moundbuilders of the Amazon: Geophysical Archaeology on Marajo Island, Brazil* (San Diego and New York, 1991); and *Parmana: Prehistoric Maize and Manioc Subsistence Along the Amazon and Orinoco* (New York, 1980).

Notes

PROLOGUE

xvi **rumbling the earth with great quakes** J. M. Cohen, Journeys Down the Amazon (London, 1975), 18–19.

XVI **So they built a boat** Ibid., 24–25; Brendan Bernard, *Pizarro, Orellana, and the Exploration of the Amazon* (New York, 1991), 14–16; John Hemming, *Tree of Rivers* (New York, 2008), 23–24.

CHAPTER ONE: A CONFLUENCE OF CONQUISTADORS

3 **The vast and rugged lands of Extremadura** Arthur Helps, *The Life of Pizarro* (London, 1896), 1–3; Rafael Varón Gabai, *Francisco Pizarro and His Brothers: The Illusion of Power in Sixteenth-Century Peru* (Norman, Oklahoma, and London, 1997), 3–10; Hammond Innes, *The Conquistadors* (New York, 1969), 22–23; Kim MacQuarrie, *The Last Days of the Incas* (New York, 2007), 18–22.

4 **"a gentleman of noble blood, and a person of honor"** José Toribio Medina, ed., translated by Bertram T. Lee and edited by H. C. Heaton, *The Discovery of the Amazon* (New York, 1988), 264, 36, 36n. The exact date of Orellana's birth remains unknown, but sources, including his own testimony made on the island of Margarita in 1542, generally agree that the year was 1511.

4 **Orellana claims to have arrived in the Indies in 1527** Medina, *Discovery,* 37.

4 **"he performed his first feats of arms as a conquistador"** Ibid., 37.

4 **that, after hacking their way across the brambly isthmus** Innes, *Conquistadors,* 30 and 38.

5 **"in the conquests of Lima and Trujillo"** Medina, *Discovery,* 37–38.

5 **Of this deeply loyal band of brothers** For a thorough (and in some ways exhausting and confusing) overview of the complex Pizarro family lineage, see James Lockhart, *The Men of Cajamarca: A Social and Biographical Study of the First Conquerors of Peru* (Austin, 1972), 28–35; see also Gabai, *Francisco Pizarro and His Brothers,* 3–10; Hoffman Birney, *Brothers of Doom: The Story of the Pizarros of Peru* (New York, 1942), 3; MacQuarrie, *Last Days of the Incas,* 37.

5 **skilled beyond his years** The exact date of Gonzalo Pizarro's birth is unknown. It is typically listed as c. 1502–6.

5   "the best lance in Peru" William H. Prescott, *History of the Conquest of Peru* (New York, 2005), 348–49 and 497; Michael Wood, *Conquistadors* (Berkeley and Los Angeles, 2000), 191–92; Walker Chapman, *The Golden Dream: Seekers of El Dorado* (Indianapolis, Kansas City, and New York, 1967), 142; Lockhart, *Men of Cajamarca*, 175–78.

5   Tall and well proportioned Agustín de Zárate, translated and introduced by J. M. Cohen, *The Discovery and Conquest of Peru* (Baltimore, 1968), 242–43.

6   The sight proved curious and intriguing Prescott, *Conquest of Peru* 131–33; Pedro de Cieza de León, *The Discovery and Conquest of Peru,* edited and translated by Alexandra Parma Cook and Noble David Cook (Durham, North Carolina, and London, 1998), 74–77; MacQuarrie, *Last Days,* 27–28; Innes, *Conquistadors,* 210. See also, on balsa craft, the interesting article by Thor Heyerdahl, "The Balsa Raft in Aboriginal Navigation off Peru and Ecuador," in *Southwestern Journal of Anthropology,* vol. 11, no. 3 (Autumn 1955): 251–64.

7   "They were carrying many pieces of gold" Quoted in MacQuarrie, *Last Days of the Incas,* 28; Prescott, *Conquest of Peru,* 133; Cieza de León, *Discovery,* 76.

7   "This line signifies labor" Quoted in MacQuarrie, *Last Days of the Incas,* 29; Prescott, *Conquest of Peru,* 142. Different versions of this speech exist in various translations.

8   Francisco Pizarro had discovered the Incas Prescott, *Conquest of Peru,* 133 and 145–47; MacQuarrie, *Last Days of the Incas,* 29–30; Cieza de León, *Discovery,* 76, 103–13.

8   earned him the title of Marquis de Valle Hugh Thomas, *Conquest: Montezuma, Cortés, and the Fall of Old Mexico* (New York, 1993), 597–98; Buddy Levy, *Conquistador: Hernán Cortés, King Montezuma, and the Last Stand of the Aztecs* (New York, 2008), 317–18.

9   "discovery and conquest in the province of Peru—or *New Castille*" Prescott, *Conquest of Peru,* 162–63.

10   "Some of the strangers, he was told, rode giant animals" Quoted in MacQuarrie, *Last Days of the Incas,* 53–54.

10   "such magnificent roads could be found nowhere in Christendom" Bernard, *Exploration,* 31. For a detailed description of the complex Inca road system, see Charles C. Mann, *1491: New Revelations of the Americas Before Columbus* (New York, 2005), 85–86.

10   "made water [urinated] . . . out of sheer terror" Quoted in Mann, *1491,* 80.

11   "large gold and silver disks like crowns on their heads" Quoted in John Hemming, *The Conquest of the Incas* (San Diego, New York, and London, 1970), 38.

12   Peru now lay in the hands of Francisco Pizarro For detailed analysis and descriptions of the massacre at Cajamarca, see Hemming, *Conquest of the Incas,* 35–45; MacQuarrie, *Last Days of the Incas,* 77–85; Prescott, *Conquest of Peru,* 213–29.

12   "Atahualpa said that he would give a room full of gold" Quoted in

MacQuarrie, *Last Days of the Incas,* 96; also in Hemming, *Conquest of the Incas,* 47–49, and Prescott, *Conquest of Peru,* 225–26 and 243–44. Hemming says Atahualpa claimed the rooms could be filled in two months.

12   **the greatest empire on the face of the earth** Charles C. Mann points out that in 1491 the Inca Empire was bigger than the Triple Alliance of the Aztecs in Mexico, the Ming Dynasty in China, and the Ottoman Empire. See Mann, *1491,* 64.

13   **melting down six hundred pounds of gold per day** Hemming, *Conquest of the Incas,* 72–73; John Hemming, *The Search for El Dorado* (New York, 1978), 45; Prescott, *Conquest of Peru,* 170–71.

13   **"The riches and greatness of Peru"** Quoted in Hemming, *Search for El Dorado,* 45.

14   **pay taxes to the Spaniards in the form of goods and services** Lesley Byrd Simpson, *The Encomienda in New Spain* (Berkeley and Los Angeles, 1966); Hernán Cortés, *Letters from Mexico,* edited, translated, and introduced by Anthony Pagden (New Haven, 2001), 498; and James Lockhart, *Spanish Peru, 1532–1560: A Colonial Society* (Madison, Milwaukee, and London, 1968).

15   **"having left the said cities freed from siege"** Quoted in Medina, *Discovery,* 39 and 264n.

15   **Orellana next played . . . while the Pizarro troops suffered only nine casualties** Medina, *Discovery,* 39–40; Pedro de Cieza de León, *Civil Wars in Peru: The War of Salinas,* translated by Sir Clements Markham (London, Hakluyt Society, 1923), 195–202; Hemming, *Conquest of the Incas,* 233; Prescott, *Conquest of Peru,* 329–32.

15   **"with the aid of men whom I took along"** Medina, *Discovery,* 263; Anthony Smith, *Explorers of the Amazon* (New York, 1990), 43.

16   **"the said province under the yoke of Spain"** Medina, *Discovery,* 263.

16   **"a spot so fertile and so rich"** Ibid.

16   **"procurations and appointments, making him lieutenant-governor"** Ibid., 42.

CHAPTER TWO: BIRTH OF THE GOLDEN DREAM

18   **tribes clad in golden ornamentation and jewelry** Hemming, *El Dorado,* 108; Chapman, *Golden Dream,* 140–41.

18   **His exploits included a heroic climb** Levy, *Conquistador,* 96–97; Hemming, *El Dorado,* 10.

18   **the Amazon remained entirely unexplored by Europeans** Samuel Eliot Morison, *The European Discovery of America: The Southern Voyages, A.D. 1492–1616* (New York, 1974), 213.

19   **"emeralds as big as a man's fist"** Quoted in Alexander von Humboldt and Aimé Bonpland, translated and edited by Thomasina Ross, *Personal Narrative of Travels to the Equinoctial Regions of America During the Years 1799–1804,* vol. 3 (London, 1908), 40.

19 "On going up a certain number of suns [a few days]" Ibid., 40.

19 were living among Amazonian tribes somewhere upriver Medina, *Discovery*, 210–11; Smith, *Explorers*, 71–72.

19 Ordaz landed on the island of Trinidad F. A. Kirkpatrick, *The Spanish Conquistadors* (London, 1934), 300–301; Edward J. Goodman, *The Explorers of South America* (New York, 1972), 79–80; Hemming, *El Dorado*, 10–11; Chapman, *Golden Dream*, 54–55; A. F. Bandelier, *The Gilded Man (El Dorado)* (New York, 1893), 34–35.

19 "a very powerful prince with one eye" Quoted in Chapman, *Golden Dream*, 57; Bandelier, *Gilded Man*, 36.

19 they would be forced to abandon the boats Bandelier, *Gilded Man*, 35; Chapman, *Golden Dream*, 56.

20 The Spaniards optimistically (and erroneously) interpreted this pantomime Kirkpatrick, *Spanish Conquistadors*, 301.

20 "He said that there was much of that metal" Quoted in Hemming, *El Dorado*, 15; Bandelier, *Gilded Man*, 36.

20 "less than stags, but fit for riding like the Spanish horses" Quoted in Chapman, *Golden Dream*, 57.

21 "He who goes to the Orinoco" Quoted in Gerard Helferich, *Humboldt's Cosmos: Alexander von Humboldt and the Latin American Journey That Changed the Way We See the World* (New York, 2004), 124.

21 Quesada, too, had heard stories R. B. Cunninghame Graham, *The Conquest of New Granada: Being the Life of Gonzalo Jimenez de Quesada* (Boston and New York, 1922), 90–91; Chapman, *Golden Dream*, 103–6. See also Joyce Lorimer, editor, *Sir Walter Raleigh's Discoverie of Guiana* (London, 2006), 49n, which describes the origins of the El Dorado mythology among the Misc or Chibcha around Bogotá in the late 1530s, providing the impetus and the prelude to the Pizarro/Orellana expedition.

CHAPTER THREE: INTO THE ANDES

24 "the most laborious expedition that has been undertaken in these Indies" Pedro de Cieza de León, *Civil Wars in Peru: The War of Chupas* (London, 1917), 56.

24 La Canela—the Cinnamon Valley . . . Pineda agreed to the terms Ibid., 57; Cohen, *Journeys*, 14–15; Medina, *Discovery*, 46.

24 "nobles of the highest ranks" Medina, *Discovery*, 46.

25 "carried nothing but a sword and a shield" Cieza de León, *War of Chupas*, 57. Some sources put the total number of men as high as 340, and others at 280. Similarly, the numbers of the swine and the hounds vary. Garcilaso gives 4,000 swine and a flock of llamas, and 340 men, 150 cavalry, with the remainder infantry (León claims 5,000 swine); Garcilaso de la Vega, translated and with an introduction by Harold V. Livermore, *Royal Commentaries of the Incas and General History of Peru*, Part 2 (Austin and London, 1966), 873–74; Medina, *Discovery*, 46; Cohen, *Journeys*, 15; Smith,

Explorers, 45. The number of dogs varies as well, from 900 at the lower end to 2,000 at the upper. See John Grier Varner and Jeannette Johnson Varner, *Dogs of the Conquest* (Norman, Oklahoma, 1983), 119–22.

25   ancient relatives of pines David L. Pearson and Les Beletsky, *Travellers' Wildlife Guides: Ecuador and the Galápagos Islands* (Northampton, Massachusetts, 2005), 25–26 and 252–55.

26   The Indians, apparently intimidated Vega, *Royal Commentaries,* 874.

26   Although eruptions of great magnitude were common Zárate, *Discovery and Conquest of Peru,* 192. Vega, *Royal Commentaries,* 874.

27   "We came to very rugged wooded country" Medina, *Discovery,* 245.

27   "It just rained; it never stopped" Quoted in Wood, *Conquistadors,* 195.

28   "We continued our journey" Medina, *Discovery,* 245.

30   "When Orellana's party saw him" Cieza de León, *War of Chupas,* 58.

30   "carrying only a sword and a shield" Medina, *Discovery,* 168.

31   "big leaves like laurels" Vega, *Royal Commentaries,* 875.

31   "This is cinnamon of the most perfect kind" Cieza de León, *War of Chupas,* 59. The trees were actually *Nectandra* and *Ocotea,* related to avocados, and of the magnolia family.

32   "So he [Pizarro] ordered some canes" Ibid., 60.

32   "who tore them to pieces with their teeth" Ibid.

32   "fertile and abundant province" Ibid., 61.

32   "We found the trees which bear cinnamon" Quoted in Medina, *Discovery,* 246.

33   He had found the upper reaches of the Napo Wood, *Conquistadors,* 196.

33   "ranges of forest clad and rugged mountains" Ibid. Also in Cieza de León, *War of Chupas,* 61.

CHAPTER FOUR: EL BARCO AND THE SAN PEDRO

35   "combs and knives" Cieza de León, *War of Chupas,* 62; Chapman, *Golden Dream,* 148.

36   It was an awesome, humbling spectacle Vega, *Royal Commentaries, Part 2,* 876. Vega says that Pizarro and his men could hear the San Rafael Falls from "six leagues," or more than twenty miles. See also Wood, *Conquistadors,* 197.

36   "so narrow it was not twenty feet across" Quoted in Wood, *Conquistadors,* 197. Vega claims that the gorge is closer to 1,500 feet high, though that strains credibility given the topography.

36   "rash even to look down" Vega, *Royal Commentaries,* 876–77.

36   "The rest fled in astonishment" Ibid., 876.

37   "He was fifteen days going and coming" Gonzalo Pizarro, quoted in Medina, *Discovery,* 246.

37   "As soon as he [Ribera] came with this story" Medina, *Discovery,* 246. See also Betty Meggers, *Amazonia: Man and Culture in a Counterfeit Paradise* (Washington and London, 1996), 122–30, and Hemming, *Tree of Rivers,* 30.

38   "must flow down to the Sweet Sea" Cieza de León, *War of Chupas*, 64. Also quoted in Wood, *Conquistadors*, 199.

38   "a beautiful and abundantly flowing river" Quoted in Wood, *Conquistadors*, 200.

38   "all have their homes and living quarters" Gonzalo Pizarro, letter to the king, quoted in Medina, *Discovery*, 247.

38   "reduce to a peaceful attitude of mind" Ibid.

38   "the chief wanted to plunge into the river and to take flight" Cieza de León, *War of Chupas*, 64.

39   "because there were frequently on the river" Medina, *Discovery*, 247.

39   The sickest were abandoned Levy, *Conquistador*, 213–14.

39   including Arawakan, Panoan, and Tupian Harriet E. Manelis Klein, "Genetic Relatedness and Language Distributions in Amazonia," in Roosevelt, *Amazonian Indians from Prehistory to the Present*, 343–46.

41   "I found it advisable to build a brigantine" Gonzalo Pizarro, quoted in Medina, *Discovery*, 247.

42   "showed himself more active than anyone else" Medina, *Discovery*, 54; Cohen, *Journeys*, 25; Medina, *Discovery*, 169.

42   "They set up a forge" Vega, *Royal Commentaries*, 877.

42   The Spaniards also learned from the natives Dr. Robert Carneiro, from personal notes on manuscript, August 10, 2009.

43   "water tight and strong, although not very large" Toribio de Ortiguera, quoted in Medina, *Discovery*, 314–15.

43   They christened the craft the *San Pedro* The exact dimensions of the craft are not recorded. Oviedo, in Medina, *Discovery*, 54n, claims that the boat could hold up to twenty men. See also Cohen, *Journeys*, 25.

43   "if we did not find any good country" Pizarro, letter to the king, quoted in Medina, *Discovery*, 247.

43   "which afforded no small help to [the men] in their need" Cieza de León, *War of Chupas*, 65.

44   "Continuing their journey down the river bank" Ibid.

44–45   "beginning to feel the pangs of hunger" Ibid.

45   "All of the companions were greatly dissatisfied" Friar Gaspar de Carvajal, quoted in Medina, *Discovery*, 170.

45   The friars held a somber mass Wood, *Conquistadors*, 202–3.

45   "vast one and that there was no food" Quoted in Medina, *Discovery*, 248; Vega, *Royal Commentaries*, 878; Chapman, *Golden Dream*, 148.

45   "plenty of food and rich in gold" Vega, *Royal Commentaries*, 878.

46   "Being confident that Captain Orellana would do as he said" Gonzalo Pizarro, quoted in Medina, *Discovery*, 248.

46   On board they retained most of the equipment Cohen, *Journeys*, 26–27; Smith, *Explorers*, 52; Wood, *Conquistadors*, 205.

46   (twenty-two of the worthy craft) The number of canoes varies among the sources, cited as anywhere from ten to twenty-two.

CHAPTER FIVE: THE SPLIT

49 "hauling the boat out of the water and fastening a piece of plank on it" Carvajal, in Medina, *Discovery*, 171.

49 "owing to the effect of many other rivers" Ibid.

49 "the Captain and the companions conferred" Ibid.

50 "We reached a state of privation" Ibid., 172.

50 "Our Lord deliver us" Ibid., 171.

50 "He would see fit to bring us to a haven of safety" Ibid., 172.

51 "Sick and sound alike" Quoted in Cohen, *Journeys*, 36.

51 "The Captain was the one who heard them first" Carvajal, in Medina, *Discovery*, 173; Cohen, *Journeys*, 37; Chapman, *Golden Dream*, 156; Smith, *Explorers*, 55–56.

52 "And so that night a heavy watch was kept, the Captain not sleeping" Carvajal, in Medina, *Discovery*, 173.

52 "for they had had their fill of living on roots" Ibid.

52 "We heard in the villages" Ibid.

53 manioc beer called *chicha* Linda Mowat, *Cassava and Chicha: Bread and Beer of the Amazonian Indians* (Aylesbury, UK, 1989), 45–46. See also Gonzalo Fernández de Oviedo, translated and edited by Sterling A. Stoudemire, *Natural History of the West Indies* (Chapel Hill, North Carolina, 1959), 39. It is called *masato* in Peruvian Montana.

54 "their shields on their shoulders" Carvajal, in Medina, *Discovery*, 174; Cohen, *Journeys*, 37–38; Richard Muller, *Orellana's Discovery of the Amazon River* (Guayaquil, Ecuador, 1937), 38; Chapman, *Golden Dream*, 156.

54 He asked that they take these Cohen, *Journeys*, 38; Carvajal, in Medina, *Discovery*, 174; Smith, *Explorers*, 55.

54 Orellana understood this man to be a chief Carvajal, in Medina, *Discovery*, 175; Smith, *Explorers*, 55; Cohen, *Journeys*, 38.

54 "meats, partridges, turkeys, and fish of many sorts" Carvajal, in Medina, *Discovery*, 175. Cohen, *Journeys*, 38.

55 "his knowledge of the language" Quoted in Hemming, *Tree of Rivers*, 27.

55 Seven of the Spaniards Bernard, *Exploration*, 44.

55 The people of Imara Wood, *Conquistadors*, 208.

56 Canoes were moored or beached Cohen, *Journeys*, 39.

56 Despite Orellana's linguistic skills Levy, *Conquistador*, 21.

56 "spoke to them at great length" Carvajal, in Medina, *Discovery*, 177; Cohen, *Journeys*, 39.

57 "on the subject of what steps it was proper to take" Carvajal, in Medina, *Discovery*, 176.

57 "The companions were very happy" Ibid.

57 "news of what was happening" Ibid., 178.

58 Orellana, as fair and diplomatic Cohen, *Journeys*, 42.

58 "that kind treatment was the proper procedure to be followed" Carvajal, in Medina, *Discovery*, 176.

CHAPTER SIX: THE PLIGHT OF GONZALO PIZARRO

60 "There was not even any track to follow" Cieza de León, *War of Chupas*, 67.

61 "the heavens poured down water" Ibid.

61 "personally captured . . . five canoes from the Indians" Gonzalo Pizarro, letter to the king, September 3, 1542, quoted in Medina, *Discovery*, 249.

61 "with a dozen Spaniards" Cieza de León, *War of Chupas*, 68.

62 "We were forced to eat the little buds of a plant" Quoted in Wood, *Conquistadors*, 212.

62 "wild herbs and coarse fruits" Cieza de León, *War of Chupas*, 68.

63 the Land of Cinnamon Hemming, *Search for El Dorado*, 108.

63 "without wasting any of the entrails" Cieza de León, *War of Chupas*, 68.

63 "larger and mightier than the one they had been navigating" Ibid., 69.

63 "the gold-bearer" Quoted in Wood, *Conquistadors*, 213.

63 "cuts made by wood knives and swords" Cieza de León, *War of Chupas*, 69.

64 "palm shoots and some fruit stones" Gonzalo Pizarro, letter to the king, September 3, 1542, in Medina, *Discovery*, 248–49.

64 "many very thick patches of yuca" Cieza de León, *War of Chupas*, 69; Cohen, *Journeys*, 28.

65 After the members of the scouting party were satiated The sources differ here, some saying that Pineda's men ate the yuca raw, others suggesting that Pineda took the time to cook the tubers. Since Pineda was able to successfully return to Gonzalo Pizarro with his canoes loaded with the yuca, it seems safe to assume that he indeed must have cooked the plant, or else his men would have been too sick to paddle the difficult journey back up the Napo. See Wood, *Conquistadors*, 213 (who says "Having cooked for themselves and eaten . . . "); see also Cohen, *Journeys*, 28, who says "His men . . . ate them cooked and unwashed."

65 "nothing but saddle and stirrup leathers" Quoted in Wood, *Conquistadors*, 214; Cieza de León, *War of Chupas*, 70.

65 "saw the canoes and learnt what they brought, and they all wept for joy" Cieza de León, *War of Chupas*, 69–70.

66 "I determined to take the expeditionary force" Gonzalo Pizarro, letter to the king, September 3, 1542, in Medina, *Discovery*, 249.

66 "As all came in an exhausted state" Cieza de León, *War of Chupas*, 70.

66 "root of white color, and rather thick" Ibid.

66 "lost his reason and became mad" Ibid.

66–67 "super-crop that enabled man to evolve from foraging to farming" Hemming, *Tree of Rivers*, 26.

67 "Subtle morphological traits differentiate" Quoted in Hemming, *Tree of Rivers*, 26.

67   Bitter manioc, on the other hand Mowat, *Cassava and Chicha,* 7; Hemming, *Tree of Rivers,* 26; Meggers, *Amazonia,* 47–49, 58, 60. According to Dr. Robert Carneiro, "Even in the case of 'sweet' varieties of manioc there is a small amount of prussic acid in the phelloderm, the thin, smooth, white layer that covers the tuber just below the flaky brown skin. So ingesting the phelloderm along with the rest of the tuber, as famished men would no doubt have done, especially since the phelloderm is not readily distinguishable or separable from the rest of the tuber, would very possibly have resulted in some serious symptoms." From his editorial notes on *River of Darkness,* August 24, 2009.

67   The women bend over these graters Mowat, *Cassava and Chicha,* 21–27.

68   "groundbreaking invention" Hemming, *Tree of Rivers,* 26. Dr. Robert Carneiro points out, however, "The tipiti is only the most advanced and most recent device for squeezing the juice out of poisonous manioc. Over much of Amazonia (e.g., the Upper Xingu), other squeezing devices are used, and were used well before the tipiti was invented." From editorial notes on *River of Darkness,* August 24, 2009.

68   second only to rice as a crop of global significance Hemming, *Tree of Rivers,* 26–27. See also Mowat, *Cassava and Chicha,* 7–47; and Anna Roosevelt, *Parmana: Prehistoric Maize and Manioc Subsistence Along the Amazon and Orinoco* (New York, 1980), 136–37 and 119–39; and Mann, *1491,* 297–98.

68   "very sick and sore" Cieza de León, *War of Chupas,* 70.

68   "themselves grated the yucas" Ibid., 71. Dr. Robert Carneiro notes here, "To be specific, the 'sharp thorns' are those of the spiny aerial root of the palm *Iriartea exorrhiza.* The root, cut from the palm, is used whole, without the thorns being removed from it." From editorial notes on *River of Darkness,* August 24, 2009.

68   "rested after a fashion" Gonzalo Pizarro, letter to the king, September 3, 1542, in Medina, *Discovery,* 249.

69   "Captain Orellana told me" Ibid., 248.

69   Paying no heed Ibid.

CHAPTER SEVEN: ST. EULALIA'S CONFLUENCE—THE AMAZON

71   "The Captain, seeing that it was necessary" Carvajal, in Medina, *Discovery,* 176.

72   "jewels and gold medallions" Ibid., 177.

72   "Never did the Captain permit" Ibid.

72   He said that as a boy Ibid.; Cohen, *Journeys,* 41; Wood, *Conquistadors,* 209; Smith, *Explorers,* 70–71.

72   women warriors or "Amazons" For interesting discussions of the origins of Amazonian mythology, see Jessica Amanda Salmonson, *The Encyclopedia of Amazons: Women Warriors from Antiquity to the Modern Era* (New York, 1991), ix–xii; Abby Wettan Kleinbaum, *The War Against the Amazons* (New

York, 1983), 1–38; and Lyn Webster Wilde, *On the Trail of the Women Warriors: The Amazons in Myth and History* (New York, 1999), 1–9.

73　"an island inhabited only by women" Hernán Cortés, *Letters from Mexico,* 298–300; Hemming, *El Dorado,* 90.

73　Similar tales persisted Hemming, *El Dorado,* 90.

73　"He ordered at once some bellows" Quoted in Cohen, *Journeys,* 40–41.

73　The mosquitoes were so thick Ibid., 41.

74　"two thousand very good nails" Medina, *Discovery,* 178.

74　"We laid in what foodstuffs we could" Ibid., 178–79.

75　"feared certain death" Quoted in Cohen, *Journeys,* 43.

75　"may occur and come to pass" Quoted in Medina, *Discovery,* 73.

75　"so up-hill a journey" Ibid., 254.

75　"by which at least their lives might be saved" Ibid., 74 and 74n, 178; Cohen, *Journeys,* 43.

75　"strange and hitherto never experienced voyage of discovery" Carvajal, in Medina, *Discovery,* 169.

76　Orellana directed the laden *San Pedro* Bernard, *Exploration,* 47.

76　"many Indians in canoes ready to defend the landing place" Oviedo, quoted in Medina, *Discovery,* 412.

77　"expecting never to see them again" Carvajal, in Medina, *Discovery,* 179; Oviedo, in Medina, *Discovery,* 413; Bernard, *Exploration,* 47.

77　"many hardships and extraordinary dangers" Quoted in Bernard, *Exploration,* 47.

77　"They brought back turtles" Oviedo, quoted in Medina, *Discovery,* 414.

77　"The one which came in on the right side" Ibid. There is some disagreement among the sources about the exact date of reaching the Amazon (Maranon), but Orellana and his men named the confluence St. Eulalia's Confluence, honoring their arrival at this place on February 12, 1542. A number of other sources date the arrival at February 11, 1542.

78　"It was so wide from bank to bank" Oviedo, quoted in Medina, *Discovery,* 414.

78　More than 4,500 miles long . . . it contains an island the size of Switzerland Because precise river distances are extremely difficult to measure (they are not straight lines, for one thing), the distance given here of 4,000 miles is based on sources that measure from tributary origins at the headwaters. Most serious scientific sources consider the Amazon measured from its headwaters on the Ucayali in Peru. In 2001 the National Geographic Society accepted a measurement put forth by a Polish expedition, which gave the number as 4,650 miles. See Michael Goulding, *The Smithsonian Atlas of the Amazon* (Washington and London, 2003), 23 and 99; Bernard, *Exploration,* 49; Hemming, *Tree of Rivers,* 325–29.

79　"came with peaceful intent" Carvajal, in Medina, *Discovery,* 180.

79　"The Indians remained very happy" Ibid., 181.

79　"many partridges like those of our Spain" Ibid., 181; Cohen, *Journeys,* 46.

79–80 "It was not long before we saw many Indians" Carvajal, in Medina, *Discovery,* 181; Cohen, *Journeys,* 46.

80   "The Captain leaped out on land" Carvajal, in Medina, *Discovery,* 182.

80   The overlord leapt out on land Ibid. There exist a number of feline species in this area, and all would have been hunted by the indigenous peoples. These include the puma, the jaguar, the ocelot, the margay, and the jaguarundi.

81   "worshipped a single God" Carvajal, in Medina, *Discovery,* 182.

81   "to whom belonged the territory" Ibid., 183.

82   "since there was a good supply of materials" Ibid., 184.

82   Once the Spaniards entered their realm Wood, *Conquistadors,* 218; John Augustine Zahm, *The Quest of El Dorado* (New York and London, 1917), 73.

82   "Old men and women not suited for slavery" Meggers, *Amazonia,* 130.

CHAPTER EIGHT: THE *VICTORIA*

84   He offered to serve in the role of foreman Carvajal, in Medina, *Discovery,* 184 and 239n; Cohen, *Journeys,* 47.

84   "And thereupon the Captain ordered" Carvajal, in Medina, *Discovery,* 184; Cohen, *Journeys,* 47; Wood, *Conquistadors,* 218–19.

85   "very far away" Carvajal, in Medina, *Discovery,* 184.

85   "drive the mosquitoes away from him" Oviedo, in Medina, *Discovery,* 418.

86   "There came to see the Captain" Carvajal, in Medina, *Discovery,* 186.

86   "many things to present" Ibid.; Cohen, *Journeys,* 47.

87   It has been suggested Cohen, *Journeys,* 48.

87   "misshapen hunchbacks and dwarves and albinos" Levy, *Conquistador,* 116.

87   "sorcerers, daubed with whitewash" Carvajal, in Medina, *Discovery,* 197.

87   "culture bearers" John Hemming, email correspondence with the author on February 17, 2009; Donald W. Lathrap, *The Upper Amazon* (New York, 1970), 22–44; Smith, *Explorers,* 63–64. Dr. Robert Carneiro, editorial notes on *River of Darkness,* August 26, 2009. The extent and range of the Arawak-speaking tribes is controversial; Carneiro disagrees with Hemming, suggesting that the Arawak-speaking tribes on the Ucayali— the Piro and the Campa (Ashaninka)—would be very high up the river and likely not the groups that Orellana encountered.

87   While working on the brigantine Carvajal, in Medina, *Discovery,* 69 and 186.

88   "I preached every Sunday" Ibid., 187.

88   Within minutes he had himself "elected" chief justice Levy, *Conquistador,* 41–42.

89   "cavaliers and hidalgos, comrades, able-bodied men" Scrivener Isásaga letter, quoted in Medina, *Discovery,* 258.

89   "to go and search for the Governor" Ibid.

89   "We, perceiving and realizing the evil effects" Ibid., 259.

89   "and the Holy Mary" Ibid., 262.

90   In addition to Robles Cohen, *Journeys,* 49; Hemming, *El Dorado,* 108–9.

90   "The Captain requested of me" Carvajal, in Medina, *Discovery,* 187.

90   (perhaps resin from local rubber trees or black beeswax) Dr. Robert Carneiro points out that while they might have used latex from a rubber tree, this "pitch" was "more likely from black beeswax, which the Indians use for things like caulking, etc." From Carneiro editorial notes on *River of Darkness,* August 26, 2009.

90   nineteen *joas* . . . "quite large enough for navigating at sea" Carvajal, in Medina, *Discovery,* 189 and 240n. Medina points out that the "joa" or "goa" is not exactly a unit of measure, but rather a nautical feature, an addition made to the end of the ribs to hold the rail; quoted in Smith, *Explorers,* 63. Michael Wood, in *Conquistadors,* 219, puts the boat at around twenty-four feet in length but does not explain how he arrives at that figure.

91   "ordered that all the men be ready" Carvajal, in Medina, *Discovery,* 187.

91   Aparia the Great's chiefdom Robert Carneiro, "The Chiefdom: Precursor to the State," 37–79, in Grant D. Jones and Robert R. Kautz, *The Transition to Statehood in the New World* (New York, 1981). See also Helaine Silverman and William H. Isbell, *Handbook of South American Archaeology* (New York, 2008), 10 and 371–72.

91–92   The gunpowder . . . sleek and streamlined For detailed descriptions of conquistador weaponry, see John Pohl and Charles M. Robinson III, *Aztecs and Conquistadors: The Spanish Invasion and the Collapse of the Aztec Empire* (New York, 2005), 46–51.

92   "complete this novel voyage of discovery" Carvajal, in Medina, *Discovery,* 187.

CHAPTER NINE: RIVER OF DARKNESS, BROTHERS OF DOOM

93   "a lover of warfare and very patient of hardship" Zárate, *Discovery and Conquest of Peru,* 242.

94   "swelled in such a way that they could not walk on their feet" Cieza de León, *War of Chupas,* 72.

94   "hawks' bells, combs, and other trifles" Cieza de León, *War of Chupas,* 72–73.

94   Desperate to discover Ibid., 72; Wood, *Conquistadors,* 214; Zárate, *Discovery and Conquest of Peru,* 198; Smith, *Explorers,* 78; Chapman, *Golden Dream,* 177.

95   likely of the Secoya peoples Lathrap, *Upper Amazon,* 150–53. Lathrap suggests that at this time, this portion of the Aguarico was populated by a branch of the Omagua, called the Omagua-yete, who had migrated far upriver.

95   "there were no longer any Indians" Cieza de León, *War of Chupas,* 73.

95   "he knew not in what land he was" Ibid.

95   "the worst march ever in the Indies" Quoted in Wood, *Conquistadors,* 215.

95 "mountainous, with great ranges" Gonzalo Pizarro, letter to the king, September 3, 1542, in Medina, *Discovery*, 250.

96 "In this condition they went on" Cieza de León, *War of Chupas*, 73-74.

97 "owing to the density of the forest" Ibid.; Chapman, *Golden Dream*, 177.

98 "for it had been many days" Cieza de León, *War of Chupas*, 75.

98 The river here was rapid Ibid., 75-76; Quoted in Wood, *Conquistadors*, 216.

99 The Spaniards were reduced to fantasizing Birney, *Brothers of Doom*, 256.

99 these poor animals were subjected Bernard, *Exploration*, 92; Wood, *Conquistadors*, 215.

99 All the remaining horses Gonzalo Pizarro, letter to the king, September 3, 1542, in Medina, *Discovery*, 250.

100 Amazingly, it had taken them only a day and a half Cieza de León, *War of Chupas*, 76.

100 "they would find inhabitants" Ibid., 76.

100 "armed with their swords and bucklers" Ibid., 290.

101 "a great comet traversing the heavens" Ibid., 291; Wood, *Conquistadors*, 216; Chapman, *Golden Dream*, 178-79.

101 "the object he most prized was dead" Quoted in Chapman, *Golden Dream*, 179; Cieza de León, *War of Chupas*, 291; Wood, *Conquistadors*, 216 (although Wood offers another translation of the dream, reading "Pizarro would soon learn of the death of the person nearest to his heart").

102 "They were traveling almost naked" Zárate, *Discovery and Conquest of Peru*, 198.

102 Arriving at the gates of the city Ibid., 198-99; Vega, *Royal Commentaries*, 915-16.

CHAPTER TEN: THE ASSASSINATION OF FRANCISCO PIZARRO

104 "began to eat with such a desire" Vega, *Royal Commentaries*, 915.

104 "what they had lacked most had been salt" Zárate, *Discovery and Conquest of Peru*, 198.

105 "and to govern the millions of new vassals" MacQuarrie, *Last Days*, 334.

105 Francisco loved the physicality of the work Ibid.; Zárate, *Discovery and Conquest of Peru*, 206-10.

105 Hernando arrived with a ship full of gold MacQuarrie, *Last Days of the Incas*, 336; Cieza de León, *Civil Wars in Peru: The War of Las Salinas* (London, 1923), 246-48; Vega, *Royal Commentaries*, 862-65; Zárate, *Discovery and Conquest of Peru*, 184-87.

106 So in June 1541 Cieza de León, *War of Chupas*, 96-97; Zárate, *Discovery and Conquest of Peru*, 199-200; Vega, *Royal Commentaries*, 882-83.

106 "so boyish that he was not adapted" Cieza de León, *War of Chupas*, 97.

106 spilled the entire plan to his priest Ibid., 97-98; MacQuarrie, *Last Days of the Incas*, 340.

107 "If we show determination" Cieza de León, *War of Chupas*, 103-4.

107 "Death to tyrants!" and "Long live the king!" Ibid., 104; MacQuarrie, *Last Days of the Incas,* 341; Zárate, *Discovery and Conquest of Peru,* 202–3.

108 "Arm! Arm! The men of Chile are coming to murder the Marquis!" Cieza de León, *War of Chupas,* 106; Vega, *Royal Commentaries,* 887.

108 "most of them . . . showing great cowardice" Cieza de León, *War of Chupas,* 106; Zárate, *Discovery and Conquest of Peru,* 203.

108 "He instantly fell in a death struggle" Cieza de León, *War of Chupas,* 107; MacQuarrie, *Last Days of the Incas,* 342.

109 "At them, brother!" Zárate, *Discovery and Conquest of Peru,* 204.

109 Pizarro managed to run the first man through Zárate, *Discovery and Conquest of Peru,* 204; Cieza de León, *War of Chupas,* 108.

109 "Those of Chile . . . delivered blows" Cieza de León, *War of Chupas,* 108–9.

109 "The moon, being full and bright" Ibid., 109.

110 "put on his spurs" Vega, *Royal Commentaries,* 889; Zárate, *Discovery and Conquest of Peru,* 205.

CHAPTER ELEVEN: ON THE MARANON TO THE
REALM OF MACHIPARO

111 "furthest inland deep-ocean port in the world" Mann, *1491,* 282.

112 "many painted people who flocked to the ships" Quoted in Hemming, *Tree of Rivers,* 13.

112 The tides near the river mouth Edward J. Goodman, *The Explorers of South America* (New York, 1972), 12.

112 the *maran-i-hobo* or cashew tree Cohen, *Journeys,* 52; Medina, *Discovery,* 154–63.

113 "for along the great rivers of the Old World" Cohen, *Journeys,* 53.

113 "recognized that we were now outside" Carvajal, in Medina, *Discovery,* 189.

113 "endured more hardships and more hunger" Ibid.

114 "if it had not been observed by so many witnesses" Ibid.

114 "the fish, being opened up" Ibid., 190; Cohen, *Journeys,* 54.

115 "Before we had come within two leagues" Carvajal, in Medina, *Discovery,* 190; quoted in Cohen, *Journeys,* 55.

115 Within his chiefdom Wood, *Conquistadors,* 220; Mann, *1491,* 283–84; Hemming, *El Dorado,* 116.

115 "threatening as if they were going to devour" Carvajal, in Medina, *Discovery,* 190.

116 "it seemed as if they wanted to seize hold" Carvajal, in Medina, *Discovery,* 191. Interestingly, Toribio de Ortiguera records a different opening sequence to this initial battle with Machiparo's armies. In his account, which seems to be recorded only by Hemming (among the modern historians), the initial meeting goes like this: "[A village called] Machiparo, from which a few Indians in canoes came out on the river to meet them,

and they gave them to understand that their chief and overlord desired to see them and find out of what nationality they were and whither they were bound and what they were looking for; and they indicated to them that they should leap out on land. The Spaniards moved on in their brigantines in the direction of the shore, although with considerable caution, formed in good order, their arquebuses loaded, their matches lighted, their crossbows with cords drawn back and with their arrows in them. At the time, then, that they pulled in there, as soon as they had gotten up to the village, as the chief saw them to be of different dress and aspect from all the other people that he had ever seen, and all bearded (for the Indians are not), to a certain degree he revered them, and . . . he ordered his subjects to leave a section of the village free, with all the food that was in it . . . for consumption . . ." Ortiguera, in Medina, *Discovery*, 317-18. In this version, only after the Spaniards became unruly and poor guests did Machiparo order his men to attack. There are a few significant differences and contradictions in this version—one is that Carvajal says the powder was damp, and that contradicts the above, in which they had their "matches lighted"; also, Carvajal records no direct meeting with the chief Machiparo, though Ortiguera does. See Hemming, *Tree of Rivers*, 29, and *El Dorado*, 115. Most historians seem to side with Carvajal's version, which is at any rate in keeping with what Aparia the Great predicted would happen when the Spaniards reached Machiparo's kingdom.

116   **"There were a great number of men"** Quoted in Medina, *Discovery*, 191.

117   **"the great extent of the settlement"** Carvajal, in Medina, *Discovery*, 191; Cohen, *Journeys*, 56; Ortiguera, in Medina, *Discovery*, 318; Hemming, *Tree of Rivers*, 30; Smith, *Explorers*, 66.

117   **"There was a great quantity of food"** Medina, *Discovery*, 192.

117   **"large quantities of honey from bees"** Ortiguera, in Medina, *Discovery*, 319.

117   **"with a small amount [of manatee]"** Cristóbal de Acuña, quoted in Meggers, *Amazonia*, 127.

118   **"larger than a good sized wheel"** Quoted in Meggers, *Amazonia*, 126. The turtle farming process is described in detail here also by Cristóbal de Acuña, in Meggers, *Amazonia*, 126-27; also reproduced in Hemming, *Tree of Rivers*, 30; see also Hemming, *El Dorado*, 115.

118   **He told them to hurry** Cohen, *Journeys*, 56; Smith, *Explorers*, 66.

118   **"applying to the [babies'] forehead a small board"** Samuel Fritz, quoted in Meggers, *Amazonia*, 125.

118   **"more like a poorly shaped bishop's miter"** Acuña, quoted in Meggers, *Amazonia*, 125. Also in Samuel Fritz, *Journal of the Travels and Labours of Father Samuel Fritz in the River of the Amazons Between 1686 and 1723*, translated from the Evora manuscript and edited by the Reverend Dr. George Edmundson (Hakluyt Society, London, 1922), 47. See also Hemming, *Tree of Rivers*, 56.

119   **"came back at Cristóbal Maldonado"** Carvajal, in Medina, *Discovery*, 193.

119   **"fought so courageously"** Ibid., 194.

120   One experienced fighter named Blas de Medina Cohen, *Journeys,* 57.

120   "no other remedy but a certain charm" Carvajal, in Medina, *Discovery,*
       195; Cohen, *Journeys,* 58.

121   acts of superstition and charms Medina, *Discovery,* 241n. Cohen,
       Journeys, 58. Some of the practices of Omagua religion and magic are
       described in Meggers, *Amazonia,* 130. For a fascinating, far-reaching, and
       detailed study of Amazonian witchcraft, sorcery, and shamanism, see Neil
       L. Whitehead and Robin Wright, editors, *In Darkness and Secrecy: The
       Anthropology of Assault Sorcery and Witchcraft in Amazonia* (Durham,
       North Carolina, and London, 2004).

121   "all were cured except the one who died" Carvajal, in Medina, *Dis-
       covery,* 195.

121   "recalling to them the hardships already endured" Ibid., 195.

122   "explore the country" Ibid., 195; Cohen, *Journeys,* 58.

CHAPTER TWELVE: AMONG THE OMAGUA

123   "again and again" Carvajal, in Medina, *Discovery,* 196.

123   the black wood of the chonta palm Dr. Robert Carneiro, from editorial
       notes on *River of Darkness,* September 7, 2009.

124   "the arrow is taken in the right hand" Quoted in Meggers, *Amazonia,* 127.

124   "We saw ourselves in the midst" Carvajal, in Medina, *Discovery,* 197.

125   "on the land the men who appeared" Ibid.

125   One chronicler said Medina, footnote about variant reading to Carvajal
       account, in *Discovery,* 197n. Also in Cohen, *Journeys,* 59.

126   Machiparo and his people would do whatever it took Carlos Fausto, "A
       Blend of Blood and Tobacco: Shamans and Jaguars Among the Parakana
       of Eastern Amazonia," in Whitehead and Wright, *In Darkness and
       Secrecy,* 159, 162, and 170.

126   "possess devastating power" Johannes Wilbert, "The Order of Dark
       Shamans Among the Waroa," in Whitehead and Wright, *In Darkness and
       Secrecy,* 29.

126   "To perform assaultive sorcery" Ibid., 31–32.

127   "Those on the water resolved to wipe us out" Carvajal, in Medina,
       Discovery, 198.

128   "it was all of one tongue" Ibid.

128   "all inhabited, for there was not from village to village a crossbow shot"
       Quoted in Mann, *1491,* 284; also quoted in Antonio Porro, "Social
       Organization and Political Power in the Amazon Floodplain," in Roosevelt,
       Amazonian Indians, 83.

128   "without there intervening any space" Carvajal, in Medina, *Discovery,* 198.

128   "there was a very great overlord" Ibid. Also in Cohen, *Journeys,* 60; Muller,
       Orellana's Discovery, 50. Also quoted in Chapman, *Golden Dream,* 160.

130   "bent on seizing and unmooring the brigantines" Carvajal, in Medina,
       Discovery, 199; Cohen, *Journeys,* 61.

130   "So we remained resting" Carvajal, in Medina, *Discovery*, 200; Smith, *Explorers*, 69.

130   "very fine highways" Carvajal, in Medina, *Discovery*, 200; Muller, *Orellana's Discovery*, 51.

131   well more than a thousand miles of hostile and uncharted river Wood, *Conquistadors*, 221.

131   "So wide was it" Carvajal, in Medina, *Discovery*, 200; Muller, *Orellana's Discovery*, 51.

131   "They attacked us so pitilessly" Muller, *Orellana's Discovery*, 51.

132   The few natives resisted Ibid., 52; Cohen, *Journeys*, 62.

132   "very large, with a capacity of more than twenty-five *arrobas*" Carvajal, in Medina, *Discovery*, 201; Muller, *Orellana's Discovery*, 52.

132   "Other small pieces such as plates and bowls" Carvajal, in Medina, *Discovery*, 201; Muller, *Orellana's Discovery*, 52; See also Hemming, *El Dorado*, 116; Meggers, *Amazonia*, 128; and Hemming, *Tree of Rivers*, 271.

132   on the order of hundreds of thousands of people Wood, *Conquistadors*, 221, suggests that in 1542 in Amazonia there were three or four million people all told.

132   China Town, or Pottery Village Oviedo, in Medina, *Discovery*, 425, uses the term "Loza," or "Porcelainville." Also Wood, *Conquistadors*, 221; Hemming, *Tree of Rivers*, 30.

133   "elaborate geometric patterns" Anna C. Roosevelt, "The Maritime, Highland, Forest Dynamic and the Origins of Complex Culture," in *The Cambridge History of the Native Peoples of the Americas*, vol. 3, *South America*, part 1, edited by Frank Solomon and Stuart B. Schwartz (Cambridge, 2000), 332. See also Anna C. Roosevelt, *Moundbuilders of the Amazon: Geophysical Archaeology on Marajo Island, Brazil* (San Diego, 1991), 48–49. The style is also called "Santarém."

133   These few friendly locals Carvajal, in Medina, *Discovery*, 201; Cohen, *Journeys*, 62; Muller, *Orellana's Discovery*, 52.

133   "There were two idols woven out of feathers" Carvajal, in Medina, *Discovery*, 201; Cohen, *Journeys*, 62. See also Muller, *Orellana's Discovery*, 52.

134   "When they got to a small square" Bernal Díaz, quoted in Levy, *Conquistador*, 298.

134   "in the heart of the forest" Muller, *Orellana's Discovery*, 52.

135   "our intention was merely to search" Carvajal, in Medina, *Discovery*, 202; Muller, *Orellana's Discovery*, 52.

135   "Of all the [people] who inhabit the banks of the Maranon" Quoted in Clements R. Markham, *Expeditions into the Valley of the Amazons, 1539, 1540, 1639* (New York, 1963), 175.

135   "The Omagua are the Phoenicians of the river" Ibid.

135   "the Omagua [used] elastic" Hemming, *Tree of Rivers*, 175; also Hemming, *El Dorado*, 116. Hemming here refers to the firsthand account made by French scientist Charles-Marie de La Condamine, who

descended the Amazon in 1743 and observed the Omagua and other tribes that Orellana had first seen. Also Hemming, *Tree of Rivers,* 83.

135   "more like royal highways" Carvajal, in Medina, *Discovery,* 202.

CHAPTER THIRTEEN: BIG BLACKWATER RIVER

138   "who has many subjects, and quite civilized ones" Carvajal, in Medina, *Discovery,* 202; Oviedo, in Medina, *Discovery,* 425. Also in Cohen, *Journeys,* 64; Chapman, *Golden Dream,* 160; Hemming, *Tree of Rivers,* 31.

138   "very pleasing and attractive" Carvajal, in Medina, *Discovery,* 203. Also Oviedo, in Medina, *Discovery,* 426. The reference to the llamas strains credibility, as the people of Amazonia are not known to have possessed beasts of burden, especially this far down the river. It is certainly conceivable, however, that the people of this tribe would have heard of them, as information spread far and wide throughout Amazonia by people moving up and down the many river systems.

138   "built in the trees like magpie nests" Quoted in Hemming, *Tree of Rivers,* 30–31. Details of the flooding variants are also found in Goulding, *Smithsonian Atlas of the Amazon,* 39 and 99–101.

139   "more than five hundred houses" Oviedo, in Medina, *Discovery,* 426; Muller, *Orellana's Discovery,* 53; Bernard, *Exploration,* 72.

139   Pueblo Vicioso, or Viciousville Bernard, *Exploration,* 72, and Oviedo, in Medina, *Discovery,* 426n.

139   "end of the province of the . . . overlord Paguana" Carvajal, in Medina, *Discovery,* 204. Also in Cohen, *Journeys,* 64.

139   This extraordinary flatness Meggers, *Amazonia,* 8. Also Goulding, *Smithsonian Atlas of the Amazon,* 15 and 23–24.

139   "From there on we saw indications" Oviedo, in Medina, *Discovery,* 426.

140   "We entered into another province" Carvajal, in Medina, *Discovery,* 204. Also Cohen, *Journeys,* 64.

140   linking the Orinoco and Amazon basins Of interest here is the unique river system linking the Amazon and Orinoco known as the Casiquiare Canal, which is not a man-made canal but rather a natural one. According to John Hemming, "the land here is so flat [that] part of the Orinoco's waters flow southwestwards and never rejoin the mother river. Instead, after 300 meandering kilometers, they flow into a headwater of the Negro and hence the Amazon." Hemming, *Tree of Rivers,* 131.

141   "black as ink" Carvajal, in Medina, *Discovery,* 204. Also quoted in Wood, *Conquistadors,* 221; Chapman, *Golden Dream,* 161; Smith, *Explorers,* 69–70.

141   Its distinctive character . . . "that empty into the Negro" Goulding, *Smithsonian Atlas of the Amazon,* 215. Also see Douglas C. Daly and John C. Mitchell, "Lowland Vegetation of Tropical South America," in

Imperfect Balance: Landscape Transformations in the Pre-Columbian Americas, edited by David L. Lentz (New York, 2000), 410.

141   **"There has been no exaggeration"** William Lewis Herndon, *Exploration of the Valley of the Amazon,* edited and with an introduction by Hamilton Basso (New York, 1952), 168.

142   **The Spaniards feasted** Cohen, *Journeys,* 65; Muller, *Orellana's Discovery,* 53–54.

143   **"At this gate were two towers"** Carvajal, in Medina, *Discovery,* 205. Also recorded in Oviedo, in Medina, *Discovery,* 427; Chapman, *Golden Dream,* 161; Bernard, *Exploration,* 72; Muller, *Orellana's Discovery,* 54.

143   **they were subjects and tributaries** Carvajal, in Medina, *Discovery,* 205. Also in Oviedo, in Medina, *Discovery,* 427; Muller, *Orellana's Discovery,* 54; Chapman, *Golden Dream,* 161; Bernard, *Exploration,* 72; Cohen, *Journeys,* 65; Smith, *Explorers,* 71.

144   **"which the Indians put on"** Oviedo, in Medina, *Discovery,* 427.

144   **sacrificial idols and prayer houses** For in-depth discussions of the sun in creation mythology and Amazonian cosmology, see Gerard Reichel-Dolmatoff, "Cosmology as Ecological Analysis: A View from the Rain Forest," in *Ritual and Belief* (New York, 2001), 286–95. See also Gerard Reichel-Dolmatoff, *Amazonian Cosmos: The Sexual and Religious Symbolism of the Tukano Indians* (Chicago and London, 1971), 23–37. Here, the sun, as one of the twin brothers Sun and Moon, figures prevalently in the creation myth, the sun even creating the earth.

145   **Warriors waved their arms defiantly** Oviedo, in Medina, *Discovery,* 428; Muller, *Orellana's Discovery,* 54.

146   **The Spaniards found an abundance of drying fish** Oviedo, in Medina, *Discovery,* 428.

146   **"go on as we were accustomed"** Carvajal, in Medina, *Discovery,* 207.

146   **"too kind-hearted a soul by far"** Quoted in Wood, *Conquistadors,* 220.

147   **Orellana barked orders to his lieutenants** Oviedo, in Medina, *Discovery,* 428; Muller, *Orellana's Discovery,* 55.

148   **"in order that the Indians from here on"** Carvajal, in Medina, *Discovery,* 208.

148   **they could see people massing on the banks** Oviedo, in Medina, *Discovery,* 429.

CHAPTER FOURTEEN: ENCOUNTERING THE AMAZONS

149   **"We saw emptying in on the right side"** Carvajal, in Medina, *Discovery,* 209; Oviedo, in Medina, *Discovery,* 430; Muller, *Orellana's Discovery,* 56.

150   **The muddy Madeira** Goulding, *Smithsonian Atlas of the Amazon,* 24 and 147–50.

150   **"beating their weapons together"** Quoted in Muller, *Orellana's Discovery,* 56.

150   "temperate and one of very great productiveness" Carvajal, in Medina, *Discovery*, 209.

150–51 "a fine looking settlement" Ibid. Also quoted in Cohen, *Journeys*, 71; Muller, *Orellana's Discovery*, 56. See also Markham, *Expeditions*, 36–37 and 153.

151   "In those villages they have many poles" Oviedo, in Medina, *Discovery*, 432.

151   the Province of the Gibbets Carvajal, in Medina, *Discovery*, 209; Muller, *Orellana's Discovery*, 56.

151   "roads made by hand" Carvajal, in Medina, *Discovery*, 210. Silverman and Isbell, *Handbook of South American Archaeology*, 172–74.

152   They found many turtles Ibid. Also Oviedo, in Medina, *Discovery*, 430–31; Muller, *Orellana's Discovery* 56–57.

152   Quemados Villa, the Place of the Burned People Oveido, in Medina, *Discovery*, 431 and 431n.

152   "She said that nearby" Quoted in Cohen, *Journeys*, 73. Also in Carvajal, in Medina, *Discovery*, 210–11; Muller, *Orellana's Discovery*, 57.

153   Some said it struck rocks Hemming, *El Dorado*, 11 and 146.

155   He immediately made Aguilar his translator The amazing saga of Aguilar and Guerrero is recorded variously in Levy, *Conquistador*, 12–18; Hammond Innes, *The Conquistadors* (New York, 1969), 5–52; Peter O. Koch, *The Aztecs, the Conquistadors, and the Making of Mexican Culture* (Jefferson, North Carolina, and London, 2006), 28–31; Wood, *Conquistadors*, 29–31.

155   They lived among various tribes The journey is well documented, with some recent very good works. Most highly recommended is Andrés Reséndez, *A Land So Strange: The Epic Journey of Cabeza de Vaca* (New York, 2007). Also see Álvar Núñez Cabeza de Vaca, translated by Fanny Bandelier, revised and annotated by Harold Augenbraum, introduction by Ilan Stavans, *Chronicle of the Narváez Expedition* (New York, 2002).

156   "We decided to press forward" Carvajal, in Medina, *Discovery*, 211.

156   He ordered the men to sleep Ibid.; Cohen, *Journeys*, 73; Muller, *Orellana's Discovery*, 57. Oviedo, in Medina, *Discovery*, 431. In Oviedo's version the Spaniards interpret the indications toward the interior made by the two Indians in the canoe to also be references of communication regarding the shipwrecked members of Diego de Ordaz's party.

157   "buried in ashes" Oviedo, in Medina, *Discovery*, 432; Muller, *Orellana's Discovery*, 57; Smith, *Explorers*, 72.

157   "storehouse filled with liquor" Muller, *Orellana's Discovery*, 57.

157   "many military adornments" Oviedo, in Medina, *Discovery*, 432. Also in Muller, *Orellana's Discovery*, 57. Carvajal says that the miters or hats were of neither cotton nor wool, but of some other, unknown fabric.

157   "their houses were glimmering white" Carvajal, in Medina, *Discovery*, 212.

157   "During the whole day" Oviedo, in Medina, *Discovery*, 433; Muller, *Orellana's Discovery*, 58; Cohen, *Journeys*, 73–74.

158   Because it was tucked away on the river bend Oviedo, in Medina,

Discovery, 433; Carvajal, in Medina, *Discovery,* 212; Cohen, *Journeys,* 74; Muller, *Orellana's Discovery,* 58; Meggers, *Amazonia,* 133.

158 "dwellings of fishermen from the interior of the country" Carvajal, in Medina, *Discovery,* 212.

158 "Here we came suddenly upon the excellent land" Ibid.

159 "He gave orders to shoot at them" Ibid.; Muller, *Orellana's Discovery,* 58; Smith, *Explorers,* 72; Chapman, *Golden Dream,* 164.

159 "At the same moment there came out many" Oviedo, in Medina, *Discovery,* 433; Muller, *Orellana's Discovery,* 58; Chapman, *Golden Dream,* 164; Smith, *Explorers,* 72.

160 Cloudbursts of the arrows Cohen, *Journeys,* 74; Hemming, *El Dorado,* 118–19.

160 "Had it not been for the thickness of my clothes" Carvajal, in Medina, *Discovery,* 214.

160 Sparked by their captain's rallying cries Cohen, *Journeys,* 74; Muller, *Orellana's Discovery,* 58; George Millar, *A Crossbowman's Story* (New York, 1955), 284.

161 "They are very robust" Carvajal, in Medina, *Discovery,* 214; Oviedo, in Medina, *Discovery,* 434; Muller, *Orellana's Discovery,* 59; Chapman, *Golden Dream,* 165; Smith, *Explorers,* 73; Hemming, *El Dorado,* 119; Hemming, *Tree of Rivers,* 32; Millar, *Crossbowman's Story,* 283; Bernard, *Exploration,* 84.

161 the Amazons "fought so courageously" Carvajal, in Medina, *Discovery,* 214. Also in Muller, *Orellana's Discovery,* 59; Chapman, *Golden Dream,* 165; Smith, *Explorers,* 73; Bernard, *Exploration,* 81–83.

161 "for these we actually saw" Carvajal, in Medina, *Discovery,* 214.

162 Orellana ordered a seized Indian trumpeter . . . down this magical waterway Ibid.; Muller, *Orellana's Discovery,* 59; Chapman, *Golden Dream,* 166; Smith, *Explorers,* 73; Hemming, *El Dorado,* 121–22; Millar, *Crossbowman's Story,* 385.

162 "The Captain told them that he did not want to" Carvajal, in Medina, *Discovery,* 215.

163 The arrow had pierced one eye and exited the opposite cheek Ibid.; Cohen, *Journeys,* 76; Muller, *Orellana's Discovery,* 60; Oviedo, in Medina, *Discovery,* 435. The Oviedo version offers a different version of Carvajal's report, in which Carvajal speaks of the arrow passing "through my head and sticking out two fingers' length on the other side behind my ear and slightly above it."

163 they managed another hasty retreat Carvajal, in Medina, *Discovery,* 216; Oviedo, in Medina, *Discovery,* 435; Muller, *Orellana's Discovery,* 60; Cohen, *Journeys,* 76; Millar, *Crossbowman's Story,* 287–88.

164 *terra preta* or "Amazonian dark earth" See Mann, *1491,* 306–10. See also Hemming, *Tree of Rivers,* 383–84; Roosevelt, *Moundbuilders of the Amazon,* 128–29; and Meggers, *Amazonia,* 134. Also Dr. Robert Carneiro, editorial notes on *River of Darkness,* September 7, 2009.

164　The open savannas they imagined filled with game, too While Carvajal described "many kinds of grass," in actuality two main grass types predominate the central Amazon River floodplains. These are *Paspalum repens* and *Echinochloa polystachya*. The Spaniards could certainly have seen other herbaceous species that they considered to be "grass," however. See Goulding, *Smithsonian Atlas of the Amazon*, 51; Oviedo, in Medina, *Discovery*, 435.

164　they reached an uninhabited island Oviedo, in Medina, *Discovery*, 436; Carvajal, in Medina, *Discovery*, 217; Muller, *Orellana's Discovery*, 60; Cohen, *Journeys*, 76; Millar, *Crossbowman's Story*, 288–89.

CHAPTER FIFTEEN: THE TRUMPETER'S TALE

166　"When they saw us" Carvajal, in Medina, *Discovery*, 218. See also Oviedo, in Medina, *Discovery*, 436; Muller, *Orellana's Discovery*, 60–61; Chapman, *Golden Dream*, 167; John Hemming, *Red Gold: The Conquest of the Brazilian Indians* (New York, 1978), 194.

167　"greatest of all riverbank chiefdoms, the Tapajos" Hemming, *Tree of Rivers*, 33.

167　It was the twenty-fifth of June, 1542 Oviedo, in Medina, *Discovery*, 436; Muller, *Orellana's Discovery*, 61; Chapman, *Golden Dream*, 167.

168　"The Indian answered" Quoted in Cohen, *Journeys*, 79–80. Alternate versions of this text, all very similar in their details, can be seen in Carvajal, in Medina, *Discovery*, 219–22, and in Oviedo, in Medina, *Discovery*, 437; Carvajal, in Medina, *Discovery*, 222; Cohen, *Journeys*, 80; Muller, *Orellana's Discovery*, 63.

170　"and anyone who should take it into his head" Carvajal, in Medina, *Discovery*, 222.

170　"because he was an Indian of much intelligence" Ibid.

170　"Amazon in the Greek language" Oviedo, in Medina, *Discovery*, 437.

171　"the islands of California" Anthony Pagden, in Cortés, *Letters from Mexico*, 298–300 and 502n.

171　"When we saw all those cities and villages" Bernal Díaz del Castillo, *The Conquest of New Spain*, translated with an introduction by J. M. Cohen (New York, 1963), 214.

172　"To a large extent people are only capable of perceiving" Alex Shoumatoff, *In Southern Light: Trekking Through Zaire and the Amazon* (New York, 1986), 19–20.

172　"It is unnecessary and probably unfair" Ibid., 19 and 23. Shoumatoff's journey and remarkable essay about it are well worth the read. See Alex Shoumatoff, "A Reporter at Large: Amazons," *The New Yorker*, March 24, 1986. Also see Hemming, *Red Gold*, 224–25; Cristóbal de Acuña, in Clements R. Markham, *Expeditions into the Valley of the Amazons, 1539, 1540, 1639* (New York, 1963), 121–22; Gerard Helferich, *Humboldt's Cosmos: Alexander von Humboldt and the Latin American Journey That*

Changed the Way We See the World (New York, 2004), 160–61; Victor Wolfgang von Hagen, *South America Called Them: Explorations of the Great Naturalists La Condamine, Humboldt, Darwin, Spruce* (New York, 1945), 249–58. Another fascinating book for further inquiry and background is Abby Wettan Kleinbaum's *The War Against the Amazons* (New York, 1983). For origins and antiquity, going as far back as the Scythians and the steppes of Asia Minor and the Black Sea, consult Lyn Webster Wilde, *On the Trail of the Women Warriors: The Amazons in Myth and History* (New York, 1999). Finally, fascinating and informative is the excellent chapter on the Amazons called "The Women Warriors of the Amazon: A Historical Study," in Richard Spruce, *Notes of a Botanist on the Amazon and Andes* (London, 1908), 456–73. Spruce cites numerous credible and dependable firsthand sources who make direct references to the Amazon women warriors and their location, many of which confirm the locations generally described by Orellana and Carvajal (consensus is north of the main Amazon, up the Trombetas and/or Nhamunda river).

172   "scholars who have tried to reconstruct the journey" Shoumatoff, *In Southern Light,* 18.

172   One of his hearty men, Bernard O'Brien Hemming, *Red Gold,* 224–25.

173   "The proofs of the existence of the province of the Amazons" Cristóbal de Acuña, in Markham, *Expeditions,* 121–22.

173   "Could it have been [he wondered]" Helferich, *Humboldt's Cosmos,* 160–61.

173   The French scientist and naturalist La Condamine Von Hagen, *South America Called Them,* 249–58.

173   "I myself have seen Indian women" Spruce, *Notes of a Botanist,* 458.

173   "Those traditions must have had some foundation in fact" Spruce, *Notes of a Botanist,* 470.

CHAPTER SIXTEEN: TIDES OF CHANGE AND A SWEETWATER SEA

175   "pleasantest and brightest land" Carvajal, in Medina, *Discovery,* 223; Cohen, *Journeys,* 82; Muller, *Orellana's Discovery,* 63; Chapman, *Golden Dream,* 170.

175   "There came out toward us" Carvajal, in Medina, *Discovery,* 223; Oviedo, in Medina, *Discovery,* 438; Muller, *Orellana's Discovery,* 63.

176   "they came forth very gaily decked out" Carvajal, in Medina, *Discovery,* 223.

176   "ruled over a great expanse" Ibid.

176   The interpreter added Ibid. Some scholars, including the well-respected J. M. Cohen, interpret this to mean that these men were almost positively Caribs, "of the kind that the Spaniards had already encountered in the Caribbean and on the shores of the mainland." See Cohen, *Journeys,* 83. See also the case of Hans Staden, the German-born soldier of fortune who was shipwrecked in 1550 with Portuguese and then held captive by the

Tupinamba tribe of Brazil, where he was ritually and ceremonially prepared to be eaten and witnessed much cannibalism. Hans Staden, *The True History of His Captivity 1557*, translated and edited by Malcolm Letts, with an introduction and notes (New York, 1929), 7–8, 92, and 99.

177 **"the wound turned very black"** Oviedo, in Medina, *Discovery*, 438.

178 **"railings on the brigantines in the manner of fortifications"** Medina, *Discovery*, 224; Muller, *Orellana's Discovery*, 64.

178 **"like a rim . . . as high up as a man's chest"** Carvajal, in Medina, *Discovery*, 439.

178 **"tied to the oars"** Medina, *Discovery*, 224.

178 **"The flowing of the tide"** Carvajal, in Medina, *Discovery*, 226.

179 **"With a very great clamor and outcry"** Ibid.

179 **The canoes impeded even the movement of the oars** Muller, *Orellana's Discovery*, 65; Cohen, *Journeys*, 85. In another version the overlord is referred to by the lengthy name of Nurandaluguaburabara.

180 **None of those who fell into the water** The harquebusier referred to as Perucho (both Carvajal and Oviedo mention him by this first name only, which is a diminutive and informal expression for "Pedro") might well have been a man named Pedro de Acaray, who was listed as a soldier of Gonzalo Pizarro's at the beginning of the voyage. See Medina, *Discovery*, 242n; Oviedo, in Medina, *Discovery*, 440.

180 **"The Indian men kept uttering cries"** Oviedo, in Medina, *Discovery*, 440.

180 **In less than twenty-four hours** Soria Millar, *Crossbowman's Story*, 304. On poison dart frogs, see David L. Pearson and Les Beletsky, *Travellers' Wildlife Guides: Brazil—Amazon and Pantanal* (Northampton, Massachusetts, 2005), 91–93. Also Dr. Robert Carneiro, editorial notes on *River of Darkness*, October 8, 2009. Carneiro is of the opinion that, based on their location on the Amazon at the time of being struck with poisoned arrows, "the poison that killed Orellana's men was very likely derived from the sap of the manchineel or manzanilla tree, *Hippomane mancinella*. It was more commonly used by the Indians of the Caribbean coast. The Spaniards were in great dread of it, saying that someone hit by a manchineel-poisoned arrow was 'moria rabiando,' [pretty much what] Carvajal observed." (Translated, "moria rabiando" means "he died raging.")

Curare—a generic term used to describe many types of poison—was (and is) used for both warfare and hunting, but in different ways. The curare for blowgun darts is primarily employed for hunting animals and is associated with the plant vine *Strychnos toxifera* and its bark. Also used among some tribes (almost exclusively for hunting) is the poison from the glands of certain species of frogs that bear the apt and rather obvious name of poison dart frogs. Most notable of these is the deadly *Phyllobates terribilis* (terrible golden poison dart frog), whose toxicity is extraordinary: the poison from this frog is among the most lethal substances on earth, one small frog carrying sufficient poison to kill ten human beings. To harvest the frog poison, some frogs are roasted on a stick, the flames inducing the secretion of the poison. In the case of the deadliest *Phyllobates terribilis,* the hunter simply rubs the dart on the back of the frog and transfers the poison, and the live frog is released.

Curare was only rarely used for arrows in warfare, and when employed was more often distilled from the bark of *Strychnos toxifera.* In either case, the making of curare was and is an elaborate production, often attended to or orchestrated by a special tribal member called a "poison master." The poison master harvests the bark in the forest, then pounds the bark into fibers, which is filtered as yellow liquid through palm or plantain leaves, then boiled and distilled into a black, bitter liquid. Alexander von Humboldt witnessed the process and ceremony during his time on the Amazon, amazed to discover that the toxins worked only when they came into contact with the bloodstream; one could drink the curare liquid (indeed, the poison master tasted it as he added water throughout the distillation process, and it was also drunk as a palliative, for stomachaches) with no harmful effects. For this description, see Alexander von Humboldt, *Views of Nature: Or, Contemplations on the Sublime Phenomena of Creation, with Scientific Illustrations,* translated by E. C. Otte and Henry G. Bohn (London, 1850), 151–52. Also described in Helferich, *Humboldt's Cosmos,* 170–71.

180 **This line of flat-topped hills** Wood, *Conquistadors,* 224.

180 **The land here was savanna** Spruce, *Notes of a Botanist,* 457.

181 **"We struck out among islands"** Oviedo, in Medina, *Discovery,* 441; Millar, *Crossbowman's Story,* 310–11.

181 **"flesh roasted on barbecues"** Oviedo, in Medina, *Discovery,* 442; Cohen, *Journeys,* 86. On the practice of cannibalism among the various Carib tribes, see also Oviedo, *Natural History of the West Indies,* 32–33. He says, "The bow-using Caribs . . . and most of those who live along that coast, eat human flesh. They do not take slaves, nor are they friendly to their enemies or foreigners. They eat all the men that they kill and use the women they capture, and the children that they bear—if any Carib should couple with them—are also eaten. The boys that they take from foreigners are castrated, fattened, and eaten." For initial (earliest) contact with the Carib people and their cannibalism practices, see Irving Rouse, *The Tainos: Rise and Decline of the People Who Greeted Columbus* (New Haven and London, 1992), 22–23. According to Rouse and others, the word "cannibal" is derived from a corruption of the Spanish word *caribal,* which was used to describe the practice by Island-Carib warriors of biting the flesh from their enemies in order to consume and garner their opponents' powers. See also Hans Staden, *True History of His Captivity.*

182 **"with the thread and brass sheath"** Oviedo, in Medina, *Discovery,* 441–42.

182 **"A thing well worth seeing"** Ibid. See also Silverman and Isbell,

Handbook of South American Archaeology, 350–55, and Roosevelt, *Mound-builders*, 30–51.

183   "make a very good showing" Oviedo, in Medina, *Discovery*, 442; Silverman and Isbell, *Handbook of South American Archaeology*, 352–53; Roosevelt, *Moundbuilders*, 80–85. Roosevelt's estimate of "tens of thousands of square miles in size" is the most ambitious among scholars sizing such chiefdoms. For a fascinating argument that contests some of her claims, see Robert Carneiro, "The History of Ecological Interpretations of Amazonia: Does Roosevelt Have It Right?" in *Indigenous Peoples and the Future of Amazonia*, edited by Leslie E. Sponsel (Tucson, 1995), 45–70.

183   "Marajoara culture was one of the outstanding nonliterate complex societies of the world" Roosevelt, *Moundbuilders*, 1.

183   "territories tens of thousands of square kilometers in size" Quoted in Hemming, *Tree of Rivers*, 282. See also Roosevelt, *Moundbuilders*, 1–7, and Mann, *1491*, 288–300.

184   "until there remained only four finger widths" Oviedo, in Medina, *Discovery*, 442; Cohen, *Journeys*, 86; Millar, *Crossbowman's Story*, 312.

184   "Here we saw ourselves" Carvajal, in Medina, *Discovery*, 229.

184   The Spaniards loaded what foodstuffs Oviedo, in Medina, *Discovery*, 442–43; Cohen, *Journeys*, 87; Millar, *Crossbowman's Story*, 314–15; Muller, *Orellana's Discovery*, 66–67; Chapman, *Golden Dream*, 170–71.

185   "We ate maize in rations counted out by grains" Carvajal, in Medina, *Discovery*, 230.

185   "had been dead for only a short time" Ibid.

185   They consumed every ounce of it, entrails and all Cohen, *Journeys*, 88; Oviedo, in Medina, *Discovery*, 443; Muller, *Orellana's Discovery*, 67; Millar, *Crossbowman's Story*, 317.

186   "toiled with no little amount of endeavor" Carvajal, in Medina, *Discovery*, 230.

186   so on about July 25 This date is approximate. Carvajal (and Oviedo) say that they departed from "Starvation Island" on August 8, and most sources say that they had been there for two weeks.

186   Anticipating the very high likelihood of taking on water Millar, *Crossbowman's Story*, 318; Wood, *Conquistadors*, 225.

186   "for we did not eat anything" Carvajal, in Medina, *Discovery*, 231; Oviedo, in Medina, *Discovery*, 444; Muller, *Orellana's Discovery*, 68; Wood, *Conquistadors*, 225; Chapman, *Golden Dream*, 171; Smith, *Explorers*, 76.

187   Couple all this with the very real fact A fascinating study on starvation is summarized and used to compare the test subjects to the crew members of the whaleship *Essex* in Nathaniel Philbrick's excellent book *In the Heart of the Sea: The Tragedy of the Whaleship* Essex (New York, 2000), 158–59 and 166–67.

187   "What grieved us most" Carvajal, in Medina, *Discovery*, 444.

188 As they zigzagged . . . without food Pearson and Beletsky, *Travellers' Wildlife Guides: Brazil*, 314–19; Medina, *Discovery*, 232; Muller, *Orellana's Discovery*, 68; Millar, *Crossbowman's Story*, 320; Oviedo, in Medina, *Discovery*, 444.

188 But to the Spaniards' great relief Cohen, *Journeys*, 87; Carvajal, in Medina, *Discovery*, 232; Muller, *Orellana's Discovery*, 68.

189 "not far away from there" Oviedo, in Medina, *Discovery*, 445; Pohl and Robinson, *Aztecs and Conquistadors*, 40–41.

189 "In this manner we got ready to navigate by sea" Carvajal, in Medina, *Discovery*, 232; Cohen, *Journeys*, 89; Muller, *Orellana's Discovery*, 68–69; Chapman, *Golden Dream*, 172; Smith, *Explorers*, 76–77; Millar, *Crossbowman's Story*, 322.

190 "I am telling the truth" Carvajal, in Medina, *Discovery*, 430.

190 What Orellana would not have known For locations and early descriptions of the Pearl Islands, see Bartolomé de Las Casas, *A Short Account of the Destruction of the Indies*, edited and translated by Nigel Griffin with an introduction by Anthony Pagden (New York, 1992), 86–94.

191 Most fortunate, though Goulding, *Smithsonian Atlas of the Amazon*, 28–29.

191 "had been navigating along the most dangerous and roughest coast" Oviedo, in Medina, *Discovery*, 447.

192 "When we found ourselves within it" Carvajal, in Medina, *Discovery*, 233; Muller, *Orellana's Discovery*, 69; Cohen, *Journeys*, 89; Morison, *European Discovery of America*, 144–57.

192 After a week of constant struggle . . . cracked and bleeding Millar, *Crossbowman's Story*, 335.

193 "something more than a journey" Quoted in Wood, *Conquistadors*, 226. Another version of this quote appears in Hemming, *El Dorado*, 123, in which the journey is described as "something more than a shipwreck, more a miraculous event."

193 "So great was the joy" Carvajal, in Medina, *Discovery*, 234.

193 Only three had been killed in battle Smith, *Explorers*, 82; Cohen, *Journeys*, 90. Gonzalo Pizarro, in his return expedition to Quito, lost about ten times as many men.

CHAPTER SEVENTEEN: THE HOMEWARD REACH

194 Father Carvajal also discovered Prescott, *Conquest of Peru*, 378–79; Medina, *Discovery*, 16; Lockhart, *Men of Cajamarca*, 205–6.

195 "I, Brother Gasper de Carvajal" Quoted in Medina, *Discovery*, 235.

196 Nearly all of these men eventually sailed Ibid., 124; Cohen, *Journeys*, 91; Smith, *Explorers*, 82.

197 Maldonado, a driven and ambitious conquistador . . . a trusted leader and fearless soldier Medina, *Discovery*, 121 and 125; Cohen, *Journeys*, 91; Hemming, *El Dorado*, 92; Bernard, *Exploration*, 97.

197 "Item, whether they knew that" Quoted in Cohen, *Journeys*, 92; Medina, *Discovery*, 87 and 269; Bernard, *Exploration*, 97–98.

198 His responsibilities in Hispaniola Oviedo, *Natural History of the West Indies*, ix–xvii. Oviedo is credited, among many other early observations, with being the first European to describe in detail the pineapple, the hammock, and tobacco.

199 "letters written in August, 1542" H. C. Heaton, in Medina, *Discovery*, 384.

199 The court historian Cohen, *Journeys*, 93.

199 "other hidalgos and commoners" Heaton, in Medina, *Discovery*, 383–84. Also Medina, *Discovery*, 27–28 and 28n.

199 "one of the greatest things that have happened to men" Oviedo, *Historia general y natural de las Indias*, vol. 4, 384.

199 Oviedo deemed the discovery of the world's largest river Medina, *Discovery*, 27.

200 Treaty of Tordesillas Henry Kamen, *Spain's Road to Empire* (London, 2002), xvi, 42, and 199; J. H. Parry, *The Spanish Seaborne Empire* (New York, 1974), 47; C. H. Haring, *The Spanish Empire in America* (New York, 1947), 9n7, 17, and 98; Hemming, *Tree of Rivers*, 18–19.

200 "acquainting himself in very great detail" Quoted in Medina, *Discovery*, 125; also *Orellana's Petition and Opinions of the Council of the Indies,* in Medina, *Discovery*, 323. See also Bernard, *Exploration*, 97; Cohen, *Journeys*, 93–94.

CHAPTER EIGHTEEN: THE LAST STAND OF THE LAST PIZARRO

203 "[displayed] toward the whole expeditionary force" Gonzalo Pizarro, letter to the king, September 3, 1542, in Medina, *Discovery*, 248.

203 "Orellana had gone off and become a rebel" Ibid., 249.

203 "previous royal concession" Lockhart, *Men of Cajamarca*, 16.

203 "return to his estates" Birney, *Brothers of Doom*, 259.

203 Gonzalo Pizarro had been dismissed Ibid. Also Lockhart, *Men of Cajamarca*, 184–85 and 188; Vega, *Royal Commentaries*, 900; Philip Ainsworth Means, *Fall of the Inca Empire and the Spanish Rule in Peru: 1530–1780* (New York and London, 1932), 82.

204 By 1542 he had been back to Spain Bartolomé de Las Casas, *History of the Indies*, translated and edited by Andrée Collard (New York, Evanston, and London, 1971), ix–xxvi; Haring, *Spanish Empire*, 11–14. Also Hemming, *El Dorado*, 138–39. For Las Casas and the New Laws, see also Vega, *Royal Commentaries*, 935–39. An interesting analysis of the man and his thinking is also Anthony Pagden, *The Fall of Natural Man* (Cambridge, London, and New York, 1982).

204 "branding of Indians" Haring, *Spanish Empire*, 56. On the practice of branding prisoners as slaves, see Levy, *Conquistador*, 208. See also William H. Prescott, *History of the Conquest of Mexico* (New York, 2001), 634.

205 If carried out, the New Laws Haring, *Spanish Empire,* 56–57; Birney, *Brothers of Doom,* 262–63; Means, *Fall of the Inca Empire,* 82–86. For a full analysis and explanation of the complicated *encomienda* system, see Lesley Byrd Simpson, *The Encomienda System in New Spain: Forced Native Labor in the Spanish Colonies, 1492–1550* (Berkeley and Los Angeles, 1929) and James Lockhart, *Spanish Peru, 1532–1560: A Colonial Society* (Madison, Milwaukee, and London, 1968), 11–33.

205 "[Spain wishes] to enjoy what we sweated for" Quoted in MacQuarrie, *Last Days,* 350. Also in Sarah de Laredo, editor, *From Panama to Peru: The Conquest of Peru by the Pizarros, the Rebellion of Gonzalo Pizarro, and the Pacification by La Gasca* (London, 1925), 328.

206 "Anyone who spoke favorably of Gonzalo Pizarro" Birney, *Brothers of Doom,* 267; Means, *Fall of the Inca Empire,* 89.

206 It was, in effect, a declaration of war Cieza de León, *The War of Quito by Pedro de Cieza de León and Inca Documents,* translated and edited by Clements R. Markham (London, 1913), 90–91.

206 "See here," he railed, "I am to be Governor" Quoted in MacQuarrie, *Last Days,* 350; also in Laredo, *From Panama to Peru,* 416–18.

207 "set astride mules" Birney, *Brothers of Doom,* 271; Means, *Fall of the Inca Empire,* 90.

207 Clearly Gonzalo had no scruples Vega, *Royal Commentaries,* 1009.

208 "because they were skilled" Ibid., 1053.

208 "which was stuck on a pike" Birney, *Brothers of Doom,* 275; Vega, *Royal Commentaries,* 1055.

208 By late January 1546 Vega, *Royal Commentaries,* 1056–57; Zárate, *Discovery and Conquest of Peru,* 243; Hemming, *Conquest of the Incas,* 267–68; Prescott, *Conquest of Peru,* 427–33; Lockhart, *Men of Cajamarca,* 127.

208 In a drunken and raucous postvictory celebration Prescott, *Conquest of Peru,* 437; Means, *Fall of the Inca Empire,* 91; Birney, *Brothers of Doom,* 275–76.

209 "A procession was formed" Prescott, *Conquest of Peru,* 434–35.

209 The vein was so rich Ibid., 436, 436n, and 450; Vega, *Royal Commentaries,* 1068; Birney, *Brothers of Doom,* 291.

211 his title of President of the Royal Audience of Lima carried with it unprecedented powers Vega, *Royal Commentaries,* 1085–86; Prescott, *Conquest of Peru,* 446; Birney, *Brothers of Doom,* 283; Means, *Fall of the Inca Empire,* 93; Hemming, *Conquest of the Incas,* 270.

212 "If this is the sort of governor" Quoted in Prescott, *Conquest of Peru,* 449.

212 "new conquests . . . and future discoveries" Vega, *Royal Commentaries,* 1095.

213 He ended by appealing to Pizarro's honor Ibid., 1094–96; Means, *Fall of the Inca Empire,* 94; Birney, *Brothers of Doom,* 286; Prescott, *Conquest of Peru,* 451.

213 "If but ten only remain true to me" Quoted in Prescott, *Conquest of Peru,* 463.

214 "on the side of the heaviest artillery" Birney, *Brothers of Doom,* 295.

214 By the end of the day . . . inhospitable place Prescott, *Conquest of Peru,* 471; Means, *Fall of the Inca Empire,* 94; Birney, *Brothers of Doom,* 295–99; Vega, *Royal Commentaries,* 1139–48.

214 "Insignificant as I am" Quoted in Means, *Fall of the Inca Empire,* 95; also quoted in Birney, *Brothers of Doom,* 301 and 301n.

215 "an exquisite place" Means, *Fall of the Inca Empire,* 96.

215 "coat of mail" Vega, *Royal Commentaries,* 1193; also quoted in MacQuarrie, *Last Days,* 351; Birney, *Brothers of Doom,* 307.

216 Almost instantly . . . devoid of a worthy fighting force Prescott, *Conquest of Peru,* 486–87; Means, *Fall of the Inca Empire,* 96; Birney, *Brothers of Doom,* 308; MacQuarrie, *Last Days,* 351.

216 "What shall we do, my brother?" Vega, *Royal Commentaries,* 1193.

216 "Better to die like Christians" Ibid. Also in Prescott, *Conquest of Peru,* 488; Clements R. Markham, *History of Peru* (New York, 1968), 132.

216 "a military cloak of yellow velvet" Zárate, *Discovery and Conquest of Peru,* 275; Prescott, *Conquest of Peru,* 495.

217 "do his duty with a steady hand" Quoted in Prescott, *Conquest of Peru,* 496.

217 "[It was] hung on the royal pillory" Quoted in Zárate, *Discovery and Conquest of Peru,* 275.

217 "the worst march ever in the Indies" Quoted in Wood, *Conquistadors,* 215.

217 "the worst traitor that ever lived" Ibid., 226.

217 "Here dwelled the traitor and rebel Gonzalo Pizarro" Quoted in MacQuarrie, *Last Days,* 352. Also in Zárate, *Discovery and Conquest of Peru,* 275; Prescott, *Conquest of Peru,* 497. The death and demise of Gonzalo Pizarro also in Cieza de León, *Discovery,* 13. See also Markham, *History of Peru,* 133.

CHAPTER NINETEEN: THE EXPEDITION TO NEW ANDALUSIA— RETURN TO THE AMAZON

219 Gonzalo's letter, written in September 1542 Cohen, *Journeys,* 95; Medina, *Discovery,* 128.

219 His tale, his descriptions of the people Lorimer, editor, *Sir Walter Raleigh's Discoverie of Guiana,* 45.

220 "performing many services for the King" Medina, *Discovery,* 126 and 126n. Medina, in this note, suggests that Orellana may even have taken some part in the latter stages of the conquest of Mexico.

220 "I beseech Your Majesty" From *Orellana's Petition to Council of the Indies,* in Medina, *Discovery,* 126 and 321.

221 "some three or four years earlier" *Opinions of the Council of the Indies,* in Medina, *Discovery,* 127 and 323.

221   "It also seems quite likely to us" Ibid.; also in Cohen, *Journeys*, 96.

221   "According to the said account" *Opinions of the Council of the Indies*, in Medina, *Discovery*, 128–29 and 323–24.

222   Prince Philip on February 14, 1544, signed into law Muller, *Orellana's Discovery*, 77; Cohen, *Journeys*, 96; Chapman, *Golden Dream*, 175; Smith, *Explorers*, 84.

222   "the regions that stretched towards the south" Medina, in *Discovery*, 129 and 328–34; Cohen, *Journeys*, 96.

222   "a sufficiently large number and force" Articles of Agreement, Valladolid, February 13, 1544, in Medina, *Discovery*, 329.

223   "so that there may be avoided" Ibid., 330.

223   "at your own expense" Ibid., 329.

224   To hamper matters further Bernard, *Exploration*, 99.

224   "this man talks less intelligently" Orellana, quoted in Medina, *Discovery*, 131n.

225   He had the power of final oversight Bernard, *Exploration*, 99; Cohen, *Journeys*, 100; Medina, *Discovery*, 132; Smith, *Explorers*, 84.

225   "a worm within our midst" Bernard, *Exploration*, 99; Medina, *Discovery*, 133; Cohen, *Journeys*, 101.

225   Merchants selling gear and rigging Bernard, *Exploration*, 99. Quoted in Medina, *Discovery*, 133. Also quoted in Bernard, *Exploration*, 101.

225   "secret and sly factions" Bernard, *Exploration*, 101; Medina, *Discovery*, 136.

226   "The Adelantado has married" Quoted in Medina, *Discovery*, 137; also quoted in Cohen, *Journeys*, 103. See also Bernard, *Exploration*, 102.

227   The inspectors noted the lack of rigging Cohen, *Journeys*, 106; Medina, *Discovery*, 141.

227   "as thoroughly dismantled" Quoted in Cohen, *Journeys*, 106. See also Bernard, *Exploration*, 102.

228   Orellana did . . . shepherds seriously wounded Medina, *Discovery*, 144; Cohen, *Journeys*, 107.

229   His stop at the Cape Verde Islands . . . to set sail for the coast of Brazil Muller, *Orellana's Discovery*, 78.

230   "seventy-seven colonists, eleven horses" Quoted in Chapman, *Golden Dream*, 175. Also in Bernard, *Exploration*, 103, and Smith, *Explorers*, 87.

230   "And amidst this hardship" Quoted in Medina, *Discovery*, 147–48n.

230   "We went and reconnoitered the shoals" Quoted in Medina, *Discovery*, 359. From *Record of the Statement of Francisco de Guzmán, One of Those Who Went Away with the Adelantado Orellana*.

231   The men also pointed out Ibid.

232   Still, Orellana stopped, figuring Ibid. Also in Chapman, *Golden Dream*, 176; Smith, *Explorers*, 87; Cohen, *Journeys*, 110; Muller, *Orellana's Discovery*, 79; Bernard, *Exploration*, 103.

233   "country so poor that little food was to be had in it" Guzmán, in Medina, *Discovery*, 359.

233 "Their efforts were fruitless" Medina, *Discovery,* 148. Also in Chapman, *Golden Dream,* 176; Smith, *Explorers,* 87–88.

233 He left behind at the island camp Medina, *Discovery,* 149–50; Guzmán, in Medina, *Discovery,* 360; Cohen, *Journeys,* 111.

234 Juan Griego told the others From Juan Griego, in Medina, *Discovery,* 149n and 369–74; Cohen, *Journeys,* 111; Smith, *Explorers,* 88; Chapman, *Golden Dream,* 176. There are two distinct and contradictory versions of what happened after Orellana returned to the shipwreck at this point. One account is given by Francisco de Guzmán and the other by Juan Griego, both of whom survived the ordeal and later reported officially on it. According to Guzmán, on Orellana's return to the shipwreck camp, the thirty or so men he had left were still there building their boat, but he left them again, saying that he "felt ill" and that he "wanted to go back again to look for the branch of the river and go up as far as the point of San Juan" (St. John, the realm of the Amazons). According to Juan Griego's account, on their return from seeking the main branch of the Amazon, they failed to find the others they had left behind. Scholars are divided on which of the two versions is the more reliable, but we do know that the men did in fact construct a boat and sail away to safety, for a number of them survived.

234 "He went off again saying that he was ill" Guzmán, in Medina, *Discovery,* 360.

235 The Indian guides led them well upriver Ibid.

235 "because they considered the country to be a good one" Ibid., 361.

236 "[She] told us that her husband had not succeeded" Ibid.

236 He died, she said in a whisper, "from grief" Ibid.

EPILOGUE

239 "Because of these impious and ignominious deeds" Quoted in Las Casas, *Short Account of the Destruction of the Indies,* xxviii.

239 Such persuasive rhetoric Las Casas, *Short Account of the Destruction of the Indies,* xiii–xli; Las Casas, *History of the Indies,* xiv; Hemming, *Tree of Rivers,* 33–34; Hemming, *El Dorado,* 138–39; Wood, *Conquistadors,* 268–71. For an excellent, heady, and philosophical analysis of this debate, see Pagden, *Fall of Natural Man,* 109–45.

240 Their journey of migration had consumed ten years Cieza de León, *The Travels of Pedro de Cieza de León, First Part of His Chronicle of Peru,* translated and edited with notes and an introduction by Clements R. Markham (New York, 1964), 281 and 281n. Also in William Bollaert, translated from Fray Pedro Simón's "Sixth Historical Notice of the Conquest of Terre Firme," with an introduction by Clements R. Markham, *The Expedition of Pedro de Ursúa and Lope de Aguirre in Search of El Dorado and Omagua in 1560-1* (New York, 1961), xxviii–xxix.

240 "They emphasized the variety and multitude of the tribes" Quoted in Hemming, *Tree of Rivers,* 35. Quoted in Hemming, *El Dorado,* 141. See

also Stephen Minta, *Aguirre: The Re-Creation of a Sixteenth-Century Journey Across South America* (London, 1993), 8–9. Also Chapman, *Golden Dream,* 204.

240 **Those enticing descriptions** Bandelier, *Gilded Man,* 90–91; Hemming, *El Dorado,* 141; Goodman, *Explorers of South America,* 71; John Silver, "The Myth of El Dorado," *History Workshop No. 34, Latin American History* (Autumn 1992), 1–15.

241 **Ursúa's personal transport barge** Minta, *Aguirre,* 61.

241 **in official calculations of its length** Most serious scientific sources measure the Amazon from its headwaters on the Ucayali in Peru. In 2001 the National Geographic Society accepted a measurement put forth by a Polish expedition, which gave the number of 4,650 miles. See Goulding, *Smithsonian Atlas of the Amazon,* 23 and 99.

241 **On New Year's Day 1561** Bollaert, *Expedition,* 136–37; Bandelier, *Gilded Man,* 96–97; Cohen, *Journeys,* 146; Hemming, *Tree of Rivers,* 38; Hemming, *El Dorado,* 142.

241 **Aguirre defiantly inscribed "Lope de Aguirre: TRAITOR"** Bandelier, *Gilded Man,* 97; Cohen, *Journeys,* 150.

242 **Before witnesses . . . throughout the camp** Cohen, *Journeys,* 159; Bandelier, *Gilded Man,* 100; Hemming, *Tree of Rivers,* 39.

242 **"gentlemen or persons of quality"** Richard Hakluyt, quoted in Hemming, *Tree of Rivers,* 39.

243 **"Men of the Amazon," and himself "the Wrath of God"** Cohen, *Journeys,* 164; Chapman, *Golden Dream,* 230–32; Hemming, *Tree of Rivers,* 39.

243 **Aguirre and his horsehide-covered crews arrived on the island of Margarita** Smith, *Explorers,* 118–20; Chapman, *Golden Dream,* 235–39.

243 **"This river has a course of over two thousand leagues"** Aguirre, quoted in Smith, *Explorers,* 134. Also quoted in Chapman, *Golden Dream,* 254. A slightly different translation of this passage is found in Hemming, *Tree of Rivers,* 40, and Hemming, *El Dorado,* 144.

244 **They beheaded the traitor** Bollaert, *Expedition,* 226–27; Chapman, *Golden Dream,* 260–61; Cohen, *Journeys,* 196–97; Smith, *Explorers,* 131–32; Minta, *Aguirre,* 185–86.

244 **"most appalling in the annals of Spanish enterprise"** Clements R. Markham, in Bollaert, *Expedition,* i; Markham, quoted in Smith, *Explorers,* 132.

244 **By 1595, using his significant powers of rhetoric** Raleigh, *Discoverie,* translated and edited by Neil L. Whitehead, 71–75; Chapman, *Golden Dream,* 315 and 337. Raleigh's expedition to Guiana is covered in detail in Raleigh Trevelyan, *Sir Walter Raleigh* (New York, 2002), 215–50.

245 **"They say that once this lake is crossed"** Quoted in Hemming, *El Dorado,* 153. See also Chapman, *Golden Dream,* 279–306, on the journeys of Antonio de Berrio.

245 **"to lie in the rain and weather"** Raleigh, *Discoverie,* 135. Also Raleigh, quoted in Chapman, *Golden Dream,* 321.

245 "I know all the earth doth not yield" Raleigh, quoted in Hemming, *El Dorado,* 167.

246 "We passed the most beautiful country" Raleigh, *Discoverie,* 163. Quoted also in Chapman, *Golden Dream,* 324. See also Raleigh, quoted in Hemming, *El Dorado,* 168.

246 "There was nothing whereof I was more curious" Raleigh, *Discoverie,* 170–71 and 170–71n.

247 The curious villagers laid out a feast Ibid., 172.

247 "The birds towards the evening" Ibid., 176.

247 These would prove impassable Ibid. Also in Chapman, *Golden Dream,* 328, and Hemming, *El Dorado,* 170.

247 "most of the gold" Raleigh, *Discoverie,* 185. See also Chapman, *Golden Dream,* 331.

249 "fear not, but strike home" Quoted in Hemming, *El Dorado,* 193. See also Chapman, *Golden Dream,* 386. The details surrounding Raleigh's imprisonment, his failed return to Guiana, and his execution are covered at great length in Trevelyan, *Sir Walter Raleigh,* 371–553.

250 once sustained tremendous numbers of people Hemming, *Tree of Rivers,* 287–88. Here Hemming concisely summarizes and weighs in on the controversial "Meggers-Roosevelt" debate. He suggests an estimate, at the height of the Amazon Basin chiefdom populations, of between 4 and 5 million inhabitants spanning the entire region, with the densest populations in the "chiefdoms of the great rivers and surrounding savannahs," which is precisely what Orellana saw and Carvajal recorded. See also Mann, *1491,* 310. Woods McCann, of the New School, suggests that based on pottery findings in the lower Tapajos drainage alone, "you'd be talking about something capable of supporting about 200,000 to 400,000 people." This would make it at the time, according to Charles Mann, "one of the most densely populated places in the world." For a concise and cogent theory of the definition of and origins/development of chiefdoms, see Robert L. Carneiro, *The Muse of History and the Science of Culture* (New York, 2000), 182–86.

Bibliography

PRIMARY SOURCES AND FIRSTHAND ACCOUNTS

Acosta, Father José de. *The Natural and Moral History of the Indies,* vol. II. Reprinted from the English translated edition of Edward Grimston, 1604, and edited, with notes and an introduction, by Clements R. Markham. New York, 1939.

Acuña, Cristóbal de. *Descubrimiento del Amazons.* Buenos Aires, 1942.

———. *Nuevo descubrimiento del gran rio de las Amazonas.* Madrid, 1891.

———. *Voyages and Discoveries in South America.* Printed for S. Buckley, 1698.

Bates, Henry Walter. *The Naturalist on the River Amazons: A Record of Adventures, Habits of Animals, Sketches of Brazilian and Indian Life, and Aspects of Nature Under the Equator, During Eleven Years of Travel.* London, 1892.

Cabeza de Vaca, Álvar Núñez. *Chronicle of the Narváez Expedition.* Translated by Fanny Bandelier, revised and annotated by Harold Augenbraum, introduction by llan Stavans. New York, 2002.

Carvajal, Friar Gaspar de. *Discovery of the Amazon River According to the Account Hitherto Unpublished of Friar Gaspar de Carvajal with Other Documents Relating to Francisco de Orellana and His Companions, Put into Print at the Expense of the Duke of T'Serclaes de Tilly, with an Historical Introduction and Illustrations by José Toribio Medina.* Seville, 1894.

Cieza de León, Pedro de. *The Discovery and Conquest of Peru: Chronicles of the New World Encounter.* Edited and translated by Alexandra Parma Cook and Noble David Cook. Durham, North Carolina, and London, 1998.

———. *The Travels of Pedro de Cieza de León, A.D. 1532–50, Contained in the First Part of His Chronicle of Peru.* Translated and edited with notes and an introduction by Clements R. Markham. New York, 1964.

———. *The Second Part of the Chronicles of Peru.* Translated and edited with notes and an introduction by Clements R. Markham. New York, 1964.

———. *Civil Wars in Peru: The War of Las Salinas.* Translated and with an introduction by Sir Clements Markham. London, 1923.

———. *Civil Wars in Peru: The War of Chupas.* Translated and with an introduction by Sir Clements Markham. London, 1917.

———. *The War of Quito.* Translated and edited by Sir Clements Markham. London, 1913.

Cobo, Bernabé. *History of the Inca Empire*. Translated and edited by Roland Hamilton. Austin and London, 1979.

Cortés, Hernán. *Letters from Mexico*. Edited, translated, and introduced by Anthony Pagden. New Haven, 2001.

Díaz del Castillo, Bernal. *The Conquest of New Spain*. Translated by J. M. Cohen. New York, 1963.

Edwards, William. *A Voyage up the Amazon, Including a Residence at Para*. New York, 1847.

Fritz, Father Samuel. *Journal of the Travels and Labours of Father Samuel Fritz in the River of the Amazons Between 1686 and 1723*. Translated from the Evora manuscript and edited by the Reverend Dr. George Edmundson, with two maps. London, 1922.

Herndon, William Lewis. *Exploration of the Valley of the Amazon*. Edited and with an introduction by Hamilton Basso. New York, 1952.

Herrera y Tordesillas, Antonio de. *The General History of the Vast Continent and Islands of America, Commonly Call'd the West-Indies, from the First Discovery Thereof: With the Best Accounts the People Could Give of Their Antiquities*. London, 1725.

Humboldt, Alexander von. *Views of Nature: Or Contemplations on the Sublime Phenomena of Creation; with Scientific Illustrations*. Translated from the German by E. C. Otte and Henry G. Bohn. London, 1850.

———. *Aspects of Nature in Different Lands and Different Climates*. Philadelphia, 1850.

Humboldt, Alexander von, and Aimé Bonpland. *Personal Narrative of Travels to the Equinoctial Regions of America During the Years 1799–1804*, vol. 3. Translated and edited by Thomasina Ross. London, 1908.

Lange, Algot. *The Lower Amazon*. New York and London, 1914.

Laredo, Sarah de. *From Panama to Peru: The Conquest of Peru by the Pizarros, the Rebellion of Gonzalo Pizarro, and the Pacification by La Gasca. An Epitome of Original Signed Documents to and from the Conquistadors Francisco, Gonzalo, Pedro, and Hernando Pizarro, Diego de Almagro, and Pacificator La Gasca*. London, 1925.

Las Casas, Bartolomé de. *A Short Account of the Destruction of the Indies*. Edited and translated by Nigel Griffen, with an introduction by Anthony Pagden. New York, 1992.

———. *History of the Indies*. Translated and edited by Andrée Collard. New York, Evanston, Illinois, and London, 1971.

Martyr, Peter (Pietro Martire d'Anghiera). *The Decades of the New Worlde or West India*. Ann Arbor, 1966.

Oviedo, Gonzalo Fernández de. *Writing from the Edge of the World: The Memoirs of Darien, 1514–1527*. Translated and with an introduction by G. F. Dille. Tuscaloosa, Alabama, 2006.

———. *Natural History of the West Indies*. Translated and edited by Sterling A. Stoudemire. Chapel Hill, North Carolina, 1959.

———. *La historia general y natural de las Indias Occidentales*, vol. 4. Madrid, 1851.

Pizarro, Pedro. *Relation of the Discovery and Conquest of the Kingdoms of Peru.* 2 vols. Translated into English and annotated by Philip Ainsworth Means. New York, 1921.

Raleigh, Sir Walter. *Sir Walter Raleigh's Discoverie of Guiana.* Edited by Joyce Lorimer. London, 2006.

———. *The Discoverie of the Large, Rich, and Bewtiful Empyre of Guiana.* Transcribed, annotated, and introduced by Neil L. Whitehead. Norman, Oklahoma, 1997.

Spruce, Richard. *Notes of a Botanist on the Amazon and Andes.* London, 1908.

Staden, Hans. *The True History of His Captivity, 1557.* Translated and edited by Malcolm Letts, with an introduction and notes. New York, 1929.

Vega, Garcilaso de la (El Inca). *Royal Commentaries of the Incas and General History of Peru.* 2 vols. Translated and with an introduction by Harold V. Livermore. Austin and London, 1966.

Wallace, Alfred Russel. *A Narrative of Travels on the Amazon and Rio Negro, with an Account of the Native Tribes, and Observations on the Climate, Geology, and Natural History of the Amazon Valley.* London, New York, and Melbourne, 1889.

Zárate, Agustín de. *The Discovery and Conquest of Peru.* Translated with an introduction by J. M. Cohen. Baltimore, 1968.

BOOKS AND ARTICLES

Albornoz, Miguel. *Hernando de Soto: Knight of the Americas.* Translated from the Spanish by Bruce Boeglin. New York and Toronto, 1986.

Arens, William. *The Man-Eating Myth: Anthropology and Anthropophagy.* New York, 1979.

Aronson, Marc. *Sir Walter Raleigh and the Quest for El Dorado.* New York, 2000.

Bandelier, A. F. *The Gilded Man (El Dorado): And Other Pictures of the Spanish Occupancy of America.* New York, 1893.

Bernard, Brendan. *Pizarro, Orellana, and the Exploration of the Amazon.* New York, 1991.

Betanzos, Juan de. *Narrative of the Incas.* Translated and edited by Roland Hamilton and Dana Buchanan from the Palma de Mallorca manuscript. Austin, 1996.

Birney, Hoffman. *Brothers of Doom: The Story of the Pizarros of Peru.* New York, 1942.

Bollaert, William. *The Expedition of Pedro de Ursúa and Lope de Aguirre in Search of El Dorado and Omagua in 1560–1.* Translated from Fray Pedro Simón's "Sixth Historical Notice of the Conquest of Tierra Firme," with an introduction by Clements R. Markham. New York, 1861.

Boorstin, Daniel J. *The Discoverers: A History of Man's Search to Know His World and Himself.* London, 1983.

Bray, Warwick. *Gold of El Dorado.* From the exhibition *Gold of El Dorado: The Heritage of Colombia.* New York, 1979.

Camerini, Jane R. *The Alfred Russel Wallace Reader: A Selection of Writings from the Field*. Baltimore and London, 2002.

Campbell, David G. *A Land of Ghosts: The Braided Lives of People and the Forest in Far Western Amazonia*. New York, 2005.

Canedo, Lino G. "New Data Regarding the Origins of the Franciscan Missions in Peru, 1532–1569." *The Americas*, vol. 9, no. 3 (January 1953): 315–48.

Carneiro, Robert L. *Evolutionism in Cultural Anthropology: A Critical History*. Boulder, Colorado, 2003.

———. *The Muse of History and the Science of Culture*. New York, 2000.

———. *Anthropological Investigations in Amazonia: Selected Papers*. Greeley, Colorado, 1985.

———. "Hunting and Hunting Magic Among the Amahuaca of the Peruvian Montaña." *Ethnology*, vol. 9, no. 4 (October 1970): 331–41.

———. "On the Relationship Between Size of Population and Complexity of Social Organization." *Southwestern Journal of Anthropology*, vol. 23, no. 3 (Autumn 1967): 234–43.

———. "The Amahuaca and the Spirit World." *Ethnology*, vol. 3, no. 1 (January 1964): 6–11.

Carneiro, Robert L., Bill Cohen, Robert A. Ibarra, Sven-Erik Isacsson, and Carl E. Batt. *Anthropological Investigations in Amazonia: Selected Papers*. Greeley, Colorado, 1985.

Castro, Eduardo Viveiros de. *From the Enemy's Point of View: Humanity and Divinity in an Amazonian Society*. Translated by Catherine V. Howard. Chicago and London, 1992.

Chapman, Walker. *The Golden Dream: Seekers of El Dorado*. Indianapolis, Kansas City, and New York, 1967.

Clark, Leonard. *The Rivers Ran East*. New York, 1953.

Clayton, Lawrence A., Vernon James Knight, Jr., and Edward C. Moore. *The De Soto Chronicles: The Expedition of Hernando de Soto to North America in 1539–1543*. 2 vols. Tuscaloosa, Alabama, and London, 1993.

Cleary, David. "Towards an Environmental History of the Amazon: From Prehistory to the Nineteenth Century." *Latin American Research Review*, vol. 36, no. 2 (2001): 65–96.

Cohen, J. M. *Journeys Down the Amazon*. London, 1975.

Cook, Noble David. *Demographic Collapse: Indian Peru, 1520–1620*. Cambridge, London, and New York, 1981.

Cortesão, Armando. "Antonio Pereira and His Map of Circa 1545: An Unknown Portuguese Cartographer and the Early Representation of Newfoundland, Lower California, the Amazon, and the Ladrones." *Geographical Review*, vol. 29, no. 2 (April 1939): 205–25.

Crosby, Alfred W. *The Colombian Exchange: Biological Consequences of 1492*. Westport, Connecticut, 1972.

———. "*Conquistador y Pestilencia:* The First New World Pandemic and the Fall of the Great Indian Empires." *Hispanic American Historical Review*, vol. 47, no. 3 (August 1967): 321–37.

Cutright, Paul Russell. *The Great Naturalists Explore South America*. New York, 1940.

Dalby, Andrew. *Dangerous Tastes: The Story of Spices*. London, 2000.

Davis, Dave D., and R. Christopher Goodwin. "Island Carib: Evidence and Nonevidence." *American Antiquity*, vol. 55, no. 1 (January 1990): 37–48.

De Bry, Theodor. *The Discovery of the New World*. Amsterdam, 1979.

De Kalb, Courtney. "The Great Amazon: Personal Investigations on the River, and in Its Upper Valley." *Journal of the American Geographical Society of New York*, vol. 23 (1891): 1–46.

Derr, Mark. *A Dog's History of America: How Our Best Friend Explored, Conquered, and Settled a Continent*. New York, 2004.

Dickenson, John. "The Naturalist on the River Amazons and a Wider World: Reflections on the Centenary of Henry Walter Bates." *Geographical Journal*, vol. 158, no. 2 (July 1992): 207–14.

Duncan, David Ewing. *Hernando de Soto: A Savage Quest in the Americas*. New York, 1995.

Dyott, G. M. *On the Trail of the Unknown: In the Wilds of Ecuador and the Amazon*. New York, 1926.

Ewan, Joseph. "Who Conquered the New World? or Four Centuries of Exploration in an Indehiscent Capsule." *Annals of the Missouri Botanical Garden*, vol. 78, no. 1 (1991): 57–64.

Fausto, Carlos, and Michael Heckenberger. *Time and Memory in Indigenous Amazonia: Anthropological Perspectives*. Gainesville, Florida, 2007.

Favier, Jean. *Gold and Spices: The Rise of Commerce in the Middle Ages*. New York and London, 1998.

Ferguson, Brian R. "Blood of the Leviathan: Western Contact and Warfare in Amazonia." *American Ethnologist*, vol. 17, no. 2 (May 1990): 237–57.

Fernandez-Armesto, Felipe. *Pathfinders: A Global History of Exploration*. New York and London, 2006.

Fisher, William H. *Rainforest Exchanges: Industry and Community on an Amazonian Frontier*. Washington and London, 2000.

Gabai, Rafael Varón. *Francisco Pizarro and His Brothers: The Illusion of Power in Sixteenth-Century Peru*. Norman, Oklahoma, and London, 1997.

Galloway, Patricia. *The Hernando de Soto Expedition: History, Historiography, and "Discovery" in the Southeast*. Lincoln, Nebraska, and London, 1997.

Gibbons, Ann. "New View of Early Amazonia." *Science*, new series, vol. 248, no. 4962 (June 22, 1990): 1488–90.

Goodman, Edward J. *The Explorers of South America*. New York, 1972.

Goulding, Michael, and Efrem Ferreira. *The Smithsonian Atlas of the Amazon*. Washington and London, 2003.

Graham, R. B. Cunninghame. *The Conquest of New Granada: Being the Life of Gonzalo Jimenez de Quesada*. Boston and New York, 1922.

Graham, Stephen. *In Quest of El Dorado*. New York, 1923.

Hardwick, Lorna. "Ancient Amazons: Heroes, Outsiders, or Women?" *Greece and Rome*, vol. 37, no. 1 (April 1990): 14–36.

Haring, C. H. *The Spanish Empire in America*. New York, 1947.

Heckenberger, Michael J. *The Ecology of Power: Culture, Place, and Personhood in the Southern Amazon, A.D. 1000–2000*. New York, 2005.

Helferich, Gerard. *Humboldt's Cosmos: Alexander von Humboldt and the Latin American Journey That Changed the Way We See the World*. New York, 2004.

Helps, Arthur. *The Life of Pizarro*. London, 1896.

Hemming, John. *Tree of Rivers: The Story of the Amazon*. New York, 2008.

———. *Oxford Atlas of Exploration*. New York, 1997.

———. *Amazon Frontier: The Defeat of the Brazilian Indians*. Cambridge, Massachusetts, 1987.

———. *The Search for El Dorado*. New York, 1978.

———. *Red Gold: The Conquest of the Brazilian Indians*. New York, 1978.

———. *The Conquest of the Incas*. San Diego, New York, and London, 1970.

Herrmann, Paul. *The Great Age of Discovery*. Translated by Arnold J. Pomerans. New York, 1958.

Heyerdahl, Thor. "The Balsa Raft in Aboriginal Navigation off Peru and Ecuador." *Southwestern Journal of Anthropology*, vol. 11, no. 3 (Autumn 1955): 251–64.

Hobhouse, Henry. *Seeds of Change: Five Plants That Changed Mankind*. New York, 1985.

Holloway, H. L. "East of Ecuadorian Andes." *The Geographical Journal*, vol. 80, no. 5 (November 1932): 410–19.

Innes, Hammond. *The Conquistadors*. New York, 1969.

Jones, Grant D., and Robert R. Kautz. *The Transition to Statehood in the New World*. New York, 1981.

Kamen, Henry. *Spain's Road to Empire: The Making of a World Power, 1492–1763*. New York and London, 2002.

Kane, Joe. *Savages*. New York, 1995.

Kirkpatrick, F. A. *The Spanish Conquistadors*. London, 1934.

Kleinbaum, Abby Wettan. *The War Against the Amazons*. New York, 1983.

Koch, Peter O. *The Aztecs, the Conquistadors, and the Making of Mexican Culture*. Jefferson, North Carolina, and London, 2006.

Kubler, George. "A Peruvian Chief of State: Manco Inca (1515–1545)." *Hispanic American Historical Review*, vol. 24, no. 2 (May 1944): 253–76.

Kunze, Albert F. "The Amazon—Has It Been Fully Discovered?" *Scientific Monthly*, vol. 58, no. 1 (January 1944): 16–23.

Kurlansky, Mark. *Salt: A World History*. New York, 2002.

Lathrap, Donald W. *The Upper Amazon*. New York, 1970.

Lauer, Robert A. "The Iberian Encounter of America in the Spanish Theater of the Golden Age." *Pacific Coast Philology*, vol. 28, no. 1 (September 1993): 32–42.

Lentz, David L. *Imperfect Balance: Landscape Transformations in the Pre-Columbian Americas*. New York, 2000.

Levy, Buddy. *Conquistador: Hernán Cortés, King Montezuma, and the Last Stand of the Aztecs*. New York, 2008.

Lockhart, James. *The Men of Cajamarca: A Social and Biographical Study of the First Conquerors of Peru.* Austin, 1972.

———. *Spanish Peru, 1532–1560: A Colonial Society.* Madison, 1968.

———. *Spanish Peru, 1532–1560: A Social History.* Madison, 1968.

Loriot, James. "A Selected Bibliography of Comparative American Indian Linguistics." *International Journal of American Linguistics,* vol. 30, no. 1 (January 1964): 62–80.

MacQuarrie, Kim. *The Last Days of the Incas.* New York, 2007.

Mann, Charles C. *1491: New Revelations of the Americas Before Columbus.* New York, 2005.

Markham, Clements R. *A History of Peru.* New York, 1968.

———. *Expeditions into the Valley of the Amazons, 1539, 1540, 1639.* New York, 1963.

———. "A List of the Tribes in the Valley of the Amazon, Including Those on the Banks of the Main Stream, and of All Its Tributaries." *Transactions of the Ethnological Society of London,* vol. 3 (1865): 140–96.

Maynard, Theodore. *De Soto and the Conquistadors.* London, New York, and Toronto, 1930.

McEwan, Gordon. *The Incas: New Perspectives.* Santa Barbara, 2006.

McMahon, Dorothy. "Sidelights on the Spanish Conquest of America." *The Americas,* vol. 18, no. 1 (July 1961): 19–31.

Means, Philip Ainsworth. "Gonzalo Pizarro and Francisco Orellana." *Hispanic American Historical Review,* vol. XIV, no. 3 (August 1934): 275–95.

———. *Fall of the Inca Empire and the Spanish Rule in Peru: 1530–1780.* New York and London, 1932.

———. *Ancient Civilizations of the Andes.* New York and London, 1931.

Medina, José Toribio. *The Discovery of the Amazon.* Cited and translated by Bertram T. Lee and edited by H. C. Heaton. New York, 1988.

———. *The Discovery of the Amazon.* American Geographical Society Special Publication no. 17, translated from the Spanish by Bertram T. Lee and edited by H. C. Heaton. New York, 1934.

Meggers, Betty J. "The Continuing Quest for El Dorado: Round Two." *Latin American Antiquity,* vol. 12, no. 3 (September 2001): 304–25.

———. *Amazonia: Man and Culture in a Counterfeit Paradise.* Washington and London, 1996.

———. *Ecuador.* New York, 1966.

Meggers, Betty, and Clifford Evans. *Archaeological Investigations at the Mouth of the Amazon.* Washington, 1957.

Merchant, Frank. "Legend and Fact About Gold in Early America." *Western Folklore,* vol. 13, no. 2/3 (1954): 170–83.

Métraux, Alfred. "Twin Heroes in South American Mythology." *Journal of American Folklore,* vol. 59, no. 232 (April–June 1946): 114–23.

Millar, George. *A Crossbowman's Story.* New York, 1955.

Millard, Candice. *The River of Doubt: Theodore Roosevelt's Darkest Journey.* New York, 2005.

Minta, Stephen. *Aguirre: The Re-Creation of a Sixteenth-Century Journey Across South America*. London, 1993.

Moore, Robert T. "Gonzalo Pizarro's Trail to the Land of Cinnamon and Its Denizens." *The Condor*, vol. 36, no. 3 (May–June 1934): 97–104.

Moran, Emilio F. *Through Amazonian Eyes: The Human Ecology of Amazonian Populations*. Iowa City, 1993.

Morison, Samuel Eliot. *The European Discovery of America: The Southern Voyages, A.D. 1492–1616*. New York, 1974.

———. *The European Discovery of America: The Northern Voyages, A.D. 500–600*. New York, 1971.

Mowat, Linda. *Cassava and Chicha: Bread and Beer of the Amazonian Indians*. Aylesbury, UK, 1989.

Muller, Richard. *Orellana's Discovery of the Amazon River*. Guayaquil, Ecuador, 1937.

Murphy, Robert Cushman. "The Earliest Spanish Advances Southward from Panama Along the West Coast of South America." *Hispanic American Historical Review*, vol. 21, no. 1 (February 1941): 3–28.

Myers, Thomas P. *Sarayacu: Ethnohistorical and Archaeological Investigations of a Nineteenth-Century Franciscan Mission in the Peruvian Montaña*. Lincoln, Nebraska, 1990.

Naipaul, V. S. *The Loss of El Dorado: A History*. New York, 1970.

Newson, Linda. "The Population of the Amazon Basin in 1492: A View from the Ecuadorian Headwaters." *Transactions of the Institute of British Geographers*, new series, vol. 21, no. 1 (1996): 5–26.

O'Leary, Timothy J. *Ethnographic Bibliography of South America*. New Haven, 1963.

Overing, Joanna, and Alan Passes. *The Anthropology of Love and Anger: The Aesthetics of Conviviality in Native Amazonia*. London and New York, 2000.

Pagden, Anthony. *The Fall of Natural Man: The American Indian and the Origins of Comparative Ethnology*. Cambridge, New York, and London, 1982.

Palmatary, Helen Constance. "The Archaeology of the Lower Tapajós Valley, Brazil." *Transactions of the American Philosophical Society*, new series, vol. 50, no. 3 (1960): 1–243.

———. "The Pottery of Marajó Island, Brazil." *Transactions of the American Philosophical Society*, new series, vol. 39, no. 3 (1949): 261–470.

Parry, J. H. *The Spanish Seaborne Empire*. New York, 1974.

Pearson, David L., and Les Beletsky. *Travellers' Wildlife Guides: Ecuador and the Galápagos Islands*. Northampton, Massachusetts, 2005.

———. *Travellers' Wildlife Guides: Brazil—Amazon and Pantanal*. Northampton, Massachusetts, 2005.

Philbrick, Nathaniel. *In the Heart of the Sea: The Tragedy of the Whaleship Essex*. New York, 2000.

Pohl, John, and Charles M. Robinson III. *Aztecs and Conquistadors: The Spanish Invasion and the Collapse of the Aztec Empire*. New York, 2005.

Prescott, William H. *History of the Conquest of Peru*. New York, 2005.

———. *History of the Conquest of Mexico.* New York, 2001.

Raffles, Hugh. *In Amazonia: A Natural History.* Princeton, 2002.

Reed, Robert. *Amazon Dream: Escape to the Unknown.* London, 1977.

Reeve, Mary-Elizabeth. "Regional Interaction in the Western Amazon: The Early Colonial Encounter and the Jesuit Years, 1538–1767." *Ethnohistory,* vol. 41, no. 1. (Winter 1993): 106–38.

Reichel-Dolmatoff, Gerard. "Cosmology as Ecological Analysis: A View from the Rain Forest." *Ritual and Belief: Readings in the Anthropology of Religion,* edited by David Hicks. New York, 2001.

———. *Rainforest Shamans: Essays on the Tukano Indians of the Northwest Amazon.* Devon, UK, 1997.

———. *The Forest Within: The World-View of the Tukano Amazonian Indians.* Devon, UK, 1996.

———. *Beyond the Milky Way: Hallucinatory Imagery of the Tukano Indians.* Los Angeles, 1978.

———. *The Shaman and the Jaguar: A Study of Narcotic Drugs Among the Indians of Colombia.* Philadelphia, 1975.

———. *Amazonian Cosmos: The Sexual and Religious Symbolism of the Tukano Indians.* Chicago and London, 1971.

Reséndez, Andrés. *A Land So Strange: The Epic Journey of Cabeza de Vaca.* New York, 2007.

Restall, Matthew. *Seven Myths of the Spanish Conquest.* Oxford, 2003.

Roosevelt, Anna Curtenius. *Amazonian Indians from Prehistory to the Present: Anthropological Perspectives.* Tucson and London, 1994.

———. *Moundbuilders of the Amazon: Geophysical Archaeology on Marajo Island, Brazil.* San Diego, 1991.

———. *Parmana: Prehistoric Maize and Manioc Subsistence Along the Amazon and Orinoco.* New York, 1980.

Rouse, Irving. *The Tainos: Rise and Decline of the People Who Greeted Columbus.* New Haven and London, 1992.

———. *Migrations in Prehistory: Inferring Population Movement from Cultural Remains.* New Haven and London, 1986.

Salmonson, Jessica Amanda. *The Encyclopedia of Amazons: Women Warriors from Antiquity to the Modern Era.* New York, 1991.

Shoumatoff, Alex. *The World Is Burning: Murder in the Rain Forest.* Boston, Toronto, and New York, 1990.

———. *In Southern Light: Trekking Through Zaire and the Amazon.* New York, 1986.

———. "A Reporter at Large: Amazons." *The New Yorker* (March 24, 1986), 85–110.

———. *The Rivers Amazon.* San Francisco, 1978.

Silver, John. "The Myth of El Dorado." *History Workshop,* no. 34, *Latin American History* (Autumn 1992), 1–15.

Silverman, Helaine, and William H. Isbell. *Handbook of South American Archaeology.* New York, 2008.

Simpson, Lesley Byrd. *The Encomienda in New Spain: Forced Native Labor in the Spanish Colonies, 1492–1550.* Berkeley and Los Angeles, 1966.

——. *The Encomienda in New Spain: Forced Native Labor in the Spanish Colonies, 1492–1550*. Berkeley, California, 1929.

Sinclair, Joseph H. "In the Land of Cinnamon: A Journey in Eastern Ecuador." *Geographical Review*, vol. 19, no. 2. (April 1929): 201–17.

Smith, Anthony. *Explorers of the Amazon*. New York, 1990.

Solomon, Frank, and Stuart B. Schwartz, editors. *The Cambridge History of the Native Peoples of the Americas*, vol. 3: *South America*, part 1. Cambridge, UK, 2000.

Sponsel, Leslie E. *Indigenous Peoples and the Future of Amazonia*. Tucson, 1995.

Steward, Julian H. *Handbook of South American Indians*, vol. 3: *The Tropical Forest Tribes*. New York, 1963.

——. *Native Peoples of South America*. New York, 1959.

Thomas, Hugh. *Conquest: Montezuma, Cortés, and the Fall of Old Mexico*. New York, 1993.

Tiffany, Sharon W., and Kathleen J. Adams. *The Wild Woman: An Inquiry into the Anthropology of an Idea*. Cambridge, Massachusetts, 1985.

Trevelyan, Raleigh. *Sir Walter Raleigh*. New York, 2002.

Turner, Jack. *Spice: The History of a Temptation*. New York, 2004.

Urton, Gary. *Animal Myths and Metaphors in South America*. Salt Lake City, 1985.

——."Animals and Astronomy in the Quechua Universe." *Proceedings of the American Philosophical Society*, vol. 125, no. 2 (April 30, 1981): 110–27.

Varner, John Grier. *El Inca: The Life and Times of Garcilaso de la Vega*. Austin and London, 1968.

Varner, John Grier, and Jeannette Johnson Varner. *Dogs of the Conquest*. Norman, Oklahoma, 1983.

Vassberg, David E. "Concerning Pigs, the Pizarros, and the Agro-Pastoral Background of the Conquerors of Peru." *Latin American Research Review*, vol. 13, no. 3 (1978): 47–61.

Villena, Guillermo Lohmann. "Notes on Prescott's Interpretation of the Conquest of Peru." *Hispanic American Historical Review*, vol. 39, no. 1 (February 1959): 46–80.

Von Hagen, Victor Wolfgang. *South America Called Them: Explorations of the Great Naturalists La Condamine, Humboldt, Darwin, Spruce*. New York, 1945.

Waller, Gregory A. *"Aguirre, The Wrath of God:* History, Theater, and the Camera." *South Atlantic Review*, vol. 46, no. 2 (May 1981): 55–69.

Whitehead, Neil L. *Histories and Historicities in Amazonia*. Lincoln, Nebraska, and London, 2003.

Whitehead, Neil L., and Robin Wright. *In Darkness and Secrecy: The Anthropology of Assault Sorcery and Witchcraft in Amazonia*. Durham, North Carolina, and London, 2004.

Whitmore, Thomas M., and B. L. Turner II. "Landscapes of Cultivation in Mesoamerica on the Eve of the Conquest." *Annals of the Association of*

American Geographers, vol. 82, no. 3, "The Americas Before and After 1492: Current Geographical Research" (September 1992): 402-25.

Wilde, Lyn Webster. *On the Trail of the Women Warriors: The Amazons in Myth and History.* New York, 1999.

Wolf, Eric R. "Unforeseen Americas: The Making of New World Societies in Anthropological Perspective." *Proceedings of the National Academy of Sciences in the United States of America,* vol. 93, no. 6 (March 19, 1996): 2603-7.

Wood, Michael. *Conquistadors.* Berkeley and Los Angeles, 2000.

Zahm, John Augustine. *The Quest of El Dorado.* New York and London, 1917.

———. *Along the Andes and Down the Amazon.* New York and London, 1911.

Acknowledgments

There are many people to thank for their contributions to the life of *River of Darkness*. I owe gratitude to editor John Flicker, who had the good sense to wave off another proposal of mine and send me back to the idea trenches, and there I discovered Orellana and his Amazonian journey. A tip of my conquistador's helmet goes to my editor, Tracy Devine at Ballantine Bantam Dell. I have been impressed by her strong-armed line-editing skill, her perceptive queries, her great ear and attention to pacing, and her playful sense of imagination and adventure. Thanks, too, go to assistant editor Angela Polidoro for her careful and thoughtful editorial contributions.

My agent, Scott Waxman, has been there for me since circa 2003, and it is hard to believe that soon we will reach a decade of collaboration. We have shared the wide gamut of emotions that the book-writing and publishing trade doles out, and it has been a tremendously fulfilling and educational experience to work with him. From the beginning, his belief in me seems never to have wavered. Scott involves himself deeply from the earliest idea stages of a book, bringing his considerable experience and wisdom and his profound understanding of what makes a good story to bear on every project. Scott—here's to another random early-May meeting in New York and another Yankees–Red Sox game with Schaapy! Pretty amazing.

I must give a nod to three scholars who generously took time out of their very busy careers to talk with me, listen to me, and share their knowledge and sagacity about the Amazon Basin with me—all of which was instrumental in my understanding of the people and the region and in my writing of *River of Darkness*. First of all, thanks to Anna Roosevelt, with whom I spent a lovely, fascinating, and mind-expanding evening at Russian Tea Time in Chicago in February 2008. Anna's

archaeological and anthropological work in the Amazon Basin is legendary, and I was humbled that she would take the time to meet with me
and discuss my project and then follow that up with multiple email cor-
respondences and a nearly two-hour phone interview. Here's to the
Blinchik s Lososinoi I s Ikroisalmon—Anna—and to matriarchal and ma-
trilineal societies (and Amazonian women) the world over.

Thanks, too, to Robert Carneiro, another scholar of the highest magnitude who met personally with me. On a rainy day in early May 2009,
Bob Carneiro invited me to his office above the American Museum of
Natural History, an office in which he has been producing remarkable
scholarship for more than five decades. We spent more than three hours
talking about everything from his theory of circumscription and the role
of chiefdoms to his personal experiences doing fieldwork in the Amazon
Basin, and I was bowled over and humbled by the scope of his learning
and the sharpness of his wit. Poring over his large and detailed nautical
charts of the Amazon River on the tables in the conference room was
absolutely engaging. I also wish to extend my deepest appreciation to
Professor Carneiro for his generous reading of my manuscript and his
tremendous insight, observations, and opinions on the text. His notes
were remarkably detailed and discerning. I learned a great deal from
him, and the text benefited in numerous ways from his erudition, depth
of knowledge, and decades of experience traveling on the Amazon and
living among its people. Thanks so much, Bob. I owe you a pisco sour.

Finally, I must thank the illustrious historian John Hemming, former
director and secretary of the Royal Geographical Society in London and
the Amazon's greatest historian. Though I have yet to have the pleasure
and privilege of a personal meeting with Dr. Hemming, he has been swift
and forthright in written correspondence, answering multiple email
questions and directing me toward avenues of further study and inquiry.
His breadth of scholarship on the Amazon spans some forty years, and
his writings have contributed considerably to my understanding of the
history of South America and the Amazon. I hope, the next time I am in
London, to pay him a proper visit.

In May and June of 2008 I took a research trip to Ecuador and Peru,
spending a few days in archives, museums, and colonial buildings in

Quito before following the route of Orellana and Pizarro (the Way of the Conquistadors) over the Andes, down through the cloud forest, and onto the rivers. My two-week river, rain forest, and jungle journey was among the most interesting and adventurous of my life. With Wildlife Amazon Adventures and their two highly skilled guides, José Shiguango and Sandro Ramos, I traveled by canoe down the Napo River all the way from Coca, Ecuador, to Iquitos, Peru, camping for nearly a week in the Yasuni National Park. José's lifetime of knowledge about the flora and fauna was evident on every jungle trek and canoe excursion, and I especially appreciated his shared love of bird behavior and identification. Thanks, Sapo—from Hoatzin!

My Amazon excursion culminated in the remarkable city of Iquitos, Peru, and there I had the great fortune of staying at the lovely and historic Casa Fitzcarraldo. The house is a jungle oasis of sublime calm amid the Iquitos chaos (think thirty thousand whining *motocarros*). Owned by Micaela McPhale (daughter of Walter Saxer, producer of the Werner Herzog films *Fitzcarraldo* and *Aguirre: The Wrath of God*) and run by Micaela and her husband, David McPhale, La Casa Fitzcarraldo was a perfect end to my river journey, the walls rich with images depicting the history of Iquitos as well as the Herzog films. Micaela and David's hospitality, local knowledge, and quiet graciousness (and excellent cooking!) made me vow to return to sleep on the top floor of the five-story tree house.

For a third consecutive book I owe deep appreciation to my intrepid first readers, my dear and trusted friends John Larkin and Kim Barnes. John, here's to many more adventures and thousands of cycling miles together. Kim: a clink of the wineglass to the elusive and illusory narrative arc, with deep appreciation for your ability to help tell the story that's trying to be told. As always, a group hug to the Free Range Writers—Kim Barnes, Collin Hughes, Lisa Norris, and Jane Varley. Write onward! And a special mention to Melissa Rockwood of Rdesign for her help with the map and other design problems over the years—Missy rocks!

Finally and forever, my deepest gratitude to my lovely wife, Camie, and my beautiful children, Logan and Hunter, who give me the latitude to pursue these wild adventures.

Illustration Credits

Francisco Pizarro (litho) by Spanish School Private Collection/
    Bildarchiv Steffens/ Henri Stierlin/ The Bridgeman Art Library

Francisco de Orellana (litho) by Spanish School Private Collection/ Index/
    The Bridgeman Art Library

The Battle of Cajamarca, 1532 (engraving) (b/w photo) by Theodore de Bry
    (1528–98) Private Collection/ The Bridgeman Art Library

El Dorado: akg-images

The dogs of Vasco Nunez de Balboa (1475–1571) attacking the Indians
    (engraving) (b/w photo) by Theodore de Bry (1528–98) Bibliothèque
    Nationale, Paris, France/ Giraudon/ The Bridgeman Art Library

Crossing the Cordillera on 1st June, from "Travels in South America" by
    Alexander Caldcleugh, 1825 (litho) (b/w photo) by English School
    (19th century) Private Collection/ The Bridgeman Art Library

Our First Interview with Caripuna Indians, from "The Amazon and Madeira
    River" by Franz Keller, 1874 (engraving) by American School
    (19th century) Private Collection/ The Bridgeman Art Library

The Heart of the Andes (engraving) by Frederic Edwin Church (1826–1900)
    © Butler Institute of American Art, Youngstown, OH, USA/ The Bridgeman
    Art Library

Jaguar Hunt, from "Bresil, Columbie et Guyanes" by Ferdinand Denis and
    César Famin 1837 (engraving) (b/w photo) by French School (19th century)
    Private Collection/ The Bridgeman Art Library

Scene in a Brazilian Forest engraved by J. Bishop (engraving) (b/w photo) by
    Henry George Hine (1811–95) (after) Private Collection/ The Bridgeman Art
    Library

Bridge of Ropes, near Penipe, from Vol. II of "Researches concerning the Institutions and Monuments of the Ancient Inhabitants of America with Descriptions and views of some of the most Striking Scenes in the Cordilleras," pub. 1814 (lithograph) by Friedrich Alexander Humboldt, Baron von (1769–1859) (after) © Royal Geographical Society, London, UK/ The Bridgeman Art Library

Crossing a Stream along a Fallen Tree, engraved by C. Laplante, page 79 from "Voyages in South America" by J. Crevaux, 1883 (engraving) by Edouard Riou (1833–1900) (after) Natural History Museum, London, UK/ The Bridgeman Art Library

Caripuna Indians with tapir, from "The Amazon and Madeira Rivers," by Franz Keller, 1874 (engraving) by American School (19th century) Private Collection/ The Bridgeman Art Library

Cannibalism, engraved by Theodor de Bry (1528–98) (engraving) by John White (fl. 1570–93) Private Collection/ The Stapleton Collection/ The Bridgeman Art Library

Moonlight Effect on the Lake Juteca, page 457 from Vol. 2 of "Journey Across South America" by P. Marcoy, 1873 (engraving) by Edouard Riou (1833–1900) (after) Natural History Museum, London, UK/ The Bridgeman Art Library

Meandering river (aerial), Tambopata National Reserve, Peru © Frans Lanting/www.lanting.com

Index

ABOUT THE AUTHOR

Buddy Levy is the author of *Conquistador: Hernán Cortés, King Montezuma, and the Last Stand of the Aztecs* and *American Legend: The Real-Life Adventures of David Crockett.* His first book was *Echoes on Rimrock: In Pursuit of the Chukar Partridge.* As a journalist, Levy has covered adventure sports and lifestyle around the world. In 2010–11, he co-hosted the ten-episode series *Decoded* on the History Channel. He is a clinical associate professor at Washington State University and lives in Moscow, Idaho, with his wife and two children.

ABOUT THE TYPE

This book was set in Bulmer, a typeface designed in the late eighteenth century by the London type-cutter William Martin. The typeface was created especially for the Shakespeare Press, directed by William Bulmer; hence, the font's name. Bulmer is considered to be a transitional typeface, containing characteristics of old-style and modern designs. It is recognized for its elegantly proportioned letters, with their long ascenders and descenders.